Island Practice

Island Practice

PAM BELLUCK

COBBLESTONE RASH,

UNDERGROUND TOM,

and

OTHER ADVENTURES

of a

NANTUCKET DOCTOR

PUBLICAFFAIRS
New York

PublicAffairs books are available at special discounts for bulk purchases in the U.S. by
corporations, institutions, and other organizations. For more information, please
contact the Special Markets Department at the Perseus Books Group, 2300 Chestnut
Street, Suite 200, Philadelphia, PA 19103, call (800) 810-4145, ext. 5000, or e-mail
special.markets@perseusbooks.com.

Book Design by Timm Bryson

Library of Congress Cataloging-in-Publication Data
  Belluck, Pam.
  Island practice / Pam Belluck.—1st ed.
    p. ; cm.
  ISBN 978-1-58648-751-5 (hardback)—ISBN 978-1-61039-017-0 (electronic)
  I. Title.
  [DNLM: 1. Lepore, Timothy J. 2. Physicians—Atlantic Ocean—Biography. 3.
Physicians—Massachusetts—Biography. 4. Rural Health Services—Atlantic Ocean—
Biography. 5. Rural Health Services—Massachusetts—Biography. WZ 100]
  LC Classification not assigned
  vii610.92—dc23
  [B]
                                                    2011053117

First Edition
10 9 8 7 6 5 4 3 2 1

For my mother and father,
whose extraordinary love, encouragement, emphasis on honest effort,
and empathy and respect for others inspire me to strive for originality
and integrity and to approach the world with wonder, laughter,
a sense of adventure, and the hope of making a difference.

CONTENTS

FOREWORD

In the decade before the American Revolution, the writer St. Jean de Crèvecoeur traveled to the island of Nantucket, which was already on its way to becoming the whaling capital of the world. Despite being well removed from the eastern seaboard, Nantucket was a place of intense economic activity, sending out whaleships as far as the west coast of Africa and the Falkland Islands. Crèvecoeur spoke with the leading physician on Nantucket, Doctor Benjamin Tupper, who claimed that most of the women on the island, whose husbands and sons were often away for months if not years at a time, used opium. Tupper was himself a user and told Crèvecoeur that without his morning jolt of the drug, he would not be able to "transact any business."

Two hundred and fifty years later, Nantucket has a doctor who is also an addict. But unlike Tupper, Dr. Timothy Lepore, the subject of this book and my personal physician for the last twenty-five years, is a teetotaler. Instead of drugs and alcohol, Tim is addicted to being a doctor, and he is always, and I mean always, on call.

Being a writer with an interest in history who doesn't get out very much, I tend to know more about the past than I do about the present day, especially when it comes to the island I call home. Much in this book by Pam Belluck comes as a revelation. Some of it is fascinating; some of it is hilarious; and some of it is sad and very troubling. In *Island Practice*, Belluck has created a remarkable portrait of a physician and the island community to which he remains steadfastly devoted.

Islands have a way of exaggerating life. When things are good, they are great. When they are bad, they are terrible. The middle ground—the emotional range where most of us prefer to spend our daily lives—is harder to hold on to in a place like Nantucket, where fog can transform a crystal blue sky into a blanket of gray in a matter of seconds.

The Wampanoag Indians who named the island Nantucket (which means "faraway land") attributed its discovery to a mythic giant named Mashop. Mashop, it was said, pursued a huge bird that had scooped up a child in its talons and flown out across the waters to the south of Cape Cod. After wading through the shallows of Nantucket Sound, Mashop came upon an island he'd never seen before. Underneath the branches of a large tree he found the whitened bones of the dead child. Mashop sat down for a contemplative smoke and created the fog that still frequents the island to this day.

I live fairly close to the hospital on Nantucket, and I often hear the rotors of the MedFlight helicopter as it hovers over the church spires and roof walks of this historic town before descending into the sprawl of nondescript buildings that comprise the island's one and only medical facility. Soon the helicopter is climbing back into the sky and is gone. Inevitably, I think of Tim, the physician who, in all likelihood, made the decision to summon the helicopter and has already turned his attention to the next patient. This is the story of Nantucket's modern-day Mashop.

—Nathaniel Philbrick
Nantucket Island, February 2012

CHAPTER I

A Nice Quiet Island

"There's a trail somewhere," Dr. Timothy J. Lepore huffs. "I know there's a trail." A seemingly impenetrable forest rises on all sides, and Lepore, sixty-seven and battling bad knees, is submerged in tangled branches and tightly twisted trunks. He can't see anything beyond the brambles, and from the dirt-and-sand road near Hidden Forest, it is impossible to see him. But he can be heard coughing and breathing heavily.

"You all right?" a companion calls. "Yeah, I'm just bushwhacking," Lepore barks, swinging at the forest with his fists. His shoes are untied. His bald head is swamped in sweat. He peers through perspiration-fogged glasses. "Stay right there until I see if there's a trail."

Lepore is on a house call—not your average house call, even for doctors who still make them. But he is determined to find the home of one of his patients, and if this is what it takes, this is what it takes. Finally, Lepore manages to force some branches apart and locate the remnants of an overgrown path. Slivers of water from Stumpy Pond can be seen at the bottom of a ridge, and turtles sunning themselves on rocks pull their heads in at the commotion.

Lepore trudges up a hill, clambers over roots, tears through thickets of scrub oak, and stops.

"Come up," he calls with triumph in his voice. "What do you see?"

At first there is nothing but forest. Then, through the trees, light glints on a dark green plastic tarp. Underneath is what looks like an igloo that has been intricately woven out of tree branches, grapevines, and reeds. It is about eight feet long, barely five feet wide, and a little over six feet tall. There is a door—wood framed with a large pane of one-way mirrored glass—and Lepore has a key.

"Tom," Lepore calls as he cracks open the door. Calling out is hardly necessary—it's a tiny structure—but it represents a touch of conventional good manners in this very unconventional setting.

Lepore may be the only person who has been invited to visit this house and one of the few people aware that its owner, one Thomas Johnson, has not completely fled the island.

Most people here know of Johnson as Underground Tom, and they think he is long gone, chased away after the discovery of another one of his secret lairs—dug deep under land that belonged to a Boy Scout camp. It was revealed only after a deer hunter stumbled on the black tip of a stove pipe sticking out of the ground.

That home, too, was a phenomenon of makeshift engineering, Lilliputian craftsmanship, and camouflage. It was also quite illegal, so Underground Tom was uprooted. After authorities discovered a tree house and a brush-covered log cabin he had built in other trespassed patches of land, he was, as far as most people knew, driven off the island.

Lepore's island, Nantucket, is much more than a charming tourist destination or a summer haven for the exceedingly wealthy. It may draw more than a million visitors a year, and be known the world over for its cobblestone streets, lovely beaches, and whaling industry nostalgia.

It may be a magnet for hedge fund managers, media personalities, and the political elite.

But its roughly 10,000 year-round residents experience Nantucket in an altogether different way. They know the allure and liabilities of living in a place that is not always easy to get to or to get away from. Mystery has a way of drifting ashore, like the scrim of fog that can crease Fat Ladies Beach. And longtime residents are the first to say that this boomerang-shaped island—just fourteen miles long and three-and-a-half miles wide at its widest point—seems to host more than its per capita share of outliers: eclectic, independent-minded, occasionally slippery or up to no good, often just aiming for a little reinvention.

"If you're going to make it here, you've got to have something that's different. People have to be characters who live here," asserts Peter Swenson, who runs Family and Children's Services of Nantucket. It's a quality many islanders acknowledge with shrugged shoulders and a touch of pride.

"Nantucket attracts the kind of person who has some flaws, who in the real world would become a problem, but here they're welcome," explains Chris Fraker, Lepore's longtime neighbor. "It's safe out here. You're one step removed."

A sign in the Nantucket town clerk's office puts it plainly: "Thank You for Not Discussing the Outside World." "We print it up on fancy, bordered paper," the town clerk, Catharine Flanagan Stover, pointed out to Lepore one day.

Thirty capricious miles of Atlantic Ocean stretch between Nantucket and its closest contact with the continent, the southern base of Cape Cod, Massachusetts. But the metaphorical distance can feel much greater.

Some people here call the mainland "America"—not wistfully, or in any way unpatriotically, but as a place they have happily, if only slightly and inconsequentially, seceded from.

"I spent ten years in America; I paid my dues," says Richard Ray, a native Nantucketer who heads the health department for Nantucket, which, including the tiny islands of Tuckernuck and Muskeget, has the unusual distinction of being both its own town and county.

Lepore himself decamped nearly three decades ago from Rhode Island. An emergency room doctor tired of shots being fired outside his Providence hospital and the nightly parade of urban gore gracing his gurneys, he was tantalized after a summer shift at Nantucket's bite-sized hospital. With its rows of cedar shingles and white-railed widow's walk coordinating neatly with the island's graceful architectural simplicity, the hospital seemed quirky without being chaotic. Nantucket would offer an easier lifestyle and would be a great place to raise kids, he and his wife, Cathy, a nurse and school counselor, reasoned.

Lepore became the island's general surgeon, the head of medicine at the island's hospital, and the island's medical examiner. "So maybe I can cover up my mistakes," he suggests archly. He is the school physician and the high school football team doctor, and he has been reelected to serve on the school committee for more than twenty years straight. He has bootstrapped himself into becoming a nationally recognized expert on tick diseases, a special scourge on Nantucket.

Although he has no psychiatric training, he provides cut-to-the-chase, profanity-perfused psychological counseling. He acts as an occasional Dr. Doolittle, treating a run-over deer, an ailing sea gull, a postpartum sheep.

When crisis has enveloped the island, as with a string of teenage suicides in recent years, he is one of the people called upon to try to hold things together. And he and his wife have repeatedly taken in teenagers who are in trouble and others needing a place to stay, sometimes fraying the fabric of the Lepore family in the process.

Lepore's family practice accepts all comers. He is not just a sawbones to the summer rich. Sure, he'll handle Jet Ski collisions and overboard yachtsmen. Even a little Botox now and then. Once in a while, a vacationer will show up dangling a bluefish from his head or torso, the hook having snagged not only the fish, but the fisherman. But Lepore also sees many working-class people and foreign laborers whose jobs undergird the luxury life: construction workers with sawed-off fingers or ears, lobstermen with chests crushed by winches, the firefighter's son who shattered a finger launching fireworks.

An equal opportunity malady is something Lepore calls "cobblestone rash"—injuries from falling (or stumbling drunk) on Nantucket's picturesquely uneven streets. There are also moped injuries galore, described with delicacy and decorum by the island doctor: "I've told people if they wanted the moped experience they could just let me hit them with a bat and then go over them with a sander." Bedside manner á la Lepore.

Driven by his own irrepressible volition, Lepore works constantly, never drinks on-island so as not to blunt his reaction time, and rarely goes off-island. "Hundreds of people would have died if he wasn't there, if not thousands," claims Richard H. Koehler, a surgeon on the mainland who comes over to cover for Lepore if he steps off Nantucket for even a day. Koehler figures Lepore "must have coronary arteries the size of the Holland Tunnel"—surgeon-speak for a big heart. "Literally, I don't know how he does it."

There are a handful of other year-round doctors, including three family practitioners, an internist, an orthopedist, a radiologist, and an emergency department director. And there are off-island specialists who visit at various times. But islanders, including other physicians, routinely describe Lepore this way: If you are sick or hurt on Nantucket, Lepore is the person most likely to be there to keep you alive. He is everywhere, and one of a kind.

"His is a job that very few people want to do, and nobody's doing it like he's doing it," says Diane Pearl, an internist on the island, who grew up here. "The fact of being limitless like Tim is—I couldn't do that. This is his kingdom."

Still, to the extent that Lepore is a medical monarch of sorts, he can be controversial. He can talk in brash assertions or unfiltered barbs that he sees no point in editing into more anodyne expressions. He can irritate or confound people who expect him to advocate a particular position. He has a passion for guns, hunting, and other conservative and libertarian issues, but will also perform abortions and supply patients with marijuana cookies. He has stirred tension by proclaiming that the only way to solve Nantucket's tick disease problem is to kill more deer. And he is not known for an especially cuddly bedside manner.

The story of Tim Lepore is in part a tale of a most unusual person who is central to the health and life of a community in ways that rarely occur these days. (Even the pronunciation of his last name is unexpected—not for him the more common "LehPOOR." Lepore rhymes his name, appropriately enough, with "peppery.") Against the background of a changing, churning American medical landscape, a physician like Lepore has become an outlier and a maverick.

His patient-focused approach, once much more the norm, now strains to survive in towns and cities across the country as health care costs skyrocket, medicine becomes more corporatized and monetized, and extended face time with doctors is an increasingly vanishing commodity. This is true in Lepore's own community as well. Nantucket's small hospital was recently swallowed by a big hospital company, forcing Lepore to struggle, not always successfully, to continue practicing medicine his way.

Lepore's island practice also provides a glimpse of the inner life of a place famous for its elite reputation but rarely understood in the human, warts-and-all way that Lepore experiences it every day.

There are many such places in America, some literally islands, others isolated by other geographical realities or by demographic transformations. They might be vacation havens like the Outer Banks or Aspen, Stowe or Sun Valley, places with hardy year-round populations that take on a different identity when visitors flood in each year. They might be the hundreds of less notable small towns dotting the Midwest, the Plains, the South, and the Northeast that have seen their populations whittled as industries leave or contract, or have confronted change as immigrants or other newcomers move in. They might even be neighborhoods in tourist cities like New Orleans or San Francisco, places that outsiders surmise to be a certain way but can never really understand as the locals do.

Lepore's Nantucket, with its saltbox houses, windy moors, and sea-stung sands, may be more offbeat than people would expect. Yet it is also more emblematic of America—in all its diversity, social strain, and economic division, but also in its scrappiness, creativity, and gumption.

Nantucket turned out to be a place that would let Lepore be Lepore. His idiosyncrasies and hobbies are quixotic even by island standards. Anyone for Siberian throat-singing or dog-hair knitting? How about scooping up roadkill or carving prehistoric spear-throwers? His comments, whether uttered in public meetings or patient exam rooms, can be just as colorful: a shot-from-the-hip political incorrectitude here, an arcanely acerbic aphorism there.

"He's peculiar," observes Jim Lentowski, who heads the Nantucket Conservation Foundation, "but we all are peculiar living on this island."

Pam Michelsen, a friend who teaches high school English, particularly Emerson and Thoreau, thinks Lepore could have "walked off the pages of Walden Pond. He is a nonconformist." In fact, both of these nineteenth-century Transcendentalist thinkers gave lectures on the island, which Emerson dubbed the "Nation of Nantucket." Notes Michelsen: "Emerson said, 'What I must do is all that concerns me, not what people think.' Well, that's Tim Lepore."

Part of the island's attraction for personalities of this sort stems from the challenge of living here year-round. Sure, Nantucket has some of the most expensive houses in the country—the median home price in 2011 was $1 million, making Nantucket the only U.S. county with half the homes costing at least seven figures. But those houses belong mostly to summer visitors. For the people who live and work there—teachers, police officers, waitresses, landscapers—those seven-digit numbers serve mostly to make everything, from gasoline to groceries, a lot more expensive.

There are no big-box discount stores, no Wal-Mart or Target. And because rain, wind, or hurricanes can suddenly make it impossible to leave the island, there's no guarantee that provisions from the mainland will always be accessible. Or that someone needing medical care could get off-island to receive it. "There's a certain amount of risk inherent in living on Nantucket, enshrouded in fog sometimes to where even the Coast Guard can't get in," Lentowski explains.

Sean Kehoe, who spent his teenage years on the island, leaving for New York as an adult, feels that "the amount of work that's involved, and sacrifice just to live here, after a while it's just exhausting. You see people move away. You see people just recede into themselves." But "people like Lepore who occupy the character role, who are a little bit eccentric, who are not flamboyant—people are just glad he's here. They trust him because he just wants people alive."

Indeed, much of Nantucket has to trust Lepore at one time or another. "When you're up to your ass in alligators, Tim Lepore is one of the people you want to have with you," says Margot Hartmann, the chief executive officer of Nantucket Cottage Hospital. "He is gutsy. He does not run. That's why he's become the backbone of the island."

And why he can end up stepping into almost any delicate situation, strictly medical or not.

Billy Dexter got to know Lepore in the late 1980s. He began visiting the doctor's office for routine things, but found Lepore good to chat with. And they shared an interest in hunting; Dexter liked black-powder rifles, and he once carved Lepore a squawking duck call. He would drop by Lepore's house with a black Labrador retriever three times the normal size, and when Lepore's children saw him approaching, they would hide in the bushes and yell: "Billy Dexter's here, and he's got a warthog with him."

"Tim was the only person who was kind to him," recalls Michelsen. "Tim thought he was interesting."

But Billy Dexter had a problem—and a predilection. As Lepore described it, Dexter was "a nice guy, but when he drank, he went off the radar."

And, apparently, into someone else's barn. On October 7, 1988, the owner of a Madaket Road stable called the police to say that she had noticed a water pail had been removed from one of her horse stalls and that the horse kept rubbing its hind quarters against the stall, according to a Nantucket police report. The woman believed "that the horse had been sexually assaulted" and "also observed a pair of black Farah pants at the back of the stall. The pants were placed into evidence."

The following day, a second police report was filed: "William Dexter called the station to inquire about some pants that he was missing."

Officers put two legs and four legs together, went to Dexter's Cliff Road house, and arrested him on two counts of sodomy. "Suspect has a history of similar crimes," police records stated, "and is familiar" with the barn owner "and her stables."

The court case caused a stir. Lepore's neighbor Chris Fraker expressed the island's and Lepore's dilemma succinctly: "What do you do with the town weirdo that's doing horses and sheep? Tim's view was 'I don't give a flying Friday what you do; just don't get caught.'" But "people didn't like it anymore, so it went to court."

The assistant district attorney asked Lepore to recommend whether Dexter was criminally liable. Lepore could have taken a hard line. After all, he didn't know the forty-four-year-old Dexter especially well, and no one would say there was an advantage in defending a guy who was into bestiality. But Lepore's judgment was that Dexter did not deserve to be vilified. "At heart he was a very sad, depressed guy. He would drink and have a dalliance with a horse. I knew Billy Dexter, and he was no stallion."

So Lepore wrote a letter to the district attorney and scheduled an appointment for Dexter with a therapist at Nantucket Counseling Services.

According to the Nantucket *Inquirer and Mirror*, the therapist, Truman Esau, testified that Dexter should be hospitalized, not jailed, because he suffered from chronic alcohol dependence and zoophilia, having "admitted that having sex with animals is his personal preference."

Lepore acknowledges that Dexter's behavior was "a distasteful thing. This wasn't a guy who was going around knocking over mailboxes." But "I didn't think he represented a clear and present danger to the island." Dexter was eventually sentenced to a hospital instead of jail. A year later, though, he was arrested on federal firearms charges for having a sawed-off shotgun. It was a weapon that Lepore believed Dexter used for shark fishing, but this time Lepore didn't get involved. "I don't write many letters for felons," he said. But he doesn't throw patients overboard either. When, a few years later, Dexter suffered fatal heart failure, "I took care of him."

Dexter's brand of deviance may have been unusual, but Lepore has treated any number of Nantucket's odder ducks. "Not every miscreant is mine," he insists. "Just most."

Lepore has been pulled into some of the island's most notorious criminal cases. He's the person who pronounces murder victims dead, fixes people who are stabbed or shot, analyzes alcohol and drug levels in passed-out substance abusers, and helps evaluate whether crime suspects are mentally sound enough to go to jail.

Thomas Shack, chief of operations for the Cape and Islands District Attorney's office, remembers a recent high-profile case in which a woman seriously injured another woman in a bar fight. Shack's job was to undercut Lepore's testimony about the victim's intoxicated state.

"He has this sort of 'aw shucks' manner—you come in contact with that pretty quickly when he's on the witness stand," Shack observed. "Here I am, having to cross-examine him and kind of be tough on him, keeping in mind that this person might end up saving my life one day."

To do the work that Lepore does, for as long as he has done it, an understanding of the island is imperative. While Nantucket nurtures an affable feeling of community, it can also be a place of individual isolation. The transparency of a small town coexists with a pointed respect for privacy. And an attitude of irreverence vies with a realization that islands can, in a quicksilver second, leave people uniquely vulnerable or make their lives utterly unpredictable.

"People don't realize things happen on Nantucket," says Janine Mauldin, an island police officer. "They think it's a nice quiet island."

For one thing, there is the influence of the sea, the surf, and the sand. Collapsed sandbars can alter the channels that sea water moves through, creating sudden strong currents in unanticipated places. That can endanger swimmers and boaters, causing accidents or drownings.

Jet Ski collisions, man-overboards, and other watery mishaps land in Lepore's lap, like the time the singer Jimmy Buffett's seaplane flipped over as Buffett, an experienced pilot, was trying to take off from Madaket Harbor. The plane was badly damaged, but Buffett managed to swim to shore, where Lepore X-rayed him, identified minor injuries, and released him so he could go on to waste away again in many a Margaritaville.

Natural calamities can instigate human mischief, like the disturbing act of the unknown marauder who committed the federal crime of mutilating the tail of a dead humpback whale that beached in the summer of 2011.

And one fall day in 2010, the bones of a human leg, still in a sock and work boot, surfaced on the sand at Great Point. Police called Lepore. "Tim is the guy that I'm going to bring the bones to," notes Steve Tornovish, a detective. "He's the absolute master of the universe down here."

Lepore immediately sized things up: "A left tibia and fibula. No cut marks or bullet holes. It hadn't been gnawed on. The boot had barnacles on it. The bones had been cleaned of flesh. It had been in the water awhile."

More than a year later, verifying suspicions of many Nantucketers, state authorities determined the leg belonged to Jonathan Hemingway, a Nantucket landscaper who had disappeared one night in March 2010, when he was sailing his powerboat from Hyannis to Nantucket with his family and apparently fell overboard while his wife and children slept below.

The severed leg closed the book on one island mystery. But there is always another.

In July 2011, Lepore found a plastic bag on his desk with another human tibia inside. Someone had found it on the beach near Coatue and brought it—where else?—to Lepore. "Semifresh," he said. "Still smelled." It came from an adult over thirty, he deduced, noting that the bone's growth plates had fused, making it too developed to belong to a child. He sent it to Boston. No idea to whom it belonged, but on this island, "there's always folks missing."

What's never missing on the Nantucket that Lepore encounters every day is a spirit of individuality some people take to stubborn extremes. Gene Ratner gained national attention for his drive to save the four-bedroom home he built more than thirty-five years ago perching just above the great sweep of water off Madaket Beach. As wind, water, and time eroded shards of Nantucket's fragile coast, Ratner's house was increasingly in the crosshairs as the steps he took to protect it clashed with island environmental rules. Finally, in September 2010, after a hurricane left the house crumpled but standing, officials condemned it, and Ratner, by then eighty-five, was forced to take it down.

A few months later, in another Nantucket-versus-nature moment, came a showdown with Joe Dooley, a scalloper living with a passel of dogs on a thirty-year-old fishing boat he had bought for $10 and moored in Nantucket harbor in 2007. The boat, the *Miss China*, had a broken engine and was unable to move under its own power.

Nantucket officials once had to rescue six Dooley dogs that jumped overboard, and the Coast Guard once had to pump thousands of gallons of fuel out of the boat so it wouldn't sink. Then, in December 2010, a pounding winter storm swept the *Miss China* off its mooring and beached it in the sand near Nantucket's Brant Point lighthouse. Officials tried to get Dooley and his dogs off the boat, afraid it would break loose and sink or crack up, creating a navigational disaster for other ships.

Dooley refused. "They want to get me off the boat so they can claim it for salvage," he told the *Inquirer and Mirror*. "I'll freeze to death or starve to death before I give them that satisfaction." It was nearly a week before he finally gave in.

The miles of ocean between Nantucket and America make some people feel invisible, undetected, and emboldened. Perhaps that's why, on the Friday of Memorial Day weekend in 2010, Pamela Morgan committed Nantucket's first bank robbery in more than two hundred years.

There's a reason why "bank robbery hasn't caught on," notes Lepore. "They got no place to go."

This realization occurred a little too late to Morgan. But then, she had a lot on her plate. She had a ball of tinfoil full of fake identification cards with different aliases. She had a string of larceny convictions in Ohio, Oregon, and California. And in 2009, she had been arrested by the Secret Service after trying to jump the White House fence.

So who knows what she thought would happen when she walked into a Nantucket branch of the Bank of America, began chatting to the teller about letters she had written to Fidel Castro, and presented five crumpled $1 bills that were so obviously counterfeit some had George Washington on both sides. "She was telling me there were people after her, that her life was in danger, and if I knew her situation, I would know why she was doing this," the teller testified. Told her money was no good, Morgan pulled a note from her backpack that read: "I don't want to hurt anyone. Give me the money."

Morgan walked out with $3,000 but didn't get far. She crossed the street to Sheep to Shore, a knitting shop, then slipped into a post office, where a police officer confronted her. She explained, the officer recounted later, that she'd tried unsuccessfully to use the counterfeit bills at several stores, and that she'd foil-wrapped her ID cards because "the government was tracking her through microchips in her identification" and "the tinfoil didn't allow them to track her like that." Later in jail, she accused the Nantucket police and the FBI of tampering with her milk and bed sheets. Her case is pending, and she is being held in a psychiatric facility.

As an out-of-stater who'd been on the island less than twenty-four hours, Morgan was a washashore of the briefest variety. But people with deeper island roots have tried to get away with things too, often right under their neighbors' noses.

Not long after the Great Nantucket Bank Heist, one of Lepore's nurses was enjoying the evening air when a posse of local cops, state police, and federal agents tromped across her porch, barreling toward the house of her Belarusian next-door neighbor, Mikalai Mardakhayeu. Turns out he was running an international fraud conspiracy, a phishing scheme in which he and his cohorts pretended to prepare tax returns for people across the country while actually using their personal information to siphon off $200,000 in federal and state tax refunds.

That was nothing, though, compared to the scrimshaw-smuggling conspiracies. Two old-timers in two separate cases went too far in the name of art, specifically the practice, begun in the nineteenth century, of carving bones and teeth of whales, walruses, and other sea mammals. One, Charles Manghis, long a bearded and bespectacled presence at his shop on the Old South Wharf, was a scrimshander, an artisan who etched lighthouses and ships into ivory and whale teeth and had even carved presidential seals for both presidents Bush. The other, David Place, owned Manor House Antique Cooperative.

Both men were convicted of conspiring with a Ukrainian smuggler and a middleman in California to illegally import the teeth of endangered sperm whales. Manghis, who was tied to some 375 whale teeth, admitted his nautical transgression. Place, accused of smuggling $400,000 in teeth and tusks, did not, saying the Ukrainian hornswoggled him. And a handful of independence-conscious Nantucketers rose to his defense, signing a petition arguing for his sentence to be reduced.

"We have a proud history," wrote the organizer of the as yet unsuccessful effort, "of taking care of our own."

But as Lepore has learned from experience, sometimes Nantucket is unable to take care of its own. Trudie Hall was twenty-three and pregnant when she disappeared in July 2010, last seen when she left the island for what was believed to be a short trip to Cape Cod. Hall, a Jamaican immigrant, American citizen, and Nantucketer for ten years, turned out to have a secret even her mother claimed not to know. She had married two different men within six months of each other and not divorced either, possibly in an immigration scheme in which she reportedly received money to help the men get legal status.

To thicken the plot further, the father of Hall's unborn child was a third man, a former Nantucketer, now on Cape Cod, who was married and had previously been convicted of stealing $8,000 from Nantucket bus fare boxes.

After Hall disappeared, her rental car was found in a commuter parking lot, with blood and bullet casings inside. The investigation continues, although police and her mother assume she's dead.

Lepore was as fascinated as the rest of the island by Hall's uncertain fate. But he was not surprised that Nantucket formed the nexus of Hall's hidden world. He knows the island too well.

As far as most Nantucketers were concerned, Thomas Johnson, aka Underground Tom, was another mysterious disappearance, someone who fled the island more than a decade ago. Lepore, however, knew better.

Johnson grew up in Binghamton, New York, one of seven children of a city judge. As a teenager, he built his first log cabin in the Pennsylvania woods, where he often retreated. He briefly attended community college, reportedly writing on every test and assignment, "When Johnny comes marching home again, hurrah, hurrah."

When he was twenty, his father died in his arms of colon and liver cancer. Soon Johnson, who stayed home to care for his mother, developed a drug habit and hired himself out as an international drug courier. In 1983, he was arrested in Italy for trying to smuggle in more than $2 million of Thai heroin, stitched into the lining of a suitcase he was supposed to deposit in a train station locker in Rome.

After two and a half years in an Italian prison, he was released on house arrest, but escaped, began kiting checks, and eventually came to Nantucket, where he said he scoped out the site for his underground home by spending "a month of Sundays" sitting in a nearby tree on Boy Scouts land near Lovers Lane. In just five weeks, he dug a hole with a shovel, paid less than $150 for materials, stole or "liberated" other supplies, and built what he described as his "self-help tank," saying, "I've gone into the earth, almost like a seed, to germinate."

Johnson germinated largely in solitude, weathering hurricanes and snowstorms underground, his house insulated with rubber and covered with topsoil and sand. Its portal, camouflaged by limbs and dead leaves, was a hatch inlaid with a small glass window.

Inside, a ladder descended eight feet into the earth, which opened into a three-room chamber outfitted with a striking array of comforts: cedar paneling, a Belgian stone floor, a stained glass skylight obscured by a patch of blueberry bushes, a homemade chemical toilet, a battery-powered television, and a shower made from a plastic tube hooked to a water jug. A cubby cut into one wall served as a pantry, keeping bottles of milk and cups of Jell-O pudding cool even in summer.

At first Lepore didn't know where Johnson lived. He'd see him riding around on his bike or picking up scrap wood. Johnson supported himself as one of Nantucket's legion of part-time carpenters and painters who build and maintain summer people's homes. He drank at bars in town and occasionally got in fights.

Johnson went to tremendous lengths to conceal his house, using what might be called sleight of foot. He created shoes that made impressions that looked like deer hooves, placed his feet down as he walked in the linear pattern that resembles deer tracks, and varied the path he took to his door by taking one of fifteen different trails. He dismantled deer stands that hunters erected in the scrub pine forest to discourage them from hanging around, lest they spy his six-foot-four-inch frame lumbering toward his lair.

But Underground Tom had medical issues, including joint and back pain, and he sought out Lepore. No doubt he considered the doctor something of a kindred spirit. Lepore's office is as intricately decorated and anti-establishment as Johnson's belowground bunker.

There are skulls, arrowheads, snake skin, turtle shells, fish jaws, and antlers. Books include *Latrinae et Foricae: Toilets in the Roman World* and Philip Roth's *The Plot Against America*. And some of Lepore's many signs would appeal to his iconoclastic patient: "It could be that the purpose of your life is only to serve as a warning to others" and "*Carthago delenda est*" (Carthage must be destroyed), the famous phrase by the Roman leader Cato, which often signifies a single-minded intensity for total victory against one's enemies. In his waiting room, Lepore has posted a reference to America's favorite fantasy tale: "Nobody gets to see the wizard. Not nobody. Not no how."

Lepore never billed Underground Tom for his visits. Fascinated by weapons ancient and contemporary, Lepore allowed Johnson to pay his medical "fee" by providing informal advice about fashioning arrowheads. He tried to get Johnson to protect himself from the island's disease-carrying ticks, but Johnson refused to be tested for Lyme disease. Nor would he let Lepore repair his hernia. He allowed hardly anyone to visit him underground, although he told Lepore that at one point he had a girlfriend who would join him in the pull-down queen-sized bed he had notched into one subterranean wall.

Then, in November 1998, a hunter, Jack Hallett Sr., was searching for a deer stand, crawling under a low branch, when he happened upon the stove pipe and the trapdoor. Hallett deliberately left a footprint so the occupant of the underground house would know he had been discovered. The next day, over breakfast, Hallett told Paul Johnson, an X-ray technician and reserve police officer, what he had seen.

"You're going nowhere until you prove to me that this is true," Paul Johnson asserted. Hallett led him to the spot, and they knocked on the hatch. "I was expecting you ten years ago," Underground Tom intoned. He was cordial, but his hand trembled so much coffee sloshed out of his cup. The hermit gave his name as Tom Underwood, one of his smart-alecky aliases; Dick Human and Forest Green are others.

Although many islanders would have just as soon left him be, the jig was up for Tom. Nantucket officials worried that allowing him to remain an illegal squatter, especially in a community with sky-high rents and property values, would set a dangerous precedent. Paul Johnson worried that the disguised trapdoor was "a death trap for some kid running and falling through the window and landing on the stone floor."

The health department cited Underground Tom for multiple violations. Richard Ray, the department's director, described the dwelling as "wonderful and marvelous and purely functional, but it was without question unfit for human habitation because of state sanitary guidelines. It didn't have anywhere near the requisite natural lighting, electric, refrigerator hookup, no bathroom, no hot or cold running water. He was very proud of it, as well he should have been. He showed me around, he had books, clothes, radio. It looked to me like he was a voracious reader."

He was also a collector. Agents from the U.S. Fish and Wildlife Service and the state environmental police, one of them packing a gun, ordered Johnson to fork over the hawk claws and great horned owl's wing he used as wall decorations and the dream catcher he had made from peregrine falcon feathers. He said he hadn't killed the birds; they were roadkill.

Lepore spoke out in Johnson's defense. "He should be left alone," he told reporters. "I don't think he represents a threat to the community or the environment. If you want an archetypal low-impact guy, he's the one."

Lepore was so impressed with the underground house that he told Johnson he could build another in his backyard. "I would have moved in there," Lepore proclaimed. "The temperature's always right, cozy. I could have all my books down there." But Cathy Lepore was not thrilled, nor would island officials have been.

Underground Tom clearly wanted to stay ahead of authorities. When Ray went to the bunker a second time, everything was gone, and so was Johnson. Soon, though, other Johnson-built structures were discovered. A brush-covered log cabin made from pine trees notched by hand was found on land owned by the town's water agency. A tree house, eight feet off the ground with a bed cut into one wall, was discovered on state park land near Old South Road. Ray heard that "when they dug the foundation for the new police station on Fairgrounds Road, they found remnants of an underground house."

Tom himself had vanished. Few people knew where. Maybe to his old log cabin in Pennsylvania or one of the other habitations he'd reportedly built in Colorado, Delaware, New York, and Hawaii.

But before he left, he took Lepore to another hideaway: the vine-and-twig igloo. If the underground house was a place where, as Johnson once said, "I can hear the heartbeat of the island," the dome-shaped home near Hidden Forest was like a tiny thumb stealthily slipped atop the island's primal pulse.

The floor was paved partly with ceramic tiles and partly with glass bottles embedded in clay and dirt, the round bottle bottoms producing an inlaid stained-glass effect. A fireplace was fashioned from cement and clay, shaped to look like a tree trunk with a face sculpted in it. There was a skylight with a screen, quahog shell shelves, a towel rack, a fire extinguisher, a candle holder, an alarm clock, frying pans, and a car's side-view mirror affixed to the interior branches with a bungee cord. The bed was a wooden bunk supported by branches, with a sleeping bag and foam mats.

Lepore didn't know how often Johnson stayed on-island, but he would periodically materialize at Lepore's office. On one such visit, Johnson was covered in tick bites, and as he left, he handed Lepore his house key. "He's a few clicks off," Lepore ventured as a diagnosis.

Lepore was entranced by what Johnson called his "twigloo," to the point where he suggested to Cathy that they spend a night there. She demurred.

The day of Lepore's unannounced house call, he has not seen Johnson in about eight months. It is time, he decides, to check on his phantom patient. At the dome home, clues suggest Johnson has been around. Greenish-yellow mosquito netting is draped over the door, something that had not been there the last time Lepore had seen the place.

There is an empty beer can, a drained Cup Noodles soup container, and fragments of fire-starter logs. And there are provisions: instant coffee, black pepper, lamp oil, a bleach stick, matches, a fork, a knife, charcoal in a tin can, Coppertone sun block, and two sample-size bottles of Augmentin, an antibiotic Lepore had no doubt given him as a prophylactic against infection from his tick bites. There is a pair of work boots and a denim shirt lined with red-and-black checks splayed on the bunk, unfolded.

There is, however, no Underground Tom. The only living thing Lepore spies is a snake wriggling through the vines that form one of the house's walls. As the doctor watches, it shimmies toward the bed, slithering near a cache of Tom-thumbed reading material: *Where Nights Are Longest*, *The Importance of Innovation*, *Stone Circles Ancient and Modern: How to Build Your Own*, and a well-worn copy of Ralph Ellison's *Invisible Man*.

CHAPTER 2

WHY ARE WE LEAVING?

On New Year's Day in 1983, the noon boat out of Hyannis, Massachusetts, pulled into Nantucket Harbor, and a doctor, his wife, and their three young children stepped off the ferry and clattered down the ramp to the pier. They were pulling up stakes from the mainland, taking a chance on an island they hoped was ready to take a chance on them.

Their move had come about by happenstance. This wasn't where Lepore expected he would wind up when he finished college and started on the path to becoming a doctor. And it was hardly a seamless journey. Lepore would learn that although he had strengths, there were skills he lacked, particularly in the realm of social and political finesse.

Lepore graduated from Harvard in 1966, with the Vietnam War in full swing. He was classified 1-A, available for service, but received a deferment for medical school at Tufts. In residency, he was again eligible and could have signed up to serve in the military for two years before returning to medical school. But he decided not to: "I didn't burn my draft card. I took my chances, and I didn't get drafted."

After the 1968 assassinations of Martin Luther King Jr. and Robert F. Kennedy, "half the medical school class would want to go out on strike," he says. But "I was working my ass off. I didn't see any great benefit of picketing the school."

When riots broke out in Harvard Square, Lepore went to the basement of a Baptist church in Cambridge to care for people who encountered the forceful side of the crowd-control police. "I washed tear gas out of people's faces and stuff. A line of state cops was coming up with batons, and they're whacking people. One of the cops knew me and said, 'Hey Tim, get out of here.'"

It was a tense, unsettled time: "Everybody hated everybody. There were such cliques, a right-wing group, an extreme left-wing group. The women were pissed off at everybody. There wasn't a sense of collegiality."

Lepore's personal life became unsettled too. "I had this girl I went out with all through high school," he recalls. "We were engaged. I gave her a ring over at King's Chapel Burying Ground. We had pictures and announcements." Then she went to Norway for the summer, and Lepore double-dated with her brother. "Probably wasn't a good idea. She found out, broke up with me. Wouldn't have worked. We're too much alike."

At Harvard, he dated a woman who belonged to a fairly radical organization called The People First. In medical school, after "a brief interlude for an Irish nurse," Lepore began seeing a married woman. But at graduation, "the girl I was engaged to showed up and I was spending too much time with her," so the married woman "got pissed off at me and took off with her family."

In medical school, Lepore's skill and work ethic landed him the position of chief resident. But he was not the easiest person to work with. Once, he wanted a patient's arterial blood gas analyzed, a measurement of how much oxygen and acid is in a person's blood. It is often ordered when a patient is having shortness of breath or vomiting. The lab technician was delaying doing the test, and Lepore was beside himself. He stormed to the lab, kicked the door open, and "I came in like Attila the Hun. If I'm taking care of a patient and I want something, I'm not making a suggestion." Lepore barked at the technician: "You're going to run this. I don't want it done tomorrow, not in an hour. I want it done now."

Subtle diplomacy was not one of his hallmarks. During a rotation in the pediatric cardiothoracic department, Lepore sat in a rocking chair all night next to a child who'd had heart surgery. He stepped away briefly to grab a sandwich in the cafeteria. When he returned, a pediatric resident had written in the patient's chart: "Dr. Lepore's taking care of this patient. He should be writing notes."

This annoyed Lepore to no end. He confronted the resident. "What am I going to be writing notes to myself all night? If I'm taking care of this kid, I don't need someone sticking their nose in."

The next day, the entire team of pediatric residents "trooped into the chief of surgery to complain about me. He looked over the note and said, 'Lepore was right.' Inappropriate, but right. I don't think he appreciated my handling of the situation, but he also thought it was a stupid note in the chart."

Lepore insisted he was not being argumentative for argument's sake. In his view, he was putting patients' interests first and others shouldn't stand in the way of what he believed was best. "I did all my scut work. If somebody gave me trouble along the way, one time is okay; two times, it's not going to happen. I had a testy attitude at times," he acknowledges now, realizing that if he were a resident adopting that kind of stance these days, "I'd probably be kicked out in thirty seconds."

Then there was the matter of the not-quite-dead guy. Lepore was watching Sunday afternoon football in the residents' dorm when he and another resident got called about a patient with severe atherosclerosis, a degenerative disease of the arteries. The patient was in his eighties, and he seemed to have breathed his last.

Lepore was matter-of-fact. "You look at them, they look pretty blue. He was not obviously breathing. I don't think we checked to listen to his heart, but I mean, he looked dead. So we pronounced him."

Lepore called the attending physician to report the patient's death. "He was not surprised. I called the family, who were not surprised. I went back to watch the game."

Not long afterward, a nurse called with a discomfiting question: "Do patients sometimes breathe when they're dead?"

Lepore hurried back, panicked. "The son of a bitch is alive!" He had to call the attending physician and the family. They were "less than pleased." The man lived for another week or so. Pronouncing a live man dead is kind of a no-no in medical circles. "It probably did reflect poorly on me," Lepore says, but it was not considered a disciplinary offense, presumably because nobody had died. Indeed that was the problem: nobody had, at that point, died. However, "You don't get gold stars for that. If the attending is not made to look good, they do not smile on you."

The one salvageable lesson for Lepore was a rule of thumb about what makes for a convincing corpse: "Call us when the body is room temperature," he told the nurses. And not a degree warmer.

In the early 1970s, Lepore spent about nine months of his residency doing rotations at Roger Williams Hospital in Providence, Rhode Island, where his reputation preceded him: "The guy before me had said I was a pain in the ass."

Cathy Clark, a nurse at Roger Williams, heard the rumors too and thought, "Oh my God, no." The scuttlebutt about the sturdily built, curly-haired doctor was hardly flattering: "His name is Lepore; they call him the leper; he's always fighting with everybody."

Still, as Lepore prepared patients for surgery, handled their postoperative care, and ultimately scrubbed in himself, he and Cathy became friends. Cathy, a tall brunette, unpretentious and down-to-earth, lived upstairs in his apartment building. She had recently lost her husband, whom she met growing up in Newport, Rhode Island. He died from aplastic anemia after two gruelingly unsuccessful bone marrow transplants.

Cathy was devastated: "I felt like I had just dropped out of society." She began dating another resident, and they got married and moved to Wisconsin. Almost immediately, she discovered it was an ill-fated choice. "I was miserable. He was just busy all of the time. On the weekends he would go play golf both days, so I would never see him. He wasn't abusive; he just was absent. It was like he all of a sudden dropped out of the marriage."

Within a year, Cathy decided to move back east and wrote Lepore, remembering that he had a big house in Brookline, Massachusetts, outside Boston, and often rented out rooms. He had moved out of the house by then but agreed to help Cathy find an apartment. Cathy met Lepore at Newton-Wellesley Hospital in suburban Boston, and an odd thing happened. "I saw him walking across the parking lot, and I got very dizzy. I thought it must be love. Then I realized I had vestibular neuritis."

Love, vestibular neuritis—why quibble? Vestibular neuritis is an inflammation of the nerve connecting the inner ear to the brain, and pretty soon Cathy began feeling nauseous. Later, at a job interview at another hospital, "I couldn't walk. It was like I was just drunk. I couldn't focus my eyes. I was just sitting on the floor of the ladies' room and vomiting my brains out."

She was sent to the emergency room, where, it turned out, an exgirlfriend of Lepore's was working. Cathy realized Lepore was the only person she knew in Boston.

"I get this phone call that she's near death," Lepore recalls. He picked her up in his truck and took her to his apartment, where she continued to throw up.

It was, Cathy remembers, "about as unromantic as it could possibly have been." To be fair, it wasn't only her fault. There was also the enchanting behavior of Lepore's dog, a slobbering bloodhound named Odie. Lepore was so convinced that Odie was a talented tracker that when his sister, Sherry Buckley, visited, Lepore had Odie sniff a pair of his sister's underwear and then "had me hiding in the woods and the dog was supposed to find me," his sister recalls. Odie "ran right by me."

While Cathy was weak with nausea at Lepore's apartment, she encountered his approach to another of Odie's shortcomings. There were "all these bowls turned over with dog turds underneath them. I mean, who does that?"

She asked the obvious question: "Why is the turd on your floor?" Lepore gave the obvious answer: "If they dry out, they're easier to pick up."

Still, somehow, a romance was ignited. "His girlfriend had left," Cathy remembers. "It was sort of like the lonely hearts' club. You can be like that with somebody when you're very comfortable with them." Lepore helped her find an apartment and invited her to his residency graduation dinner, their first official date. "He was so interesting. He was just funny. He always seemed to be able to handle everything."

When Lepore's residency was ending in June 1975, he wanted one of Tufts's fellowships in thoracic surgery. But the attending physician "didn't support me," recommending that he work at another hospital for a year first. "The hell with that," Lepore thought, and returned to Roger Williams instead, which offered him a job working in the emergency room and handling the surgical side of the intensive care unit.

In August 1976, Cathy went to the Dominican Republic to get a divorce from her second husband. In September, on a Wednesday, Lepore said, "Let's get married." Cathy said okay. That Saturday they went to a justice of the peace they found in the phone book.

In retrospect, Cathy explains her thinking: "My first husband died; my second one I got divorced from. After that, I said, 'I just don't want to be bored. I want to have someone interesting.'" She pauses. "I think I went over the top."

Their wedding was as briskly functional as Lepore's description of it: "There was no ring. Her parents, my parents, two of her sisters, my buddy, Cathy's grandmother. Cathy's grandmother said the justice of the peace was a short man. We said he's in a wheelchair. No vows. Whatever he said, we said. I sweated through my $5 Salvation Army suit, we went to an omelet shop for 25 bucks, and we were done by 11 and went to the Harvard-Columbia football game."

They had no honeymoon and were back at work on Monday.

Lepore's job at Roger Williams Hospital involved a gamut of cases from cancer surgery to trauma. A man fired a shotgun into his own mouth. A woman stabbed in the chest needed thoracic surgery. Another man shot his brother in the face, leaving his eye in a gruesome state. A pharmacist took a bullet on his first night on the job. A kid, twelve or thirteen years old, was shot so badly that Lepore had to elbow his way through a swarm of pediatricians to get to the boy's side.

One night, "I got five stabbings from a Star Market, and they weren't all in the same fight." A man doused his body with gasoline and set himself on fire. Another jumped off a roof, and Lepore operated on him three times in one day, peeling off dead skin from gangrene that had developed in his legs.

If the violence weren't enough, there was a constant stream of car accidents from the nearby highway. A teenager driving a station wagon struck a pole so hard that a spare tire flew forward, pinning the kid against the steering wheel and crushing his larynx. Lepore managed to get him breathing.

Calamity lurked everywhere. Christmas decorations ignited a major fire in a women's dorm at Providence College. When Lepore arrived at the hospital at 1 AM, "every stretcher had a burned or dead girl. Some had jumped; some had smoke inhalation. There were some horrendous burns. I was really the only one there. I went down the line and took care of everything, intubating people, sticking in IVs. It took about twenty minutes for anybody else to show up. After that they decided I should be head of the ER."

Lepore made a point of living about two hundred yards from the hospital so he could always get there instantly. He and Cathy bought a house, but the hospital was not situated in the safest neighborhood, something the Lepores began to worry about more after they had children: Meredith, born in 1977, the day they moved into their Providence home; T.J. in 1979; and Nick in 1982.

Cathy was flashed twice by men when she was walking with the children on the street. At an auto repair class at a nearby garage, she saw people bringing in bags of money—bookies, she assumed, or corrupt cops. People would break into the house when they saw her leave to take the kids to school. Their car was burglarized repeatedly.

Even worse was the summer night Cathy heard men arguing outside. Lepore went to investigate and see if he could help. Instead, he was shot at. For Cathy, "it was just awful. I hated living in Providence." Plus, Lepore was so busy he had little time for the family. He worked thirty-six-hour shifts and had academic responsibilities at Brown University. When Cathy went into labor with Nick, Lepore was treating a Brown urology professor who had fallen down an elevator shaft.

Then, in the summer of 1980, Lepore was invited to visit Nantucket by a medical school friend, Paul Thompson, who worked summer emergency room shifts at Nantucket Cottage Hospital. Lepore had been to the island only once before, in the fall of 1974 with a girlfriend. His main recollection was of trying to teach her to drive a stick shift there; he claimed she nearly blew out the transmission.

But when Lepore visited Thompson, he liked what he saw. The hospital was small and manageable. Cases could get wacky—water injuries, exotic diseases, a woman who brought in a rabbit with red eyes—but they were unlikely to involve gang violence or the carnal wreckage he saw in Providence. And the shifts were better: twenty-four hours on, then forty-eight hours off.

It was an appealing arrangement, recalls Jeffrey Drazen, a summer doctor from 1974 to 1979 who is now the editor in chief of the *New England Journal of Medicine*. "You worked every third day, they gave you a house, they paid you $200 a week, and you saw twenty patients a day." A head nurse staffed the door. "If you had a fishhook sticking out of your head, she'd let you in. But if you had poison ivy or something like that, she'd tell you to come back."

When the Lepores first saw it, the hospital had an exam room, a room for sewing up patients, and fifty beds (nearly three times as many as it has today). An heir to the Campbell Soup fortune, whose family had donated a lot of money, stayed in the hospital as if it were a residence. And there were free meals for the medical staff. "You could come in and order breakfast, do your rounds, and get your eggs over easy," Drazen remembers.

But despite its comfortable trappings, this was a hospital that needed to be more medically sophisticated, to learn to operate with greater urgency. Drazen recalls his first case, a thirty-year-old with serious heart problems. The physician in charge said to "just wait it out. He was into doing that for a lot of things." Drazen finally persuaded the doctor that the patient should be sent to the mainland.

With the island drawing ever-wealthier summer residents and the working-class people to support that influx, it was time to give Nantucket the sort of health care people could rely on whether they trimmed hedges or owned hedge funds.

Lepore's friend Thompson arranged for him to work in the hospital for the month of August 1981. The Lepores returned the following summer, relishing the tranquil contrast to inner-city Providence. Narrow streets, some set with brick or studded with cobblestones, made the pace of life seem more manageable. Strict building codes—pitched roofs, unpainted gray shingles—kept sprawl in check and had a way of letting the island showcase its natural surroundings: plants, birds, water. On the boat heading home the Lepores asked themselves, "Why are we leaving?"

The island had a vascular surgeon, Earl Mahoney, but he had already retired once, been pressed back into service, and wanted to retire for good. The hospital talked to Lepore about working there full-time.

"They needed somebody who was well trained, enthusiastic, had good judgment—and wanted to live on Nantucket," says Drazen, who still summers there. "Boy, they got the right person. He keeps up with what's going on. He adapts to his environment. He knows what he can't do and what he can do. He is willing to take chances when that's the only option, particularly when the weather shuts things down. He's involved in the community—to succeed on Nantucket, you have to be."

Lepore did wonder what he might be giving up at Roger Williams, but he didn't think he was going to get promoted there any time soon. He was also losing patience with the de rigueur meetings and mundane responsibilities of a big hospital; they seemed to take him away from patient care. In September, he told Roger Williams he would leave January 1. "Nobody quite believed me until December 28." Then "they put all kinds of pressure on me to stay. They said, 'It sounds nice, but you won't be happy there.' I asked for a leave of absence for six months. They wouldn't give it to me. So I said, 'Okay, guys, I'm out of here.'"

Lepore and his family didn't know exactly what they were getting into.

On a visit to the island a few months before they moved, they got blasted by a big storm. Pilot whales were beaching left and right. Boats were blocked from coming or going. The family was stuck. "There's no reason to get all heifered up," Lepore decided then. "You're either going to get off or you're not going to get off."

They stayed for the first few months in a "very fancy-dancy house on lower Main Street," but it became clear they needed something more affordable. After a stint in a tiny hospital-owned house at the bottom of a hill—"if your brakes fail, you'd run right through it"—the hospital asked if they wanted to buy the land up the hill for $75,000. It was on Prospect Street, right next to a windmill built in 1745, just a hundred-yard dash from the hospital. Meant for a mind-set like Lepore's. "It's a conscious decision that I live that close."

Cathy, who helped set up Lepore's family practice next to the hospital and worked there as a nurse for a while, hoped that Nantucket would allow her husband to relax and spend more time with the family. Reality sank in for her all too quickly: "On call twenty-four hours a day. Medically isolated when emergencies occur. You don't have a lot of backup. Here, he's sort of it."

But for Lepore, the unpredictability of Nantucket was part of the attraction. "I thought it would be an adventure. A situation where I was going to be pretty much on my own. It was, 'What the hell. Go thirty miles out to sea and see what you can do.'"

He had a chance his very first night, when a patient came in with complete heart block, needing a pacemaker, something Lepore had never put in before.

"What do I do?" he asked himself. "Oh, what the hell," he replied, since there was no one else to answer the question. He racked his brain for a few seconds before calling his friend Paul Thompson, a cardiologist, who talked Lepore through putting a line into a subclavian vein, one of two large veins that run from the ribs to the collarbone. Lepore got the pacemaker in. It was a watershed moment and a harbinger of what the next thirty years would have in store: Lepore felt "mildly totipotent after that night."

A few nights later he got another call. "Somebody had put a vegetable some place that vegetables don't usually go, and he wanted me to come and take it out." Lepore was hooked.

CHAPTER 3

CUT, SEW, AND TIE

Maybe it happened because Doug Kenward came home late and forgot the potatoes. Maybe it had more to do with how much his wife had to drink. Whatever the reason, the result on that Sunday afternoon was bloody. Kenward's wife stabbed him in the heart with a butcher knife—in front of their sixteen-year-old son.

Kenward's son struggled to get him out of the house. He tried to drive but didn't know how. He flagged down a truck, got neighbors to help hoist his father into the back, and sped Kenward to the hospital, unconscious and in shock.

There, Tim Lepore, on Nantucket barely a year, realized this was the most life-threatening case he had encountered. That's counting the gang shootings and car crack-ups whose victims had paraded like macabre mannequins onto his emergency room table in Rhode Island. Kenward was, in Lepore-speak, "making an honest attempt to die." Lepore aimed to make a liar out of him.

There was no time to transport Kenward off-island, no time to summon extra help. Kenward had a hole in his right ventricle. Fluid was building in the pericardium, the sac around the heart, making the pressure so high that the math was despairingly simple, Lepore knew: "No blood was going into the heart, so no blood was coming out. That's what kills people." Lepore had seconds to determine how to open the chest to repair the stab wound without further imperiling the heart. "The decision," as he put it, "was the incision."

Lepore cut into Kenward's chest and inserted spreaders to separate the ribs. He opened the pericardium, careful not to slice the vagus nerve, which stretches from brain to abdomen.

He found the hole in the ventricle and controlled the bleeding by sticking his finger in it. He asked nurses for special sutures for stitching up blood vessels, but the hospital had none. "Give me some black silk," he demanded instead, his knowledge of obscure medical facts kicking in. He knew that in the 1890s, black silk thread was used to fix a stab wound to the heart.

Lepore sewed the deep hole, then waited and watched. Kenward, forty-four and a Nantucket Electric Company worker, pulled through. Well enough that he became a swimmer; well enough that he became a marathon runner. A cousin who was a doctor later told him that the chance someone with that kind of stab wound would make it to the hospital alive was 10 percent. The chance of surviving an operation? 1 percent.

Kenward recalls that when he regained consciousness, he eyed the doctor at his bedside.

"Who are you?"

Lepore answered as if he were a gunfighter in a spaghetti western: "I run. I shoot. I fix people up."

Typical Lepore, on a not entirely atypical day. There may not be tons of stabbings on Nantucket ("stockbrokers don't usually go after lawyers," Lepore observes), but there are always people needing surgery.

Lepore doesn't have a surgical specialty, meaning that rather than having extensive experience in particular procedures, it's more like: "You name it, I've done it."

Lepore contends that the operating itself is not difficult. "Surgery—I don't want to demean it—but it really is cut, sew, and tie. In the OR, it's a controlled environment. It may look chaotic, but it isn't. The surgeon has things planned out. I like to say if you can eat in a public place without a bib, you can do surgery."

Many surgeons with perfectly adult table manners would disagree. Richard H. Koehler, a laparoscopic surgeon who comes over from Plymouth, Massachusetts, to cover for Lepore on the rare occasions he leaves Nantucket, says general surgery is "very, very, very tough. General surgery is by all measurements the worst on-call schedule you have to carry. The risk of the surgery you're doing is very high. The complications are life-threatening. Sometimes you're doing it in the middle of the night. You can't pass it off to somebody."

Still, to Lepore the issue is not whether he can handle the surgery, but whether the hospital can. It has one operating room and one person qualified to administer anesthesia at any given time (two nurse anesthetists from Cape Cod trade shifts), so if other cases arise, Lepore will anesthetize patients himself.

Even more significant, Lepore believes, is whether the hospital can provide adequate care after the patient has been cut open and stitched up. Postoperative care can be constrained in a hospital that now has just nineteen beds and no dedicated intensive care unit. And while Nantucket may encounter a wider range of cases than even some big-city hospitals—how many of them see patients with fishhooks in their eyes?—it may not see any one type of case as often as larger hospitals do.

"In medicine today, what really makes the difference is the critical care, postsurgical care, and we can't do a lot of that here," says Wayne Wilbur, one of the visiting nurse anesthetists. "We don't have the volume, and we don't have the equipment."

There is no dedicated recovery staff explicitly skilled in the kinds of things that can occur after surgical procedures.

"If we put a patient on a ventilator, we run out of people that are competent to deal with a ventilator fairly quickly," Lepore recognizes.

"Whoever happens to be there does the postanesthesia recovery," if they are certified in advanced cardiac lifesaving. "Most are, but some people just don't want to do it. It can be a little bit hairy."

Mary Murray, an obstetrician-gynecologist who spent eighteen months working on Nantucket, says the contrast with larger medical centers she has worked at can be stark. "Not that it is not a real hospital, but when something like this happens in Connecticut or New York, there's a team, they go in the OR, it's well planned, there's a board-certified anesthesiologist, and there's a postoperative nursing staff that's highly trained—all just waiting for something like this. That's what we do in hospitals that are a little more civilized."

Many postrecovery questions can arise, Lepore notes: "Are they warm enough, what's the urine output, what's the blood pressure, what's the pulse, the oxygen saturation? They have to be checked much more frequently. It can be a little bit more anxiety-provoking because it's not something the staff does every day. And if you're operating on someone with other confounding issues—diabetes, pneumonia—those factors come into play in the recovery of a patient. My concern is this: if I operate on a desperately ill patient and I don't have backup in recovery."

Another potential limitation is blood. Nantucket's hospital keeps only six units of blood in stock, an amount that could be used up for a single patient with, say, a fractured pelvis, a laceration of the cervix, or a ruptured spleen. If the supply is depleted, more must be flown in from the Red Cross in Boston. "If we run out in the morning, we could have more by the afternoon, but if we run out at night, you're not getting it. You have to husband it," Lepore knows.

The hospital's constraints constantly guide Lepore's decision making. "It's easy to operate on people; the hard thing is not to operate on people." If he thinks Nantucket is less than ideal, he will quickly move patients to hospitals in Boston or Cape Cod, rather than be "sitting here looking at my belly button—omphaloskepsis, I think it's called."

When Foley Vaughan, a Nantucket lawyer, fell to his knees and began vomiting, Lepore quickly discovered he had scar tissue blocking his colon. "Tim decided he couldn't wait," Vaughan recalls. "He cut me open, unkinked it."

But when Vaughan experienced the same problem ten years later, Lepore, evaluating the hospital's limitations and recognizing that surgery could wait a bit, flew Vaughan to Boston City Hospital in a twin-engine plane. In Boston, "they had a team of eight people doing the operation," Vaughan notes. "The country doctor did it his way, and the city doctors did it their way."

At first, Lepore had to rely on boats, often the Coast Guard, or on somebody's private plane to take patients off-island. But he worked to make arrangements with Boston MedFlight because its helicopters can make the Nantucket-to-Boston trip in less than an hour; travel by plane or ferry can take more than twice or three times as long. Also, helicopters can land just outside the hospital and are equipped with oxygen and other medical equipment.

"What I really respect about Tim is he knows what can and can't be done here," says Wilbur, the nurse anesthetist. "If he can't do it right, he's not going to do it. The real thing about saving lives here is knowing when to call that helicopter."

But sometimes the helicopter isn't flying. Fog, wind, rain, and snow can keep aircraft grounded. Then Nantucket becomes as isolated as it was before helicopters were invented. Often Lepore ends up playing chicken with the weather. One morning, he may have a patient he is confident he can operate on, but he can't be sure the patient won't develop complications that evening when a storm is scheduled to strike. "You can really get into trouble," says Koehler. "If he knows the weather is going to crap out that night, even though he could do the operation, he makes the better judgment of sending that patient off."

Although Lepore transfers many cases, the number of surgeries at Nantucket's hospital has been increasing, from 250 in 2006 to close to 400 a year. And when Lepore goes off-island, the hospital may need to bring in not only a surgeon to pinch hit, but an obstetrician too.

On days when the hospital has to fill Lepore's shoes "we all remember it," says Margot Hartmann, the hospital's chief executive officer. Those covering for him "are used to offering very different coverage than he provides. Patients are used to calling him at the drop of a hat, and people from other hospital systems may not be prepared for it."

Koehler, who practices in Plymouth, Massachusetts, and has covered for Lepore since about 2008, is not a stranger to small-town medicine, having spent about seven years doing surgery on the larger island of Martha's Vineyard. But when he fills in on Nantucket, he says, patients will come into the ER and ask, "Is Dr. Lepore here?" Told he is off-island, some will say: "Oh well, I'll check back when he comes back."

Koehler is not offended. He understands. Lepore is "like the one-man band walking down the street. If you did a cartoon of him, it would be like he's got the cymbals on the head, the syringe coming off him on one side, the stethoscope on the other side."

At least, Koehler says, so far when he has been on Nantucket, "nobody has come up to me in the supermarket and said, 'I'm rectal bleeding.'"

A few years after Lepore made a surgical splash saving Doug Kenward's life, he encountered a case that ended with the exact opposite outcome, mortifying and tormenting him for years.

One Saturday in February 1987, Michael Butler, forty, a shipyard mechanic and occasional fisherman, showed up in the emergency room. Butler reported that he had eaten some turkey and stuffing left out from the previous day and soon afterward felt stomach pain that kept worsening. Assuming food poisoning, doctors gave Butler ipecac to make him vomit, but his abdominal pain only became more severe.

The supervising physician was David Voorhees, who had been on Nantucket since the 1960s. Voorhees was not a trained surgeon, but he had handled many operations. Lepore was not supposed to work that weekend.

Butler, who was separated from his wife and daughter, told hospital staff he had been a heavy beer drinker for years but had recently started cutting back. He had broken his ankle several months earlier and had been unemployed since. Butler's brother, Chuck, recalled recently that Butler had also been beaten up several years before this hospitalization, suffering a head injury that "put him in a downward spiral," made him "emotionally unstable," and caused him to drink.

After rejecting the food poisoning idea, Voorhees indicated on the chart that Butler probably had pancreatitis—inflammation of the pancreas frequently associated with alcoholism. But he advised it would be good to "rule out appendicitis" and "rule out peptic ulcer perforation."

Butler began sweating profusely, his abdomen distended. He was fed intravenously all night, but by Sunday morning, his heart was racing, and he was bleeding internally. X-rays taken for the first time showed a hole in his gastrointestinal tract with "massive contamination." That, Lepore recalls, is when "I get a call that there's a forty-year-old guy in the ICU dying. I came in. His heart rate was 140. He had no blood pressure. He had a perforated ulcer and had sat there overnight."

Lepore acted immediately: "I called in an anesthesiologist. I called in Voorhees to come and help me. And I operated on the guy."

It was a tricky situation. "Because of the delay in diagnosis, the guy was in shock. He was a setup for multiple organ failure. If somebody had recognized it the day before . . . "

Still, Lepore thought he could handle it. "If I didn't do something, the guy would have been dead in an hour or two," so he decided sewing up the hole was worth the risk and "went ahead and fixed it."

He irrigated Butler's stomach to wash away contaminants. He found the rip—it was in the duodenum, a C-shaped tube in the small intestine that opens into the stomach. He plugged it by stringing down a piece of omentum, the fatty apron attached to the bottom edge of the stomach.

Butler's condition foiled Lepore's repeated attempts to insert a small stomach feeding tube, so he made a surgical hole in the stomach and inserted a larger tube. He sewed everything up and gave Butler cephalosporin, an antibiotic to ward against infection.

Butler began doing better. Then, late Monday afternoon, his breathing grew labored. He was given oxygen but soon became disoriented and feverish. His lungs grew wet and congested. His heart was beating too fast and then slowed to such dangerous levels that he suffered a heart attack.

Lepore was able to revive Butler and place him on a ventilator. But his white blood cell count plummeted, placing him at greater risk for infection. A chest X-ray suggested he had acute respiratory distress syndrome, meaning his lungs could not pump enough oxygen into his blood. He sank into a coma.

"I thought that we could control this in terms of multiple organ system failure, but I was wrong," Lepore recalls. "The problem was the pony was out of the barn. I don't think anybody could have put all the king's horses and king's men back together again."

On Tuesday, Butler, still comatose, was transferred to University Hospital in Boston. Several days later, he needed another abdominal operation because the site of his perforated ulcer was leaking, overwhelming his bloodstream with bacteria. He continued to deteriorate and was declared brain dead, and ten days after he entered Nantucket's emergency room, Butler's family decided to remove him from the ventilator.

Then Butler's widow, Carol, sued—at first only Voorhees, the physician that first day. But later, Lepore was added as a defendant. He was crushed and defiant.

"I did all the right things. I told the family I was concerned about this. I was out front with them. And I still got sued. If I had done nothing, I wouldn't have gotten sued because I wouldn't have had my hands on him."

The case alleged negligence and wrongful death. An expert witness for the plaintiffs, Dr. Albert Harary, wrote: "There were several departures from accepted medical practice, which contributed to the poor outcome and death of this patient."

He wrote that the X-ray was taken too late, a day after Butler came in, leading to an eighteen-hour delay in surgery and increased severity of Butler's infection. That was Voorhees's responsibility, but Harary also questioned decisions involving Lepore.

He said the antibiotic given to Butler, cephalosporin, was inadequate and probably worsened the infection. He said the staff acted too slowly to try to prevent Butler's heart attack when he exhibited respiratory failure and that they delayed checking Butler's arterial blood gas, which measures oxygen and carbon dioxide in the blood and might have indicated he needed to be on a ventilator sooner. And he said that if Butler had been put on a ventilator when CPR was begun, instead of twenty-five minutes later, he might have suffered less brain damage.

"Both Dr. David Voorhees and Dr. Timothy Lepore were involved in the deficiencies in care that resulted in the death of this patient. This patient's death was a direct result of unnecessary delay in diagnosis of the perforated ulcer, inadequate antibiotic therapy, and especially a failure to recognize and prevent the impending respiratory catastrophe despite ample warning signs. The medical care delivered to this patient was clearly below accepted standards and resulted in this patient's death."

Lepore was eager to defend himself in court but said the insurance company representing him, Voorhees, and the hospital wanted to settle. His part was settled for $100,000; the other defendants settled for more. Contacted in 2011, Carol Butler declined to discuss the case.

The lawsuit lasted three years and "was horrible for him," Lepore's wife, Cathy, recalls. He felt the settlement "was an admission of guilt. If it was a lapse of something, or if you were tired and made a mistake, that's one thing, but he would do the same thing again tomorrow."

Cathy herself felt responsible because she's answered the phone when the hospital called looking for Lepore. "If I had said, 'He's out running,' he would not have had any part of it. It wasn't his patient. And they did not call him before the patient was in really bad condition."

Lepore's son Nick remembers his father being "really depressed, kind of in a funk for months. At times he'd be angry about it. Doctors get sued all the time, but for him and for us, it was really a big moment. Nothing like that had ever happened."

In truth, in the world of medicine these days, it is almost extraordinary that Lepore, fielding such a diverse agglomeration of cases and emergency situations over three decades, has never faced another lawsuit. The only other time anything even resembling legal action came up, he says, was in Providence, where he was periodically contacted by a lawyer for a woman "until they realized that she was being guided by the Martians."

Koehler, who has been an expert witness in lawsuits against surgeons, says a single lawsuit in such a long tenure is "incredibly remarkable. The average general surgeon in this country is sued once every five years."

For years after the Butler suit, Lepore plagued himself with what ifs. "Once somebody puts that stake in that hole, even though they take the stake out, the hole's still there," Cathy notes. Lepore says he is not surprised doctors have committed suicide over such cases: "You beat yourself up. You go for a long time questioning yourself. Somebody goes into medicine trying to do good, and all of a sudden you get accused of this. You go to bed with it; you wake up in the morning with it. Did I do something wrong?"

Since Nantucket is such a small community, perhaps it was inevitable that, several years later, Lepore entered the emergency room to find that his next patient was Butler's brother, Chuck. He was a lobsterman who had collided with a piece of lobstering equipment and needed stitches in his head. "I don't try to avoid him or anything," Chuck Butler recalls. "I personally respected all the doctors here and thought they were doing the best they could in a little one-horse town, and I didn't think it was appropriate to sue. I never really blamed them for it."

But the case still haunts Lepore. After every procedure, even the simplest suturing, he revisits each step at home.

"Should I have put a stitch in there? Did I do that right? Could I have done this better?' You play these things over and over. I do, anyway."

In the mid-1990s, Lepore, as the hospital's medical director, had a decision to make. He was performing most of the surgeries, but Voorhees occasionally did some. Lepore liked Voorhees. While self-taught at surgery, he had what Lepore called "a great kinesthetic sense." He was eccentric too. His father was a musician who had conducted the "Bell Telephone Hour," and "David would walk around the halls humming the New World Symphony." Voorhees lived in a house that used to be a cow-birthing barn, and he installed operating lights over the dining room table.

Now, though, Voorhees had had several strokes, and Lepore was noticing that problems were cropping up, especially with obstetrical cases. Some Caesarean sections "went too long." Other births Voorhees presided over were risky enough to require surgery, but Voorhees delivered them vaginally. "It was obvious the skills had atrophied." Lepore fretted about what to do.

"That was hard for Tim," recalls Steve Tornovish, a police detective who is married to one of Cathy's sisters. "Tim had great respect for him."

Finally, Lepore confronted Voorhees. "Look, I think you should retire. Your skills have eroded, and you shouldn't be doing surgery."

Voorhees reluctantly accepted the verdict of the younger, newer doctor. Two years later, at sixty-five, Voorhees died of a stroke.

Lepore himself finds obstetrical cases to be some of the toughest. Not the surgery itself, usually an emergency Caesarean section, which he considers "a semimindless procedure you can do if you got opposable thumbs." But with a pregnancy, "you are dealing with two people," and "when it goes wrong in a C-section, it can go wrong very fast."

Koehler says it is almost "unheard of for a general surgeon" to do C-sections. "When I cover over there, I could do a C-section if I really, really needed to do one. But it's high-risk."

Lepore is much more comfortable if he knows the patient's health and pregnancy history, "if I have an understanding of the patient as a surgical candidate." Once, in fact, while running a half-marathon, he was tailed by a police car and stopped at mile 10 to come in and perform an emergency C-section on a patient he had been treating. He finished the race later.

But when Lepore is unfamiliar with a pregnant woman's health history, "it becomes more than cut, sew and tie." The case of Lee Ann Psaradelis was like that. In her third trimester of pregnancy, she arrived in the emergency room with massive internal bleeding. "All of a sudden, they lost the fetal heart," Lepore recalls. Despite an emergency C-section, the baby did not survive.

Psaradelis turned out to have a big tumor on her right adrenal gland, called a pheochromocytoma, which causes excess release of hormones that control heart rate and blood pressure. Psaradelis had not been Lepore's patient, and whichever doctor had been caring for her during her pregnancy had not spotted the tumor. "Going through the chart we could not find anything that would have told us it was there," Lepore recalls.

Now it was causing her to bleed so profusely that Lepore started seeking blood donors. Thirty people showed up to donate, but it was too late. "She just went downhill and died," Lepore remembers. "I can see it in my mind's eye right now."

He says he has also encountered many cases in which women needing emergency C-sections have not signed consent forms ahead of time. This disturbs him because he worries they may not be able to consider their choices in a calm and reasoned manner while in the throes of labor. "You cannot obtain informed consent on a patient who is non–English-speaking, has been medicated, and it's 3 o'clock in the morning. You tell me that that's informed consent, I'll say to you that that's bullshit."

For years, Lepore has felt "pushed into" performing such emergency Caesareans, "but that doesn't mean that I think it's right. Sometimes I'm tempted to sign my name on the chart with invisible ink." As a precaution, he will write in the patient's medical record that informed consent is needed, something that, he knows, "does not necessarily make the administrators happy" because it suggests the hospital did not follow procedures to the letter. He has also worked to persuade the hospital and family practitioners to discuss emergency Caesareans well in advance.

"I've had people tell me that the patients would be scared about it," he says. "Well, you know what? Every patient should be told about possibility of the C-section. They make great DVDs of these things in English, Spanish, and every other damn language. They should sign something ahead of time. The patient should meet the potential surgeon and understand about the procedure."

Lepore was thrilled in 2009, when he and the hospital's emergency room director recruited the island's first full-time obstetrician-gynecologist, Mary Murray, a summer visitor from Connecticut who was recently divorced with young children.

"I immediately liked him," Murray says about Lepore. "I did immediately feel like I've known him in a previous life. I could literally complete his sentences, and he could complete mine."

That Murray could perform emergency C-sections was especially important to Lepore.

"The guy had been out there for all these years handling emergencies," Murray explains. "He never trained to do a C-section. He taught himself to do it. He'd come flying in in the middle of the night to operate on a person he doesn't know, maybe a language he doesn't speak, with no backup."

Suddenly, he had someone to share obstetrical cases with. And Murray felt she "could have worked with him for twenty years. In times of stress the guy always has something in his back pocket. He's also very irreverent. You never know quite what's going to come out of his mouth."

But Murray grew frustrated with what she describes as a number of hurdles. She had trouble getting equipment and approval for procedures like minimally invasive hysterectomies. The reimbursement system and other policies made it hard for her to earn enough to live on the island, and she bridled under some restrictions set by the hospital's parent company.

Lepore tried hard to keep Murray on Nantucket, offering to invite her into his practice and even take out a home equity line on his house to help her out. But eighteen months after she arrived, Murray left and moved to Georgia. Now one of the island's newer family practitioners, Mimi Koehm, performs C-sections, but Lepore would love to have more help.

Bruce Chabner, a prominent physician at Massachusetts General Hospital in Boston, who is on the board of Nantucket's hospital, says everyone recognizes the island's need "for people that deliver babies," but "it's hard to find the right person, and people can make more money elsewhere."

So Lepore carries on, fielding obstetrical cases and their sometimes-dicey complications. One of the bloodiest was a D&C, dilation and curettage, on a woman who had just given birth. The procedure involves removing tissue and remaining fragments of placenta in the uterus, so the obstacles don't cause too much blood to be lost.

Before he could even start, "all of a sudden, we have audible bleeding—you can hear it bleed. That's exciting bleeding."

Wary of using too much of the hospital's blood supply, he transfused the woman with two units, cleaned out the uterus, packed it with absorbent material, administered medication, and "crossed my fingers and crossed my toes. It stuck. I have great respect for what can come out of the vagina: some wonderful kids, and lots of bleeding."

Richard Ray has seen a lot as director of Nantucket's health department, but even he was unprepared for what Lepore was proposing. Ray was hospitalized with pneumonia and an ear infection, and Lepore's approach was to puncture the ear drum to drain the fluid. Standard enough, but there was a catch: Lepore wanted to use a scalpel he had carved himself out of obsidian, a volcanic glass.

Lepore hit on the idea as an off-shoot of one of his many hobbies: flint knapping, the ancient art of carving stone tools. Why not make his own scalpel blades? he wondered. So what if the technique was 30,000 years old, from the Upper Paleolithic era.

He took a rock of obsidian like "a round piece of cheese, flat on the bottom, flat on the top. Now make the cheese into an octagon, with eight or maybe nine points on it. When you hit the top of one of the points, you knock off a sliver."

Using a stone, he dulled one end of a long sliver, making that part into a handle. The rest, about an inch and a half long, became a blade that he considers "as sharp or sharper than a steel scalpel. For cutting soft tissue, you can't beat it: amputating a leg, cutting at the knee joint, ligaments, tendons, muscle, fat, skin. The only drawback is obsidian blades are extremely brittle. If you try to cut against the bone, you may break it. But if it falls in, you can X-ray and see it," so the errant blade can be retrieved.

For a while, Lepore was so enamored of his obsidian creations that he tried to using them whenever he could, asking patients' permission. He did hernia operations and appendectomies. When a visiting photographer showing his work on the island developed a hernia, Lepore performed the obsidian operation for free. The photographer paid him with a photograph he had taken of a Nepalese shaman, which still hangs in Lepore's office, adding to the impression that Lepore has shamanistic powers of a sort. Or would like to.

Ray was wary about the obsidian ear drum puncture but agreed after setting some limits: "Tim wanted to just walk into my hospital room and apparently wanted me to bite down on a towel while he stuffed this thing in my ear. Our nurse anesthetist talked him into putting me under for a few minutes while he did this. Worked fine."

The obsidian era ended only when Lepore became unable to sterilize the scalpels. Obsidian cannot withstand typical high-heat steam sterilization, so Lepore sent the scalpels to Cape Cod Hospital, which would use ethylene oxide, a gas that kills microorganisms and bacteria. Unfortunately, ethylene oxide can also hurt people. Although invisible and pleasant smelling, it can be explosive, flammable, and carcinogenic. "I think it was teratogenic" (able to cause birth defects) "or something," Lepore says. "Or it killed wildebeests. I don't know—it was discontinued." And the obsidian operations had to be, too.

The enthusiasm Lepore shows for obsidian and other offbeat approaches can belie the care with which he makes medical decisions.

"When someone has that swagger and is not good, then it's empty, it's bluster," says Michelle Whelan, who runs Sustainable Nantucket, a nonprofit organization. "But when they have that excellence and integrity, you tolerate it."

In August 2011, a six-year-old boy broke his wrist, and an orthopedic surgeon visiting from New York was ready to operate. Lepore told the orthopedist he'd have to wait six hours because the boy had recently eaten, and anesthesia should be administered to a patient with an empty stomach.

The orthopedist got angry, threatening to complain to Hartmann, the CEO. But Lepore stood firm: "It's nice that he doesn't think it's unsafe. I think it's unsafe, and the anesthetist thinks it's unsafe, so it isn't going to happen. If I have a young child who gets into trouble because he ate too close to anesthesia, I don't have any backup. I'm stuck with that kid if he turns sour. So why not just try and arrange everything so it's as safe as possible?"

Hartmann says cases like this show that Lepore is "not a cowboy. You could miss that because he comes across like that. He likes to shock, and he has that kind of swashbuckling, outrageous quality to him. But inside there's really an excellent conservative clinician with very good judgment."

Still, Lepore loves a surgical challenge. Like the man with what looked like appendicitis, who neglected to mention that he had just eaten a club sandwich. Lepore discovered the man had swallowed a toothpick, which had perforated his small bowel. A toothpick-ectomy was the operation of choice. Another patient had a swollen, oozing sore that Lepore thought was "a big abscess around his anus." But "when I put my finger in to feel it, I could feel this fish bone. I had to cut it out."

Lepore's toughest surgery, from a technical standpoint, involved a woman in her sixties with diverticulitis, inflammation of pouches in the lining of the colon that can lead to serious infections, bleeding, or blockages. The woman needed to have the infected portion of the colon removed and two healthy colon sections sewn together in its place.

An imprecise surgeon might nick the tube that links the kidney to the bladder or cause the colon to dangerously leak stool into the abdomen. The patient was very overweight, making surgery riskier because excess fat can obscure what the surgeon can see while cutting. "This was not someone that I would have gone out of my way and operated on," Lepore recalls. But Diane Pearl, an internist, "pushed me into doing it."

Lepore first had to delicately remove part of the rectum. Wanting to be extra careful, he did it in the most technically difficult way, handsewing the connections between blood vessels and loops of intestine rather than using a stapler. Lepore wanted to remove the damaged piece of colon on one day and then sew the healthy pieces of colon together another day. But Pearl urged him to do a single operation. "You know, Tim," she said, correctly in this case, "Nantucketers are hard to kill."

Sometimes Lepore's patients are willing enablers, encouraging him to try something new, even when others are skeptical.

"Hey, Dr. Lepore, do you want to cut these off?" Mary Monagle called out to him one day in 2010. Monagle, then the charge nurse on the hospital's evening shift, was referring to loose flaps of skin under her arms that jiggled like Jell-O. The flaps were the result of gastric bypass surgery Monagle had undergone on the mainland to offload more than a hundred of her three-hundred-plus pounds.

When Monagle approached Lepore about removing the flaps, he was intrigued. Poking what he called her "bat wings," he sounded instantly confident. "I can do that."

"Really?" Monagle asked. The operation, a brachioplasty, is usually done by a plastic surgeon. Lepore had zero experience with it, and Monagle's friends were astounded: "Are you crazy? Are you really going to let him do it?"

"I trust him," Monagle replied simply. Lepore ordered a $400 copy of *Body Contouring After Massive Weight Loss* and set about studying. Monagle figured this could be interpreted in two very different ways: "Oh my God, you're going to let someone who needs a book do your surgery?" or "Wow. He bought a book."

"I want to do it right for you," Lepore told her.

The surgery took five hours, longer than usual because of Lepore's unfamiliarity with the procedure and trouble finding a vein in which to insert Monagle's IV. In first the left, then the right, Lepore made an incision that ran from Monagle's arm pit to her elbow. He pinned down the excess fatty skin with clamps, then cut it off. He removed a pound and a half of skin on each side, and Monagle imposed only one condition: that the excised skin not be "jerkied and given to Ajax," Lepore's red-tailed hawk.

Afterwards, Lepore was so proud of his handiwork that he had staff from all over the hospital come look. Monagle was overjoyed. "It's hard to find a surgeon that you trust. I love that man."

Still, about six months later, when Monagle decided to move to Florida and asked if Lepore would perform an abdominoplasty or tummy tuck to reduce her excess belly fat, he said no, at least not until Monagle lost some more weight. "Otherwise it won't look right," he told her. So Monagle left but planned to return for the procedure, rather than have another surgeon perform it. "I'll take a break from wherever I am and come back to have Dr. L do my abdominoplasty."

Lepore does not try everything. He usually declines, for example, to perform laparoscopic surgery, the less invasive form of operating in which a surgeon, guided by images projected from a scope onto a video screen, works through small incisions, using tools to manipulate the tissue. Laparoscopic surgery is becoming popular because it leaves less scarring and usually involves less recovery time. But it requires surgeons to use long-handled instruments instead of their hands and be good at judging how much pressure they are applying.

Lepore knows how to perform surgery laparoscopically—he took his first course in it in 1977—and he has the equipment. The problem is that he can't do it as regularly as he would like.

"Laparoscopic is fraught with problems. You have to be doing it again and again and again, and I don't have that number of cases. It's different enough that I don't think I could do it safely. Laparoscopic is sort of like putting your arm behind your back as you do it. The view on the scope can be very misleading. It's like working with chopsticks."

Lepore knows that not being able to offer laparoscopic puts him "at a disadvantage." But to feel confident, he would first want to assist on scores of laparoscopic surgeries performed by experts. And for that, he'd have to go off-island. He would feel guilty leaving Nantucket so frequently.

So when a fifteen-year-old girl came in with a perforated gastric ulcer, Lepore sent her for laparoscopic surgery at Children's Hospital Boston. "I could have done it here, but it would have been a big incision, and she would have had a six-inch scar. Now all she has is a little incision in her belly button."

Koehler, a laparoscopic surgeon to whom Lepore sometimes sends cases, says, "A regular surgeon would just say, 'Hey, you know what? You don't need a laparoscopic.' He's very, very honest and has very, very good judgment."

Lepore is acutely aware of the degree to which patients on the island must rely on his judgment. As he once told Hartmann: "You wake up in the middle of the night, and they're all around the bed, and you know who they are."

In fact, Lepore remembers not only his patients but their pathologies. It was nearly thirty years ago that he saved Doug Kenward from his stab wound to the heart, prompting what Detective Steve Tornovish says was an island-wide joke: "If you come home late, you damn well better have a bag of russets with you." (Kenward's wife received a suspended sentence in the case, Tornovish says.) But Lepore recalls much more than the joke; a veritable anatomical atlas of that case is indelibly imprinted on his brain.

And that turned out to be a lucky thing in March 2009, when Scott Bernard, a house painter, was found dead on Cato Lane.

Tornovish says police officers called to the scene couldn't tell how Bernard had been killed. "People thought he was hit by a car." But when "Tim and I were together looking at the body, Tim said, 'This is exactly what Kenward had.'"

That told police they had a murder on their hands, then only the second killing on Nantucket in a quarter-century. But who was the killer? Tornovish turned to Lepore again: How far would Bernard have been able to walk after being stabbed? "With that wound? Seventy-five yards," Lepore replied. "And he was aspirating blood the whole time."

The police returned to the spot on the shoulder of Cato Lane where the body was found. "We literally tracked the blood back about seventy-five yards, around a corner to a driveway, and right to the guy's front door." They arrested Thomas Ryan, another house painter, who pleaded guilty to the killing.

Another job had been added to Lepore's résumé: homicide detective. "He may be crazy all day long," Tornovish asserts. "But he is almost always right."

CHAPTER 4

Moby-Tick

Out of the corner of his eye, Lepore spots something: a faraway pickup truck, the driver wearing orange. Lepore's eyes light up behind his wire-rimmed glasses.

"A hunter—maybe he bagged a deer. Hey, I know that guy. It's Ronnie Conway. He works for the electric company. He's also a patient."

He whirls his boxy, green Honda Element into a U-turn and races down a looping island road toward Conway's house. He can't believe his good fortune. Inside Conway's garage, hanging upside down from triangular hooks: five slaughtered deer.

Lepore grins. "Can I?" Conway nods.

Lepore squats by one blood-dribbled head, placing his bare hands on the scruff of the neck almost tenderly, as if petting it. The deer were gutted in the field, so their rib cages splay open, and Conway has placed buckets under their mouths so blood doesn't splash all over. "After two or three days, we'll skin and quarter them," Conway enthuses, and a hunting buddy, son of the meat manager at Stop & Shop, will cut them into venison steaks.

Combing through the deer hide, Lepore hits pay dirt: a thick, round, black tick, then two, then three. He pinches them off with his fingers, beaming through his brush mustache.

Fishing in his pocket, he pulls out a glass vial with an orange top; he always keeps some handy. He pops in the squirming creatures, swollen from the deer's blood, and moves on to Conway's other carcasses. Soon Lepore's vials with their wriggling eight-legged captives will be winging their way to the mainland via Federal Express. There, they'll be sliced, diced, and tested for a rogues' gallery of diseases, diseases that have become all too familiar on Lepore's island.

"Not that it's going to get me the Nobel Prize," Lepore smirks. "I'm not going to meet the king of Sweden." But that's beside the point. This afternoon, Ronnie Conway's garage has become a beachhead in what, to Lepore, is a struggle of epic proportions: *Homo sapiens* versus *Ixodes scapularis*—man versus tick.

Like a certain fictional ship's captain obsessed with a great white whale, Lepore is out to conquer another of nature's leviathans: the wily tick. His style is somewhat different, of course. Lepore isn't the raging megalomaniac Captain Ahab was. He's more what you would expect if Ahab was played by Robin Williams. But make no mistake: Tim Lepore has a tick fixation.

Given the slightest provocation, or not, he will expound on the three main tick-borne diseases: Lyme disease and the less well known but potentially deadly babesiosis and anaplasmosis. Or one can read the squeamish details in Lepore's delightful color brochure: "The breeze blowing, the sun shining . . . the tick crawling up your leg . . . "

Lepore, who has been bitten but never infected, tracks Nantucket's tick cases with meticulous religiosity. He can list celebrities and demi-celebrities who've had tick diseases. And among his tick-themed paraphernalia are a cell-phone ring tone based on Brad Paisley's country song "Ticks" and a parody of the famous gray T-shirt from Martha's Vineyard's Black Dog tavern—Lepore's says "The Black Tick" and has a bug silhouette.

An acknowledged expert, he gets calls from doctors and researchers around the country. Some patients bring him deer they've killed so he can siphon off ticks in his own backyard.

"He has this obscene interest in it, and everybody gives him credit for that," says Jim Lentowski, who runs the Nantucket Conservation Foundation. But on Nantucket, Lepore is also controversial in his outspokenness about a highly charged topic: He believes the only way to prevent tick diseases is to kill more of the island's deer. "He really understands and is so passionate that he turns a lot of people off because they just think he's being a nut about it. He's a high-profile person on that point, and he wears a lot of people down."

On the same December day of the Ronnie Conway bonanza, Lepore is waging his tick crusade on other fronts too. It happens to be the Saturday of the Christmas Stroll, the biggest—well, pretty much the only—tourist event of the off-season, so most year-round Nantucketers are downtown reopening shops they had otherwise mothballed for the winter or helping run tourist activities.

Ferries from the mainland are filled to the gills with giddy landlubbers. On the island, they promenade in red hats and jingle bell necklaces, mink vests and Prada high-heeled boots (perhaps not optimal footgear for Nantucket's cobblestoned streets, but some folks are too well-heeled to care). As Victorian-costumed carolers sing, visitors tour gussied-up Georgian Revival mansions, imbibe generous goblets of eggnog, and fill their bags with trinkets like Christmas ornaments from the Cold Noses boutique, featuring a silhouette of any breed of dog personalized with your pet's name.

Lepore is having none of it. He has more important things to do: staking out the waste water treatment plant, for one.

The plant is drab and dank, its interior a mass of gigantic tanks and labyrinthine pipes, festooned with perky signs like "Anionic Polymer—Caution." But Lepore isn't there for the ambiance or the sewage. He is lying in wait for ticks.

During the weeklong deer-hunting season in November and December, the plant becomes a check-in station. Hunters haul in freshly killed deer and heave them onto a wooden scale, warped and reddened with years of deer blood. James Cardoza, a retired state wildlife biologist, records each deer's weight, sex, and age. Then Lepore swoops down and pores over the dead animal, scooping up blood-bloated ticks with his hands.

Hunters, usually eager to cart their deer home, can be taken aback by the bald, bespectacled man gleefully picking ticks off their conquests. But Lepore persists: "Jim lends me an aura of officialdom." Anything to get his hands on the island's prime promoter of ticks—in his view, a devil disguised as Bambi.

"The deer basically is the taxi cab for the ticks" is how Lentowski puts it. And on Nantucket, ticks have no trouble hailing a cab. Where are deer going to go, after all? They stay on-island and multiply, so that, state biologists say, there may be sixty white-tailed deer per square mile on Nantucket, the highest concentration in the state, where most counties have about ten to twenty per square mile.

Deer scamper through backyards and driveways, are spotted around Main Street and the hospital parking lot. The deer furnish adult ticks with a "blood meal," Dracula-style. The blood meal is critical to allowing ticks to reproduce. Filled with blood, a tiny tick can swell to the size of a grape and lay 2,000 eggs. "A deer could literally cause tick reproduction so that everybody would be up to their necks in ticks," says Sam Telford III, an associate professor of infectious disease at the Tufts School of Veterinary Medicine and the guy who receives Lepore's FedEx packages of neatly bottled arachnids.

Deer don't directly cause infections; baby ticks get those from feeding on mice carrying disease-causing bacteria or parasites. But deer give adult ticks the sustenance they need to have those babies, who grow up to bite and infect unsuspecting human. "A public health nightmare," Lepore contends.

That Saturday at the sewage plant, Cardoza tapes up charts showing the number of deer shot each day that week. He sits behind a desk placed incongruously among tanks and pipes, picking his teeth with a white pocket knife, munching potato chips, and nibbling from a bag of mini Oreos, the kind found in a kindergartner's lunch. Affixed to some equipment is a pencil drawing of a deer with a cartoon bubble: "I got ticks—want one?"

What with the Christmas Stroll, few deer, tick-toting or otherwise, are crossing the sewage plant threshold.

"There are not enough hunters," Cardoza laments. But then Sergeant Dean Belanger, a state environmental police officer, appears, carting a doe he'd found dead on the road. With deer so common here, "we have a lot of deer versus car," he explains. Lepore heads out to Belanger's truck for a look.

The doe has been dead several days. But Lepore runs his hand through the matted hide and smiles. "Yeah," he crows, popping his find into his orange-topped vial. "I got one."

"I'm dying," Laura Mueller kept repeating. "I'm just dying. I'm telling you that."

At seventy-one, Mueller, a summer resident and retired nurse, had barely made it to the hospital. She had excruciating chest pain spreading rapidly to her neck and shoulders, a gaping hole in her spleen, and bleeding in her belly. She could feel herself going into shock. Mueller had been struck by babesiosis, a malaria-like disease that can spike 105-degree fevers, destroy red blood cells, and cause facial paralysis, congestive heart failure, even death.

Lepore, one of the few doctors who know about babesiosis, knew that the spleen had to be removed immediately, before it filled up with too many damaged blood cells and burst. But he feared the hospital's blood supply was too limited to keep Mueller alive. And the hospital's only operating room was being used for other procedures.

Lepore called for a helicopter to take Mueller to Boston but discovered her vital signs were too unstable for her to fly. "We just have to operate right now because I don't think you'll make it otherwise."

He cleared the operating room. Moments before she passed out, Mueller summoned strength to reassure the worried-looking anesthetist: "Don't be nervous. Dr. Lepore's here."

Lepore stuck in his hand, scooped up the spleen, clamped the blood vessels. Mueller needed almost all the hospital's blood, five transfusions, and remained hospitalized for days that August, only able to return home to suburban Chicago in October. There she had to be rehospitalized, and complete recovery took ten months. But she lived.

Nantucket wasn't always swimming in ticks. If there were any, scientists say, they were in tiny pockets, in forests, surviving on small animals like rodents or rabbits. People probably never came in contact with them. Nor did deer because, for a very long time, Nantucket had no deer. Lepore says that judging from carbon dating of deer bones he has dug up at old dump sites, Nantucket may have been deer-less since 1000 CE.

Others think there were deer until the 1700s or early 1800s, when they were driven off by sheep that grazed forests into grassland, ruining deer habitat. That, and hunting by Indians, finished the deer off.

Whichever version is true, Nantucket had no deer at all for at least a century, until June 3, 1922. That day, the *Antonina*, a fishing sloop, spotted a white-tailed deer swimming—or trying to. The *Antonina* took pity, hoisted it aboard, and brought it to Nantucket. There, the deputy game warden, William H. Jones, released the deer among some pines outside town. Then he decided no self-respecting buck should have to go it alone.

"Warden Jones has suggested to the state department that a mate be sent down to keep it company," the Nantucket *Inquirer and Mirror* reported. Deer romance was apparently not the state's highest priority. It took four years, but on February 22, 1926, a huge crowd gathered on the docks, the biggest "since Clinton S. Folger brought his automobile to the island."

Two does had been imported all the way from Michigan, an arrangement "secured" by the deft negotiating skills of Breckinridge Long, a summer resident and diplomat who had helped Woodrow Wilson establish the League of Nations. Town approval was needed for this momentous step, but the "islanders took kindly to the proposition," and the selectmen voted to "formally accept the deer."

When they arrived, "there was a grand skirmish as the youngsters followed the deer along and watched the crates being lifted into Irvin Wyer's truck." Next morning, the release of the deer into the swamps drew enthusiastic onlookers, including "folks who passed their boyhood years ago, but were still boys, nevertheless." The buck "will probably deeply appreciate the companionship after his four years of loneliness," the newspaper wrote, wondering "how long it will be before he locates his new chums."

Not long, apparently. Some years later, the *Inquirer and Mirror* editorialized: "there is no telling how many deer there are here now" and "those who have occasionally caught a glimpse of one or more of the deer while out driving, have been elated and returned to town to tell their friends all about it." The editorial warned that "anyone who would dare molest or shoot one of the deer during the state's open season of two weeks in December would bring upon himself the condemnation of the entire community."

In 1932, "Old Buck, the original deer on Nantucket, met with an accident which cost him his life," hit by a car, the paper lamented. "Everybody will feel sorry, for he deserved to live to a good old age, that he might see his grandchildren, great-grandchildren, great-great-grandchildren, and a lot more grand progeny, thrive happily in the swamps and moors of Nantucket."

Nantucket was so enamored of its deer that an article described "the strange pastime known as 'deer hunting.' No, you don't take a gun with you . . . more like a sightseeing excursion at night," an "added attraction to all those couples who like to drive slowly along the 'lovers' lanes' to catch visions of the moon and all its attendant fancies and effects."

When in 1935, the state authorized a weeklong February hunt on Nantucket, the paper called it "a barbaric slaughter" with "bloodthirsty gunners from the mainland posing as 'sportsmen'" and locals "augmenting the gangs which came down from America."

It was "disgusting" to see cars "with deer carcasses lying across the engine hoods or on the running boards. . . . A car bearing Rhode Island number plates drove down into Pearl Street with four deer stretched across it and left the nauseating sight there all day and evening within the sight of passersby, many of them children, while the men 'tanked up' in a nearby emporium."

The outcry was so great that by the second day, Massachusetts's governor agreed to stop the hunt, marooning the gangs from America on the island for days until ferries could fetch them. Ten months later, the governor had to halt another hunting season when a man was killed by another hunter who had "leveled his gun and fired, thinking a deer was approaching—perhaps wishing to get in the first shot before his companions espied the supposed game."

Long before Old Buck came to Nantucket, George Hull's ancestors did. Seven or eight generations of Hulls have ironed their identities into the island. Hull's great-grandfather was fire chief, a great-uncle was a monsignor, and Alvin B. Hull held the sentinel post of Nantucket town crier.

To George Hull, that legacy bequeathed a certain perk: immunity to diseases carried by Nantucket's ticks. Never mind that Hull's wife, Diana, a nurse in Lepore's office, has seen every permutation of tick malady. Hull told Lepore: "My whole family comes from here—we're immune to it."

Three months after making this claim, Hull, an electrician, was digging trenches when he developed flu-like symptoms that mushroomed into "bad migraines and just continuous pain. By the twentieth day, I just couldn't handle it anymore."

"I swear you got a tick thing going on," his wife told him. It was babesiosis. Hull had shortness of breath, plummeting platelets, and fevers so high doctors packed ice around him.

Eventually he recovered, stunned that "anything like this could ever touch me. The last thing I remember before I lost consciousness was Tim laughing at me."

Not only is there no magical immunity, but babesiosis, while still uncommon, is spreading, "being seen in areas that it wasn't seen before," says Barbara Herwaldt, a medical epidemiologist at the Centers for Disease Control and Prevention. Up to 5 percent of patients die, with or without treatment, says Telford, the Tufts tick researcher.

Nantucket, more than any place else, has put babesiosis on the map. It began in 1969, when Nancy Gray, a fifty-nine-year-old widow from California, spent the summer in a Nantucket farmhouse on a property so heavily blanketed with trees it eventually became known as the Hidden Forest. Gray, healthy and outdoorsy, walked, cared for a neighbor's horse and donkey, and had a dachshund that brought home dead mice. She frequently checked the dog for ticks, and that May she found a tick on her own neck, plucking it off with difficulty.

Two months later, Gray was feverish, cringed from abdominal pain, and was listless and depressed. No Nantucket doctor could figure it out.

A neighbor, convinced she was dying, called a doctor he knew in New Brunswick, New Jersey—Benjamin Glasser, a colorectal surgeon who was flown to Nantucket on a private plane. Gray instructed him to let her die at home. But Glasser took her to St. Peter's Medical Center in New Brunswick, where a lab technician noticed similarities between Gray's anemic blood and that of malaria patients. The CDC got involved, and scientists peering through microscopes identified babesia parasites. Gray, given antimalaria drugs, gradually recovered.

But her case rocked the infectious disease world. Babesia parasites were thought to affect primarily animals: rodents, cattle, dogs, horses. Of the documented cases in people—a thirty-three-year-old tailor in Yugoslavia, an amateur photographer in California, a forty-seven-year-old fisherman in Ireland—all had previously had their spleens removed and therefore had problematic immune systems. The Nantucket case was the first time babesiosis was known to afflict a healthy person whose spleen was perfectly intact.

More cases cropped up on the island, to the point where the illness was christened "Nantucket fever."

One cold morning in 1973, a Harvard entomologist, Andrew Spielman, took the ferry to Nantucket with two research assistants: a Vietnam veteran whose jittery manner made Spielman think he had posttraumatic stress disorder and the veteran's girlfriend. They carried mouse traps and raccoon traps with peanut butter for bait, strapping the traps to bicycles and bumping over cobblestones until they reached a biological field station. They stayed over at the Siasconset home of Gustave Dammin, a friend of Spielman's and the chief pathologist at Boston's Brigham and Women's Hospital.

Spielman thought Nantucket fever probably originated with voles who were transmitting it through dog ticks. But the voles he trapped and tested had no babesia parasites. For kicks, he tested white-footed mice and found their blood flooded with parasites. They had hardly any dog ticks but were crawling with deer ticks.

Spielman scooped deer ticks off mice, infected them with blood from a babesiosis patient, and turned them loose on hamsters in his lab.

When the ticks bit the hamsters, the hamsters developed babesiosis, showing that deer ticks were the culprits behind Nantucket fever.

Spielman was summoned by Nantucket's board of selectmen, where the chairman, laying his great tattooed forearms on the table, grunted: "So, Doc, whadda we spray?" But there was no quick fix.

Spielman named the tick: *Ixodes dammini. Ixodes* is derived from the Greek word for sticky and is a genus of hard-bodied ticks. *Dammini* is derived from Spielman's host, Gustave Dammin. Dammin's wife, Anita June Coffin, was descended from a genus of hard-boiled Nantucketers: the Coffins, one of the island's oldest whaling families. The Coffin home took in paying guests, including dignitaries like Ernest Hemingway's mother, who painted on the moors. But to Gustave Dammin, the tick thing was the bees' knees. There was a tick naming ceremony. Dammin's wife embroidered a tick on her husband's Harvard tie. Once he thought he had babesiosis and was "very upset" when he didn't, recalls his son, Tristram Dammin, an emergency room physician in Boston.

The tick naming ignited controversy in entomology circles, however. Most experts ultimately decided it was the same species as *Ixodes scapularis*, so they have de-Dammini-ized it.

"Those young Turks at the CDC took the name away, the bastards," says Tristram Dammin. As consolation perhaps, "Andy Spielman sent me my own bottle of ticks," and his father became the namesake of a backyard antitick method: Damminix, tubes of insecticide-treated cotton balls that mice will use for nest-building, causing ticks that feed on mice to die.

Several years after the babesiosis discovery, researchers discovered that a mysterious arthritis-like disease in children in Lyme, Connecticut, was caused by the same tick. That illness became known as Lyme disease.

Then, in 1994, Genevieve Gordon, a longtime Nantucketer, started feeling funny. An energetic sixty-eight, she worked two jobs, selling tchotchkes at the John Rugge Antiques Shop and spices at Nantucket Gourmet. But, she remembers, she became disoriented, feverish, and nauseous and had "terrific diarrhea." Her grandson "found me semi-conscious" and rushed her to Lepore.

"I was sure she had babesia," Lepore recalls. But the hospital's lab "kept looking at the slide and could not find babesia." Finally, Patricia Snow, a longtime Nantucket lab technician, identified Gordon's illness as anaplasmosis, a tick-borne disease in the same family as Rocky Mountain Spotted Fever. (Initially, anaplasmosis was called ehrlichiosis, a term Lepore still uses in one of his tiny gleeful rebellions against medical convention.) Anaplasmosis had never been seen in this part of the country. And it was caused by the same deer tick that spreads Lyme disease and babesiosis.

Gordon recuperated after three months but found her dog, a French Bordeaux named Bijou, "dead in the bathroom" from anaplasmosis.

It turns out a single tick bite can cause one, two, or all three diseases. And some experts believe people on an island like Nantucket are more likely to be bitten by ticks carrying more than one disease. That could be because the sheer number of ticks increases odds that people will encounter ticks carrying multiple infections, or that the concentrated nature of the island ticks' food supply makes it easier for ticks to become co-infected.

There may also be more tick diseases than those three. In 1997, Telford discovered deer tick virus, which appears related to tick-borne encephalitis.

Telford says he and Lepore are constantly "fishing for new infections" caused by ticks. Lepore also sends Telford other insects to check for diseases. He catches greenhead flies near beaches, attracting them with the motion of a swinging rubber ball and then trapping them when they fly into a canvas cone.

At night, he sets traps for mosquitoes in Hidden Forest, an area so murky and impenetrable "you think a dinosaur is going to stick his head up." He fills a sack with sugar yeast and water to create carbon dioxide, which, circulated by a fan, entices the mosquitoes. At 5:30 AM, Lepore ventures back into the swamp, collects mosquitoes from the sacks, transfers them to plastic bags, and squirts in ether to euthanize them.

Then he deposits them in his home refrigerator. Cathy abhors finding his creatures in the kitchen, but a bag of mosquitoes draws relatively few complaints. "It doesn't have fur, doesn't have eyes," Lepore says. "Compared to the other stuff—a squirrel looking at you, a bag of dead mice—mosquitoes are pretty good."

Telford tests Lepore's greenhead flies for tularemia, a potentially fatal disease that causes skin ulcers, pneumonia, and breathing problems. Mosquitoes are checked for eastern equine encephalitis, which killed a horse on Nantucket in the 1970s and has caused outbreaks on the mainland.

Plus, there's always the possibility of discovering something new, "if Tim comes up with a mysterious disease," Telford says. "The study of tick-borne diseases has benefited greatly from the active mind of Tim Lepore."

Nantucket has been one of the top three counties for Lyme disease since 1992, according to the CDC. "Their risk is obviously among the highest," says Dr. Paul Mead, a CDC medical epidemiologist. Between 2002 and 2006, the latest county data available, Nantucket averaged an incidence rate of 357 cases per 100,000, which probably understates the actual number of cases because it only includes people diagnosed with lab tests, not clinically. Also not counted are short-term vacationers and people who get infected on Nantucket but don't discover it until they've left.

Anaplasmosis affects about fifteen to twenty people on-island each year. Babesiosis is increasing, with sixty-nine cases in 2008, nearly triple the count a few years earlier. "Nantucket is far and away the babesiosis capital of the world," asserts Telford. Fortunately, "Tim is by far the world's expert on diagnosing and treating babesiosis. He is Mr. Babesiosis."

Some of the increase might relate to better reporting, because Lepore doggedly logs any case he finds, but another reason probably lies in Nantucket's ecology. Explains Telford: "On the mainland, you have lots of other things, like fox and raccoon, that could take the ticks away. On Nantucket, ticks are stuck with deer. Biodiversity is less on the island, so the intensity of disease transmission is higher."

He thinks "there might actually be some microevolution on Nantucket that's produced a parasite that's a little more likely to cause disease." And people have "created an environment that lets deer and ticks thrive."

Lentowski, whose conservation foundation protects a third of the island's land, notes that more people are visiting Nantucket for longer stretches, coming in spring and staying until fall, allowing more time to be vulnerable to ticks. Houses are being built closer to deer and tick habitat.

"It used to be to get Lyme disease, you had to be going blueberry picking or out in the moors hiking, and not that many people did that," says Richard Ray, the health department director. Now, "deer are moving into our properties because we've taken away their feeding area."

The new houses make it harder for hunters, who can't legally hunt in residential areas, to get to places to shoot deer. And, says Rob Deblinger, a Massachusetts Division of Fisheries and Wildlife official, houses are being landscaped with "expensive ornamental plantings, rhododendron, arborvitae, all excellent deer food. People put down nitrogen in the form of fertilizer, and that's like ice cream to white-tailed deer."

Diagnosing tick diseases can be tricky. People don't always feel tick bites. Tristram Dammin says a tick secretes a kind of anesthetic when it alights, and then affixes itself stealthily with a cement-like substance and the barbs of its feeding tube. And not every tick bite resembles the classic bulls-eye.

Symptoms may not be obvious, either. Initial Lyme blood tests may be negative because it takes weeks for antibodies to develop. Anaplasmosis and babesiosis are easier to diagnose from blood tests, but doctors often don't think to test for them because the symptoms—fever, muscle aches, fatigue—are common to many conditions. And while tick diseases are treatable, they can linger for months or years, sometimes causing permanent joint damage or recurring fatigue.

Doreen Goodwin spent a year trying to determine what she had. Two Lyme disease tests came up negative. A third was positive, and the hospital gave her antibiotics, but she didn't improve. One day in the shower, soap kept getting in her eye, and she realized she could no longer close her lid. As she brushed her teeth, her mouth "wasn't working right." In the mirror, she saw that "only one half of my face smiled."

She consulted Lepore, who determined she had a double tick infection, Lyme plus babesiosis, and the illness had given her Bell's palsy. It could last, he told her, "three weeks, three months, three years."

Goodwin, then forty-three, endured an hour of intravenous treatment daily. She could only sleep at night by putting a cotton ball on her eyelid to keep it shut.

"I didn't say much anymore when I saw people. You can't really deal with people when you're self-conscious of your fallen face. My husband took me out for lunch to the Sea Grille, and the salad kept falling into my lap, so I burst into tears."

When function finally returned to her face twenty-three days later, she promised herself: "I'll never not smile at people again."

Michael Miller, a longtime martial arts instructor on Nantucket, thought a spider was biting his right thigh, killed the bug, and didn't give it a second thought. Then he landed in the emergency room with such severe internal bleeding that he used up half the hospital's blood supply before being told, by doctors other than Lepore: "Mr. Miller, you're too sick for Nantucket." He was airlifted to Boston, where doctors quarantined him, thinking the strapping Tae Kwan Do expert had malaria or tuberculosis.

Then Miller asked about tick diseases, and the Boston doctors instantly knew whom to call: a doctor on Nantucket they referred to as

Leh-Poor. "They were saying they had read some of these journals and he's very famous for his work on Lyme disease. They spoke of him as if here were a god."

They returned Miller to Nantucket, where Lepore determined he had one of the worst combinations of Lyme and babesiosis he'd seen and treated him back to health.

The mere fear of tick diseases stresses Nantucket's health system. In a recent year, about 2,500 hospital visits concerned suspected tick cases. Only about 10 percent were actually tick-borne diseases, but the hospital's resources were stretched by having to screen every patient.

So recognizing a false alarm has become Lepore's expertise too. One patient, a medical malpractice executive, was convinced he had Lyme. When Lepore, finding microscopic traces of blood in the man's urine, suggested a CAT scan, the patient protested that he'd had one nine months earlier that showed nothing. But Lepore persisted and discovered the man had a kidney tumor. He'd caught it early enough for the man to be cured.

"I knew it wasn't Lyme disease," Lepore proclaimed.

Tim Lepore was cranking out bumper stickers. They were festooned with pictures of his bloated, blood-sucking, spindly-legged nemeses and sported slogans: "Save Our Ticks!" "Honk If You Love Ticks," "(Nan)Tick(et) Advocacy Association." They bore the name of a group Lepore had just formed: The Committee to Protect Nantucket's Deer Ticks.

It was Lepore's last-ditch effort to inject some irony into an island-wide brouhaha over ticks and deer to try to persuade Nantucketers to see things his way.

The uproar had started more than a year earlier, in 2004, when Lepore, Ray, the health department director, and others proposed adding extra days for deer hunting on Nantucket. They argued that more deer had to be killed for tick diseases to decrease. Deblinger, of the Massachusetts Division of Fisheries and Wildlife, agreed. At the request of Nantucket's selectmen, he convened a public meeting and said other methods of deer control, like darts that inject deer with contraceptives or feeding stations that apply insecticide to deer as they eat, are ineffective or too expensive, so hunting was best.

Deblinger felt the only problem was "attracting hunters to Nantucket. It's not your typical trip for deer hunting purposes, where somebody jumps in a camper. It's a $200-plus ferry ride, and then you have to rent a place, and most everything's closed in the winter."

Deblinger proposed a twelve-day deer-hunting season in February, "a time when we're not competing with any other state," so hunters would find it "so tempting that it would override the expense." February is also when bucks have no antlers, so hunters, normally drawn to deer with impressive antler racks, would be as likely to shoot does, and killing breeding does is more effective for controlling deer reproduction.

But Nantucket has many hunting opponents. In fact, after complaints during the Thanksgiving hunting season about blood-stained cobblestones and cars with dead deer on Main Street, deer carcasses had to be covered to spare shoppers and visitors the sight.

The selectmen compromised with a six-day hunt and, Deblinger recalls, picked a week in "the dead of winter when the fewest number of residents of Nantucket would actually be on the island."

Leading up to the 2005 hunt, things seemed fine. More than nine hundred permits were sold, most to out-of-towners, often from places as far away as California and Texas. "All the guys who had gotten their new guns for Christmas said, 'Hey, let's go to Nantucket,'" Lentowski remembers. Restaurants and inns were enjoying a weeklong resuscitation at a time when much of Nantucket is shuttered for the off-season.

Then, trouble started. First, the week before the hunt, this island that rarely sees blizzards experienced a series of punishing snowstorms.

Two-foot accumulations made it impossible for hunters to drive to moors and forests, the normal deer-hunting locations. Recalls Telford, "All these SUVs were parked everywhere. All these guys in orange were trespassing all over the place."

Many hunters, new to Nantucket, had no idea where to go. Some asked how to avoid getting lost, and Belanger replied, "You can always follow your own blood" from the scratches the thick brush would cause.

Hunters popped up everywhere they shouldn't be. "People were going bananas thinking they were going to shoot," Lentowski recalls. "All these Rambo-type guys wandering the island with their shotguns."

An SUV was struck by a twelve-gauge shotgun. A preschool closed for the day because hunters were too close by. Three people were arrested for poaching on private property and shooting deer illegally. There were even complaints from people annoyed that their dogs had rolled in deer guts.

Some 246 deer were killed, more than double the state's expectation. State officials had counted on 100 deer being killed that week, which would have required just five to seven more years of February hunts to reduce the deer population to a safe size. But "the hunt was so successful that the new prediction was that we'd reach the goal in three to four years," Deblinger notes. The state "expected the people of Nantucket would be grateful so many hunters came to the island to help them solve their problem."

Not quite. People were furious, like 1935 all over again. At a packed Board of Selectmen meeting eleven days later, one resident, Annye Camara, called the hunt "extremely terrifying," saying she "moved here from a large metropolitan area, largely because I thought I would not be dodging bullets."

Even some local hunters, like Tony Barone, protested, claiming the out-of-towners' bad behavior gave hometown hunters "a black eye. . . . We can argue the tick thing until our heads fall off, but the majority of people don't want the hunt."

Some opponents objected because some deer were pregnant in February. Deblinger dismissed that, saying "the mating season for deer is in September and October, so if they're shot in the November archery season or the December shot gun season, they're just as pregnant as in February. That's just an animal rights, rhetoric emotional issue, something that's fun to bring up at a public hearing."

If deer are pregnant, Lepore said, "Who cares? The idea is to thin the herd. You shoot a doe and it could be a two-fer or a three-fer. These people are pro-choice for humans but pro-life for deer."

Residents formed the February Group, signing petitions, making phone calls, writing letters to newspapers. One letter, from Ursula Austin, asked, "Have we considered the litigation this town will face when someone is shot or wounded through inept hunting?"

Even Doreen Goodwin, who had gotten so ill from tick diseases, said, "I don't like it when they're making me sick, but you look at that little Bambi face."

Families were divided. Tristram Dammin, son of the namesake of the *Ixodes dammini* tick, has a second cousin with the accidentally literary name of Warren Pease. Some of the Peases, who live on Tuckernuck, a tiny island in Nantucket County, would feed the deer, Dammin says. "And then Warren Pease, he would shoot them." Dammin himself is in the middle: "I wouldn't shoot them, but I would eat them."

In November 2005, at the selectmen's request, the Division of Fisheries and Wildlife's board members returned to Nantucket for a raucous public hearing. That's when Lepore launched his sarcastic pro-tick campaign. He argued that deer hunting was so clearly the best antitick disease method that to consider scrapping the extra hunt is "like putting whether or not you get operated on for appendicitis up for a vote."

He had his backers, but ultimately the Fisheries and Wildlife board decided it had to cancel future February hunts. "Usually you bring the objective scientific observers, the boys from Harvard and people like

Lepore, and you win the day," Deblinger notes. "But something really happened over the February hunt. It wasn't just animal rights activists. People really saw it as though there were nine hundred people from off-island slaughtering their deer."

The scientists had lost, and they were completely befuddled. "It shocks me that people in that socioeconomic class will tolerate the public health problem that they have," said Deblinger, noting that the number of complaints was small compared with the number of people getting tick diseases each year. "If I could afford a house on Nantucket, I would not want to deal with not being able to walk around my property because of the fear of being bitten by a tick and contracting a very serious disease. My God, I have no idea how they tolerate that."

George Darey, chairman of the division's board, went even further: "I just feel sorry for the people who come to Nantucket and don't know it has the highest rate of Lyme disease in the country. You won't see me go there for vacation."

More than three years after the February hunt, in the summer of 2009, Nantucket's tick predicament had reached fever pitch. The previous year had seen 411 laboratory-confirmed cases of tick diseases, up from 257 in 2007.

In a survey of property owners in the island's Tom Nevers section, 61 percent said one or more people in their households have had Lyme disease. An average of 2.3 people per household, including guests and renters, had had one of the three tick diseases.

People were anxious, especially summer residents, who flocked to a select board meeting. Tom Foley, a technology executive and twenty-year summer resident, was there. He had babesiosis that summer, which dangerously ruptured his spleen. Emergency room staff immediately called Lepore, whom Foley had never met. "You could tell right off the bat he was brilliant," recalls Foley, who says doctors on the mainland later told him, "if I had walked into any other hospital, no one would have known what was wrong."

"Tim," Foley asked, "am I going to die?"

"No," Lepore assured him. "You're going to be okay."

Lepore insisted that Foley be flown to a Boston hospital so he could be watched round the clock. But the fog was so thick that the helicopter had to turn around. Eventually Foley was airlifted by jet. "Tim sat with me the whole time. And everything he said turned out to happen. I kept telling people in Boston, 'Tim says this.' I am one of few people that got to keep their spleen."

Foley told the selectmen his story. "People are going to die from this. People don't want to talk about it—they're worried it will hurt property values—but something has to be done."

The selectmen appointed a special tick committee to hold hearings and make recommendations. "We recognize that it's a big problem here," said Michael Kopko, then the board chairman, whose wife and daughter have had tick illnesses. "Those of us who live here all know someone or are related to someone or have ourselves had a tick-borne disease."

The committee met for months, hearing experts on all sides. Some members downplayed the problem. Elizabeth Trillos, a businesswoman, noted that a friend had babesiosis but said, "people understand it's a part of life of being in Nantucket."

Another member, Beverly McLaughlin, said her husband contracted Lyme and babesiosis but "didn't check himself" for ticks after being outdoors. "You know, men aren't too bright." As for Nantucket's hundreds of cases, "you know what? That's not an epidemic."

Most committee members disagreed. Noting that Nantucket has more cases of tick disease than HIV, Bruce Hopper, a doctor, declared, "This is a public health problem."

Committee members looked at trimming brush to attract fewer deer to backyards, but considered that insufficient. They evaluated spraying pesticides, but cited too many unknown health risks. They considered the "personal responsibility" approach, asking people to avoid woods and long grasses and keep skin covered with pants tucked into their socks. Dammin, a committee member, scoffed: "They all look like nitwits. Who's going to do that in the summertime?"

They discussed four-poster deer feeders, structures that entice deer with corn and spray them with insecticide. But Malcolm MacNab, a doctor and the committee chairman, said feeders would be too expensive, hundreds of thousands of dollars a year. Injecting deer with contraceptives was considered costly and impractical.

At talk of expanded hunting, McLaughlin protested: "I really love the deer, and I can't help it: My mother took me to see *Bambi*." Hunters, like Kevin Madden, a committee member, objected too, wanting deer to be plentiful enough for them to easily kill and eat. "Let them live until I need them," Madden said. "I don't want to see all the deer wiped out because some people get Lyme's disease."

Lepore, considered too dogmatic to be a committee member, suggested acidly at one meeting that the island consider "introducing a chronic wasting disease" to afflict deer so they "drop dead right on your lawn." When he testified, though, he reined himself in: "These diseases, while not necessarily the four horsemen of the apocalypse, have caused near-fatalities. This is more than just a nuisance."

The committee's final report said people needed to be educated about protecting themselves from ticks, but that more hunting had to be part of the solution. Voters, in a nonbinding resolution, approved hunting and other "deer reduction" methods by two to one. The selectmen agreed gradually to increase hunting to bring deer down to under twenty per square mile. But so far, no changes have been implemented. "Everything was put on hold," Dammin says.

"Everyone wants to get rid of the disease, but no one wants to cut down our hedges, no one wants the four-poster, no one wants to kill the deer," MacNab says. "There is no magic bullet."

So, with the bullets he has, Lepore does his part.

When a friend inquired about a place to hunt, Lepore had a tip. "The most awesome spot: the town dump." He said deer are attracted to pruned leaves and grass clippings that people discard and can't detect encroaching hunters because the dump has too many competing smells.

"I have a blind there," Lepore pointed out. "On top of the first refrigerator on the right."

CHAPTER 5

IN THE BLOOD

One frigid day, a teenage Tim Lepore was engrossed in a scrappy game of pond hockey on a lake in his hometown of Marlborough, Massachusetts. Glancing up between goals, he spotted a woman making her way toward the pond, her unsteady gait more than offset by her air of determination. Tim quickly lowered his hockey stick and skated to the pond's edge.

Tim's mother had come to fetch him because his father needed him. More precisely, Tim's father needed his son's blood.

John James Lepore was a general practitioner and a well-respected surgeon at Marlborough Hospital. To many, he was a heroic figure, the first doctor in Marlborough to enter the Army Medical Corps in World War II, returning home to become a medical mainstay of this industrial city's growing community.

On this day, John Lepore was conscripting his son as a blood donor. Tim's blood is O positive, the most common blood type, which meant that many of Marlborough's ill or injured could benefit from what flowed from his veins. And every couple of months, Tim's father would send Tim's mother out to haul him into the hospital so he could give one patient or another better odds of staying alive. "He knew where I was, and it was quick and easy," Tim recalls.

Tim would also accompany his father to the hospital every New Year's Day, where he would see trauma cases streaming into the emergency room, observe as X-rays were taken and developed by hand, and look over his father's shoulder as he performed surgery in the OR— stopping only when his father took a break for coconut cream pie.

"He could do anything," it seemed to Tim. "He could fix the damn elevator. Literally, he would work on the elevator in the hospital, and then he'd fix some tools in the OR, and then he'd operate. He was very technically and mechanically talented, and he had very fast hands. He had a great curiosity."

John Lepore loomed so large in the world Tim inhabited that the son would invariably compare himself to the father. "I have a curiosity, but sometimes I end up with a couple of screws left over," Tim thought. "He was much better than me."

It wasn't only his father's skill and reputation that made Tim feel that way. In some ways, from the moment he was born, Tim would be unable to measure up to an ideal—the angelic image of an older brother Tim would never be able to know.

The first child of John and Edna Lepore was born on the last day of 1941, a few weeks after Pearl Harbor and a couple of months before John Lepore went off to war. Captain Lepore was thirty-one, older than most soldiers, but his battlefield accomplishments quickly drew notice: He was named surgeon in chief of a field hospital in Ireland and then landed at Algiers during Operation Torch, part of the first American contingent in North Africa.

He received a commendation from the British and American armies, noting "he has apparently inexhaustible energy, has worked many long hours, has displayed very high surgical skill, has overcome difficulties which presented themselves, and altogether has shown himself to be an officer of exceptional ability." Other commendations followed, including one praising his work "under adverse conditions with lack of sufficient surgical equipment and medical supplies in such a manner as to gain the confidence and admiration of every patient and member of his command." The commendation quoted soldiers saying: "As long as officers like Captain Lepore are to be our surgeons, we don't mind taking chances of being wounded in front line duty."

Captain Lepore took chances too. He scavenged wire from the Germans to provide electricity to tents where battlefield surgery was performed. He removed a fan motor from a car to fashion it into a suction pump, which he used to pump the stomachs of soldiers with abdominal wounds.

Lepore wrote to his wife saying how much he missed baby Johnny. But in one of her letters back, when Johnny was two, Edna Lepore told her husband that their son had a bad case of measles (it would be about twenty years before the introduction of the measles vaccine). Johnny developed postmeasles encephalitis, swelling of the brain tissue as it tries to fight off an invader—it can cause brain bleeding and severe brain damage. Even today about half of all measles encephalitis cases result in death.

With fluid building up in Johnny's brain, destroying tissue and causing seizures, he was sent to Children's Hospital Boston, where Edna Lepore was allowed to visit him only once a week.

At first, John Lepore, nearing the end of his tour in North Africa, wrote his wife assuring her that "Johnny was fine," according to their daughter Cheryl, nicknamed Sherry, who was thirteen months younger than Tim. "He was assuming that my mother might be exaggerating a little bit, overly worried about her firstborn."

As things got worse, though, Lepore headed for home before his tour ended, finagling passage on a series of boats and planes. But the decorated war surgeon could do nothing to save his own son, a child he had not seen since the boy was two months old. Johnny died in February 1944.

Ten months later, Timothy James Anthony Lepore was born. When Tim was growing up in the house on Main Street, the catastrophic loss of the Lepores' firstborn child was barely mentioned. There were no mementoes of Johnny in the house, and Tim never even saw a picture of him until after his mother's death decades later. But each year, his parents visited and decorated Johnny's grave. And "the day my mother died, she was talking about it."

During Tim's childhood, the devastation of his brother's death was forever in the shadows, lurking.

"At Passover you set a place at the table for the prophet—it was sort of like that," recalls Tim, who was raised Roman Catholic. "It would come up occasionally as the great unspoken. It would come up—like a summer storm—come up and go away. My father and mother were very closed-mouthed about it. It was always there, sort of like the place setting."

Tim says he wasn't particularly conscious of being compared with his brother or of carrying the weight of having to make good. But he was aware of the idealized impression that parents carry with them of a child lost so young. "When you die at two years, two months, you're always at the top of your game. They don't want to borrow the car. They haven't screwed up in school or knocked somebody out. A two-year-old is all promise."

Bob DiBuono, Tim's closest childhood friend, who happened to have the same birthday as Johnny, says that Tim would mention Johnny, sometimes wistfully. Bob, who had an older brother, recalls that "when Tim and I would get into a fight, we used to punch each other, and when we were duking it out, Tim would say, 'Oh I wish I had an older brother like Johnny. I wish Johnny was still alive. He would beat the crap out of you.'"

And, Bob says, Tim intuitively saw the maddening irony and frustrating limitations of becoming skilled in medicine: "when your father is a doctor and he couldn't do anything about it."

The insidious power of disease colored Tim's early life in another way—this time involving his mother, Edna Lepore. Tim's first memory of his mother is of visiting her in a medical facility, a sanitarium where she spent a year when Tim was about four, causing her to miss a chunk of his early childhood.

She had severe tuberculosis, which Tim now believes she may have become vulnerable to during the postpartum depression she suffered after the births of Tim and Sherry. Because of the tuberculosis, she had one lung removed, plus the lobe of the other lung.

She would likely have died if the antibiotic streptomycin had not been discovered and made available just before she got sick. "But she was always a little deaf from it," Tim says. She was also given an infinitely refillable prescription for another drug, Isoniazid, which kills bacteria but can be toxic to the liver in large or long-term doses, especially in women. "Now, they only let you take it for six months to a year," Tim notes. "She refilled that prescription for thirty years."

While Edna Lepore was hospitalized, her husband played her wire recordings he made of Tim and Sherry talking. He played the children recordings of their mother speaking too. That was the only way they knew her for what seemed like a long time. "She was just this voice," Sherry recalls.

Then one day, a woman walked into the house and asked, "Do you know who I am?" Sherry didn't know. Tim did, though. "You're my mother."

The mother Tim knew was a shadow of the woman she had been before her illness. Pioneering and outspoken, Edna Maria Granitsas was the daughter of a man from the mountains of Greece and a woman from Sweden. The couple came to America after Granitsas's mother's father was trampled by horses. They joined a tide of Greek, Italian, and Irish immigrants who settled in Marlborough, about twenty-five miles west of Boston, a shoemaking stronghold that stayed that way long after other factory towns wilted. Marlborough, often accidentally or deliberately misspelled without the "ugh," was the hometown of Horatio Alger Jr.; perhaps Alger's up-by-the-bootstraps ethos influenced Granitsas.

She was a trailblazer early on: graduating from high school at sixteen, the youngest in her class at Boston University, racking up a master's degree before she turned twenty-one. Then, while studying for a doctorate at Radcliffe in 1935, she decided to run for school committee, the first woman ever to seek political office in Marlborough.

"Do Voters Like Blondes?" asked a headline in the *Boston Evening American*, accompanied by big photos of Granitsas in coy poses, with her dogs "Tina and Cookie and the puppies" and at the Pine Grove Inn, a roadside restaurant and dance hall her parents ran. "Five foot two eyes of blue; But, oh, what those five feet could do!"

The article about Granitsas, written by a woman, noted that "there was a young man named Peter who was constantly consulted during the interview. Naturally curious about a possible romance, I asked about it. 'Romance!,' she said, shrugging her shoulders. 'I haven't time for any.'" Asked if a woman could be as effective a school committee member as a man, Granitsas replied: "Better."

When Granitsas won, becoming the youngest woman on any school committee in the state, the *Boston Post* called her "blonde, pretty and not a grind," a woman who did not believe "Latin and solid geometry should be choked down the throats of children." She stated that "teachers should be quite as exciting to their pupils as movie actresses," and "if a child wants to yell out in class, the teacher should not throttle the child. Let the child yell until it decides not to yell."

Granitsas made her own voice heard, pledging to eradicate Communist sympathizers from the schools and pushing to require teachers to take an oath of loyalty to the Constitution. Perhaps conscious of her foreign-sounding name, she asserted: "I am 100 percent American."

And in 1938, she led the charge to remove two statues from Marlborough's high school, a copy of the Venus de Milo and a statue of Apollo, because their nakedness made them too scandalous and "indecent" and might inappropriately affect the morals of students. The removal of the statues, which had perched in front of the school's assembly hall for nearly fifty years and were nicknamed Venie and Pol, was ridiculed in newspapers and editorial cartoons.

"With the lady having no arms, it was hardly hand-in-hand, but Venus and Apollo were driven in disgrace from the old homestead," one paper wrote. "Venus and the boyfriend have suddenly become sinister threats in Marlboro High school life. . . . Venus wears the more clothing, being about 50 per cent draped, but Apollo is clad in the L street bathhouse mode."

A Boston minister came to the rescue, offering by telegram to "provide shelter and decent exposure for the ostracized Apollo and Venus" in his Congregational church. "Original Apollo statue is in the Vatican in Rome. If it is decent enough for the Vatican, it is decent enough for our young people to see and admire. . . . And as your Venus is a copy of the Venus de Milo in the Louvre, it will give me joy to present her grace and beauty to people who believe, and hope, that the human body is one of God's fairest creations."

Granitsas's blunt opinions and verve would be echoed in her son, Tim, who decades later became an unceremoniously candid member of the Nantucket school committee. Tim would also inherit Granitsas's political independence and inability to be pigeonholed; despite some staunch conservative stances, Granitsas was quoted in the papers supporting birth control, following the death of a close friend from a back-alley abortion. "It was rather scandalous at the time," Sherry notes.

In 1940, in what one paper called "a wedding of much interest," Granitsas married John Lepore. They had met in high school and dated over the objections of her father, who wanted her to marry someone Greek. If Granitsas's father hadn't died while she was still single, "he would have shot my father with a Smith and Wesson .44," Tim says.

Lepore's parents were Italian immigrants from the Adriatic village of Corfinio, where the soil was so poor that Tim described them as "rock farmers." Lepore, a surname derived from the Italian word for rabbits, was a nickname for a fleet-footed person. John was one of thirteen children who survived infancy. ("I think they had two or three Patricks and gave up on that name when they died," Sherry says.)

As a child, John Lepore loved tinkering and "almost blew his brother up" when he was playing around with blasting caps, said Tim, who would inherit his father's interest in mechanical things. And a defining moment for John Lepore occurred at sixteen, when he and some friends fell through the ice at a reservoir. Lepore managed to swim ashore and summon help, so that most of the boys could be rescued, but one, a police officer's son, drowned.

Broad-shouldered and quick, Lepore became a star Marlborough High School fullback and played semipro football in Marlborough during the summers. Helped by football and scholarships, he became the only one of his siblings to attend college; in just three years he took enough courses to qualify for medical school.

"I think my mother said he had to make something of himself," Tim said. "My mother wasn't going to marry a sluggo."

Lepore was hardly a slacker. He would spend mornings in surgery and see patients at his home office in the afternoons and evenings. In the summer, when the family rented a cottage on Cape Cod, Lepore would commute to Marlborough, a hundred miles away. Patients of limited means could pay in lasagna. Priests, rabbis, and other community leaders were treated for free.

The Lepores weren't rich, but they were comfortable enough to afford a small boat and a new Buick every couple of years. John Lepore once ordered an Alaskan dog sled, which he attached to his car to tow his children through snowy streets. They were financially generous to friends and family, sending nieces, nephews, and friends' children to college or medical school. "They helped people," Tim recalls.

To Bob DiBuono, Tim's best friend, John Lepore "could do no wrong. In my eyes, at the time, he was kind of like John Wayne." Bob considered his own father, who sold dairy equipment, was a Marlborough city councilman, and was a violinist who learned to play saxophone in a big band, to be a "dud" by comparison.

Bob experienced John Lepore's skill firsthand. Once, during one of Bob and Tim's regular frog hunting excursions, when the boys were about eleven, Bob was holding a frog the boys had shot with a bow and arrow. He was trying to saw off the back legs with a knife so the boys could bring the legs home to Bob's mother, who would cook them. "I cut the frog and my thumb at the same time."

His thumb dangling, he was rushed to the hospital, where, while "stinky, muddy water was pouring out of my boots," John Lepore stitched the thumb back on. A year later, Bob was making a knife, using another knife to pin the handle down so he could attach it to a blade. The knife slipped and tore through the back of his hand. "It was pouring blood." John Lepore came to the rescue, closing the five-inch gash on Bob's right hand.

"I have not seen another man like him," Sherry asserts. "He could sing; he could recite poetry; he was in plays; he could build a car; he did all the architectural renderings of the house we lived in; he did all the electricity. He made all of my dresses when I got married. If Timothy feels a little inadequate, it could be because they don't make people like my dad."

It could also be because John Lepore, despite being good with children in general, sometimes kept his own son at a distance. He had a huge collection of electric motors, scooped up from neighbors' junk piles, that he used to build an extraordinary American Flyer train set, rigged to run on three levels, with lights and a drawbridge. It was so impressive that it was displayed at a Shopper's World store, but so intricate that "I couldn't play with it much," Tim remembers. "My father could be a little bit cold except about electric motors. When he died he still had a wall full of electric motors that he had salvaged."

Tim found his father unsentimental about other things. For instance, "he destroyed all of his letters to my mother" that he had written during World War II. The only letter he saved was telling too: it was "pretty syrupy talking about baby John and how much he missed him." Tim was also "locked out" of his father's workshop, a paradise of salvaged metal and junk that John Lepore protected with a door with chicken wire strung over the top. Tim would "figure out ways to break into it. I used to sneak over the chicken wire, but I was always too noisy, and he could hear me."

Tim's father wouldn't run up and catch him, though. He would wait until dinner, where "my father sat at the head and I sat next to him. If I had screwed up, that was when the hand would be coming down. He'd put his finger underneath my collarbone and pull me down on the floor. It wasn't horribly painful, but it was an attention getter. It was 'This is my house, these are my rules, you do not know anything, and if I want your opinion, I'll ask for it.'"

Once, "he was giving me a shot of penicillin for something, and I can remember telling him I didn't want this injection. I got a slap in the ass, and then I got the shot. Sitting and telling my father I didn't want to do something he wanted me to do—not a good idea."

Lepore was gentler with his daughter, but he could apply his medical expertise with a kind of no-pain-no-gain approach. Sherry recalls that he "used to bring me to visit every sick person he could, saying, 'I want you to get whatever it is they have—chicken pox, mumps, measles—because someday you'll be pregnant and I want you to be exposed so things don't happen to the fetus.' And I got infected with all of it." Tim said his father's experience in World War II made him more conservative, even dogmatic about some things as time went on. "Back in the early '50s, around Korea, I can remember him suggesting that perhaps bombing them all is not a bad idea. He would talk about it at the kitchen table. My mother did not agree with him. My opinions were generally not solicited."

With only part of a lung left, Edna Lepore could not work. For a while, she stayed close to bed, and her husband built a sunroom onto the house so she could rest on the first floor.

Her mother became the children's main caregiver, coming from California "reluctantly because my mother needed her," Sherry says. "She and my mother were at odds an awful lot about us."

When Edna Lepore had more energy, she took her children to a little stream in the next town; they named it Lepore Brook. "We'd build dams, walk on rocks, look at fossils, dirt," Sherry recalls. "My mother had the spirit of being an outdoorsman. She lived vicariously through us. She couldn't participate in it much, but she made sure that we did."

She also used to pile them in the car, along with Bob DiBuono, who remembers her driving long distances and saying things like, "Let's go to New York." Bob protested: "Oh gee, Mrs. Lepore, I have to be home by 5:30." She was joking, but it hadn't seemed like it at first. Sherry says her mother was "the only one I ever knew that crossed her legs when she drove. I have no idea how she drove like that, but she did. She would say, 'Let's go down this road and that road and see what we can find.'"

Tim believes the rides may have had another motivation. His mother was convinced that his father was having an affair with his nurse. She said she got that notion because Tim, when he was about ten, had told her so, although Tim doesn't recall it that way.

"I perhaps said something innocently, that I had somehow walked in on them in flagrante delicto. I don't have a clear memory of that. But I remember being in the car with my mother when she went after my father's nurse."

With Tim in tow, his mother summoned the gumption and stubborn pride that had fueled her precocious educational and political achievements, and beamed them toward the nurse. She chased down the nurse in her car and screamed at her. "My mother was pissed off out of her head. I remember just shrinking under the dashboard."

Sherry remembers that her mother was "always tracking down" the nurse and "would talk to me about it and get me involved. My father always denied it, but my mother would have me check, and I would find evidence of them being together, spot them together." The nurse "would give us presents for Christmas, and I was in charge of returning them to her."

When she wasn't driving to find the nurse, she drove the children on trips, "lots of places, to get away," Tim recalls. "My mother had been desperately ill and between losing my brother and the TB, there were a lot of screwy dynamics going on. I think that was a very rough period for them."

Watching his mother, Tim absorbed the notion that fragility and resilience could intersect, that strength could be undermined and then rebuilt—useful observations for someone about to enter a lifesaving profession.

His mother was also someone who supported some of Tim's eccentricities and harebrained schemes, like the time in elementary school when he created his own newspaper. He would run around the neighborhood and ask people questions on the street: "What do you think about peace negotiations in Korea? Should we bomb them all to smithereens?" To print his articles, he'd use ink on a kind of paper made of gelatin and "try and sell them for a nickel. I wrote all the stories. It didn't go over well. I irritated the neighbors." He kept it up for about six months, until he ran out of ink.

Edna Lepore could draw the line, however. "She did not necessarily approve when I went out camping and I had three knives in my belt."

She also did not approve when one day Tim came home from fifth grade and said the word "fuck." Concluding that her son was not working hard enough and had gotten all he could from public school, she sent him to the private Fay School. It was a shock. The public school had been near Tim's house, and "I was sort of the cock of the walk," having read every book in the library and aced his classes.

At Fay, Tim instantly felt "at the bottom of the heap, and struggling: a square peg in a round hole. All of these guys knew each other and came from a somewhat more advantaged background. You're in your pimply early adolescence, and you're the sort of dumb one in the class."

Tim mouthed off in school and had to write a couple hundred times on the blackboard: "I must endeavor to remember that silence is golden." Homework included writing a "damn paper" every weekend, which his mother forced him to do. And every week, the headmaster announced each student's grades to the whole school. "If you didn't do well, he would speak to you directly in front of everybody. I remember sitting there and having him say 'Tim Lepore got a 3.0. You got to work harder on this.'"

In seventh grade, Tim was scheduled to compete in a public-speaking contest at school about the Civil War battle between the *Monitor* and the *Merrimack* warships, but he went out hiking and lost track of time: "I was late. I forgot my notes. My parents were pissed. I felt like I had let my dad down, and that is a much worse punishment than any they could give me. I had put work into it, I wanted to do a good job, and I screwed it up. That type of stuff I would do routinely."

After three years at Fay, Tim did not go to prep school like most of his classmates but stayed home and attended a Catholic high school. There he did better, played football, and joined the science quiz team that beat the pants off neighboring schools: "I can still remember the question I blew on the quiz team: the correct term for fish eggs. I answered too fast. 'Roe' was the correct answer. I said 'milt,'" a term for sperm. "It haunts me."

When it came time to apply to college, Tim figured he would go to St. Anselm like his father and many classmates. "To keep my mother quiet," he also applied to Harvard. Although he had good SAT scores, he never expected to be accepted.

"It was just for giggles," Bob DiBuono says. "His mother went to Radcliffe. I remember Tim saying his mother helped him with the essay." Tim got in. But after his first semester, Harvard started having second thoughts.

He had crashed in Advanced Introductory German, getting 115 wrong out of 130 questions on the exam. ("When I walked into class the first day and the bastards were all speaking German, it should have dawned on me," says Tim, who had never taken the language before.) In his freshman humanities course, "I didn't say one thing."

Biochemistry didn't go well either. And in freshman creative writing, when asked to write about how wonderful a Le Corbusier building was, Tim "didn't see any particular utility. I can't come up with this artsy-fartsy type of bullshit. I finally wrote this parody of James Fenimore Cooper, and the grad student liked it. That put me over the pass-fail line."

After a semester of getting Cs, Ds, and an E, he got a letter from the dean saying that Harvard was essentially putting him on probation and would reevaluate him at the end of the year. "I was in deep water. I was in with all of these people who were extremely bright and seemed to be much more accomplished and polished than I was. I knew I was dancing on the edge."

Thankfully, his second semester classes included anatomy and classical biology, for which Lepore found he had "a photographic memory. Plus I had every *Scientific American* reprint. So, the second half of the year, I hauled it out and ended up with Cs."

Still, Tim could get in his own way. In anthropology, he started with an advantage because of his encyclopedic childhood-learned knowledge of Native Americans, arrowheads, and fossils. "If only I hadn't slept through the first hour and a half of a three-hour final. I knew all the answers, just couldn't write them down fast enough."

Somehow, Tim pressed on at Harvard. "It took me awhile to figure things out, and it was scary. I had to figure out that I am not going to do literary commentary, that as an architectural critic I lack things. *Portrait of the Artist as a Young Man* or *Ulysses* escaped me. I prefer things to be straightforward: Jack went up the hill, not Jack has this crisis of confidence that's wrapped up in some Freudian mystery."

He did get As in public speaking and a class dealing with fairy tales. He realized he had strengths. "If you turn me loose in arcane subjects like myths, I kill. If you turn me loose in immunology and embryology, I can kick ass."

And he learned a lesson he would take to Nantucket in spades: "I could outwork anybody. I did not screw around."

Tim was also beginning to understand that if he were to succeed, especially as a doctor, he could not expect to slip blithely into his father's impressive shoes. Things did not come as easily to him in school, and they wouldn't come as easily in medicine.

One day in particular seemed to underscore that. During his residency at Tufts medical school, Tim was performing a cardiac operation, replacing a woman's heart valve. The patient, by pure coincidence, had had her gall bladder removed years earlier by John Lepore. Her heart condition was shaky, but when she saw the name on Tim's lab coat, she relaxed. Tim even looked remarkably like his father, the same curly brown hair, the same solid build.

"There's another Dr. Lepore taking care of me," the woman sighed with relief. "Everything's going to be all right."

But everything was not all right. Hearts are more serious than gall bladders. After the surgery, she was so fragile she had to be moved to intensive care while still on the operating table to avoid being shifted from one bed to another. In the ICU, she opened her eyes, appeared to look directly at Tim, and had a heart attack. Soon afterward, she died. Tim had lost his father's patient.

"I'm a tepid copy," he thought.

But things are not always as they seem. Several years later, when Tim was working at the hospital in Rhode Island, his friend Bob DiBuono bumped into John Lepore at the Marlborough dump.

"Hey, have you seen Tim lately?" John Lepore asked.

"No, geez, Doc, I haven't," Bob replied. Then the father spoke words he had never managed to say directly to his son.

"To tell you the truth, Bob," John Lepore murmured, "I think he's a better surgeon than I'll ever be."

CHAPTER 6

MUTINY ON THE
BOUNDARIES

"Uh, I just got your name from the phone book," the caller said. "It's about my son—he's eight. . . . "

It was way past midnight, and Lepore had been fast asleep. "My son, he's got a tick, and it's someplace I'm not comfortable examining," said the voice. "I don't know ticks from what-have-you. It's underneath, on his upper thigh, in the, uh, bathing suit area."

The doctor sprung awake. "Is it a black tick? When did you notice it? You don't want to grab it with your hands. Pull it out with tweezers." Sensing the caller's hesitation, he got ready to jump in his car. "What's your address?"

"Uh, I'm not really sure. I'm just here for the weekend," said the voice, mentioning some places tourists would frequent. "I think it's near Sanford Farms. I have a map here from Young's Bicycle Shop."

But as Lepore tried to figure out where to go, the voice shifted gears. "Oh, he pulled it off. Oh, that was chocolate. I'm sorry—he had a Hershey's kiss in his pocket."

The caller hung up—and dissolved in laughter. Score one for the Dr. Lepore Game. Lepore's say-no-to-almost-no-one accessibility is so well known that it inspired a teenage prank.

"The game was to see if he picked up the phone, how long you could keep him on the phone, or could you get him to offer to come out and check on you," recalls Sean Kehoe, who played the Lepore game in high school. "Those phone calls were priceless. It was 3 o'clock in the morning, and he was ready to drive out to Madaket to take care of an imaginary eight-year-old." Sometimes Lepore would smell a rat and hang up. "But," says Kehoe, now in his late twenties and a New Yorker who returns to Nantucket often, "he wouldn't lose his cool."

Health professionals who've worked with Lepore consider his approach highly unusual and sometimes maddening. "He can't say no," says Martina Richards, a nurse who worked for Lepore until moving to London. "But it's hard to complain about that because he also won't say no to you. That's why we'd all stay around, because as much as he might drive us nuts, he's the first person there if you need anything."

Lepore visits patients to save them the hassle of coming to the office or if he thinks they'd be more at ease at home. He also allows—even encourages—patients to visit his home. Rhoda Weinman, his former running partner, says that while they ran, people driving by would yell out the car window, "'I need a new prescription,' or 'I need this or that,' and he'd always say, 'Stop by the house.'"

When Pam Michelsen, who lived on Nantucket for twenty years, separated her shoulder playing softball, her friend advised, "You could go to the emergency room, or you could go to Tim's." The choice was easy. Michelsen notes, "I can't tell you the number of people who walked up on his porch. Rather than go to the emergency room, you go to Tim's. It takes you half the time and it doesn't cost you anything."

It doesn't cost anything because Lepore frequently provides care for free or allows patients to pay him in kind, whatever kind. Indeed, on an island flush with the financially fortunate, Lepore is the great leveler. A South African immigrant in need of an appendectomy had no money or insurance. "You work at a good cookie place; every week bring me a couple of cookies," was Lepore's solution. "What's more important—you have some good oatmeal raisin cookies, or you have money you have to share with the government?"

He told a patient who was a runner that he'd cut her bill in half if she ran a marathon. She did. Scores of other patients have standing treatment-in-trade deals. "In the real world, if I need more Ritalin, I have to go to a doctor, make an appointment, sit in a waiting room," says Chris Fraker, Lepore's neighbor and a builder. "I go next door, tell Tim I need a prescription, and he writes it on the kitchen table." In return, "the other day Tim's putting new mirrors on his Land Rover, but it's not working for him, so I get some tools and help them lay right. He fixes us, and I fix all of his stuff."

Paul Johnson had a .44 Magnum that "kicked like a mule" and wondered, "What can I do with this gun on Nantucket? I'll give it to Tim and trade it for medical work." That was payment enough, even when Lepore painstakingly removed a scalpel blade that an off-island orthopedist who'd operated on Johnson had accidentally left inside Johnson's knee. "It was an unsaid thing. I never got a bill." And one day, he dropped by Lepore's house, and "there's Tim and his six-year-old son, Nick, shooting that .44 Magnum."

At the other end of the spectrum Lepore gets gifts from wealthy patients who have already paid their bills. One "captain of industry" gave him a gas grill for removing his daughter's appendix. Champagne would arrive from Jane Engelhard, the wife of Charles W. Engelhard Jr., the gold mining magnate considered the inspiration for Goldfinger, the arch-nemesis of James Bond.

But when a landscape worker with a hernia offered to do yard work at Lepore's house, the doctor gently turned him down, saying: "I don't want to get the grass too nice."

Lepore's approach to money can exasperate his staff. "Someone would come into the ER in the middle of the night, and they would call him in, and he wouldn't bill for it half the time," Richards says.

Weinman, a lawyer, was astounded to learn how much work Lepore was doing without a contract with the hospital entitling him to get paid. She finally negotiated a contract, but even then, "I kept saying, 'You should get more money for this.' Money is so nonimportant to him."

Lepore believes "getting paid is like getting whipped cream. I can worry about the lady with the spleen or the guy with the hernia, or I can worry about money." His one financial concern is "if people are not going to pay me, tell me up front. It's the two bucks spent billing you that kills me."

Lepore often tries to honor patients' unusual or unorthodox requests. One patient's grandson wanted to be a fighter pilot but had a spontaneous pneumothorax, a collapsed lung, which would disqualify him— needlessly in Lepore's opinion. "We 'lost' his X-rays," Lepore says. "He's doing very well as a fighter pilot now."

Another family wanted Lepore to remove the brain of a relative who died of Parkinson's disease so they could donate the brain to research. "I did it down at the funeral parlor. They didn't have any power tools, so I used a wing saw. I kept the brain in a strawberry container, tied up by the blood vessels."

Lepore often launches on escapades like this "at the last minute," says Katie Pickman, one of his nurses. "Sometimes he doesn't tell us— he just disappears."

But occasionally Lepore figures the best thing he can do for a patient is look the other way.

Romelee Howard, a retired physician, was ninety-eight, and his condition was deteriorating. His wife, Eileen, a former nurse, was caring for him at home and says that one day she put him in the shower and left the bathroom briefly because she forgot his pajamas. When she returned, Howard "had turned the hot water on because he was a little confused, and he burned his feet."

Then Howard cut his hip, caused, his wife believes, because he "had a way of falling or crawling out of his bed." Lepore and his geriatric nurse practitioner, Laura Kohtio-Graves, wanted Howard to have a hospital bed at home, to receive more mental and physical stimulation, and to have his wound treated with vacuum assisted closure therapy using a device called a wound VAC.

Lepore struggled with what to do. "We were going to call protective services. I didn't think she would be able to handle this. I would never have believed that those wounds would heal."

But first, Lepore visited Eileen Howard. She'd respected him ever since her mother fell on their deck twenty years ago, and Lepore drove over in a pickup truck, took her mother to the hospital, and operated on her hip then and there. Now they discussed her husband, and Lepore became convinced that Eileen Howard was, in her own way, providing care. He decided not to force anything on her. He was "so patient with us, so tolerant of our being older, doing this, doing that."

Howard lived past his hundredth birthday, dying peacefully in November 2011. "I had a lot of great ideas, but she got the wound healed in spite of me," Lepore reflects. "Sometimes it's better to stand back and watch."

Senator John Kerry, Democrat of Massachusetts, was in Nantucket's emergency room. It was the fall of 2003, and Kerry, then a candidate for president of the United States, had had his flesh impaled by a blood-hungry predator: he had a tick bite. He called Lepore, who interrupted a Sunday football game he was watching at home. The senator, who has had a house on Nantucket's Brant Point for decades, was very concerned.

"He was starting to run for president, and he was telling me that he couldn't afford to get sick." It was too early to know if the bite would cause Lyme disease. But Lepore advised Kerry to take a two-pill dose of vibramycin, an antibiotic, to snuff out any potential Lyme infection. "Out here, I think you really have to be aggressive. The other option would be to do a full course of treatment" with other antibiotics for thirty days, but if, as a result, "he gets diarrhea, that's probably not a good idea, because then he gets really sick."

Kerry seemed hesitant. So Lepore baited him, mentioning one of his opponents, who happened to be a physician. "We can ask Howard Dean for a second opinion," Lepore suggested innocently. Kerry "did not think it was that funny."

Years later, Kerry vaguely recalls Lepore's wisecrack. "He did say something like that." But it didn't stop him from consulting Lepore about a subsequent case of Lyme disease and following his advice then to switch antibiotics. (Lepore told the senator the drug he had been prescribed can cause sun sensitivity, which might frustrate Kerry, an avid sailer and windsurfer.) And when Kerry came to Nantucket to recover from hip replacement surgery in 2009, he listed Lepore as his doctor "in case I keeled over and was unconscious."

Lepore has "treated any number of members of our family," Kerry says. "He's the only person who's treated me on the island. Whether it was feeling sick, or a muscle, or a tick bite. There are not a lot of doctors who readily make themselves as available to everybody—it doesn't matter who, what, how. He's the real glue to the community. He's the go-to guy."

Lepore is far from starry-eyed about these kinds of relationships. In fact, he considers his outspoken libertarian leanings to be the antithesis of much of what Kerry and most Democratic politicians stand for. He isn't shy about enunciating his own politics, sometimes landing him, colorfully or controversially, in the newspaper. But when political opponents become his patients, he keeps his views to himself. "Politically I'm not on their wavelength," but "it's not relevant usually to what I'm seeing people for. The last thing they want if they got a broken toe is some nitwit carrying on about the Democrats."

"Nitwit" is not the word Kerry uses. He calls Lepore "a character," a more neutral, senatorial term. And anyway, Kerry says, when he is on Lepore's exam table, "we never talk about anything politically."

Same thing when Chris Matthews, the MSNBC television anchor who once worked for Democrats, came to Lepore with pneumonia in 2008. Matthews says Lepore was "very generous in coming into the office off-hours to treat me. As I recall, we had a great conversation about all kinds of things."

But not a word was said about Lepore's appreciation of Sarah Palin or his preference for the punditry of Rush Limbaugh. "No reason to poke a skunk," Lepore jokes. "I'm not going to convince him and he's not going to convince me."

Of course, says Richards, his former nurse, political tiptoeing can work both ways. "You might need to seek out Tim even though you didn't vote for him for school committee."

Rhoda Weinman considers herself "a staunch Democrat. I'm anti-gun all the way, and he's such a big gun proponent and believes in the NRA and all that. Politically, we couldn't be more opposite. We fight about it all the time. We'd have screaming matches on the Milestone Road while running, and I'd say, 'We're going to run the next ten miles, and I don't want to hear a word from you.'" And yet, "people are like: 'He's your best friend?' Yeah, he is."

One particularly devoted patient belongs to one of the most prominent Democratic families: Edmund Reggie, father-in-law of the late Senator Edward M. Kennedy. Judge Reggie, as he is usually called because he was a city judge in Louisiana, has been active in Democratic politics ever since he marshaled crucial support for John F. Kennedy for president in 1960. In 1992, Reggie's daughter Victoria married Ted Kennedy.

"You go to Dr. Lepore," Reggie was told about a decade ago by a Boston urologist treating him recurrent bladder tumors. Reggie, who with his wife, Doris, lives half the year in a charming, airy house in Nantucket's Shimmo section, had no idea how significant the relationship would become. First, whenever Reggie had tumors scraped off in Boston, he visited Lepore, who administered catheters of bacillus Calmette-Guerin, BCG, an inactivated tuberculosis bacterium that triggers the immune system to battle tumors. Lepore used the occasions to "talk to him about Huey Long."

Then, when a New Orleans doctor perforated Doris's intestine during a colonoscopy and sewed the tear with heavy sutures, she, in extreme pain, "immediately went to see Tim." Lepore removed the sutures, joking that they were of such a heavy gauge they "could have landed a fish."

Next, Edmund came in with chest pains, "trying to have a heart attack," as Lepore put it. Lepore wanted to get him to Massachusetts General Hospital but was told no beds were available. "If I want something, that's not an answer I want. Whatever I have to do to get the answer I want, I'll do."

"Do you know who he is?" he prodded the hospital. Then he informed Ted Kennedy's office, and eventually, "mirabile dictu, they found a bed."

Remarks Doris: "Once you're his patient, you're his patient forever."

But, says Edmund, "the big enchilada was what he did for me on my crucial night." It was July 2009, and the Reggies had been entertaining friends, including Louis Susman, the Democratic fundraiser who was the new ambassador to the United Kingdom. That night, Reggie recalls, he felt "extreme back pain. I got up in the night, and my legs were weak, shaking. A little while later, around 3:30 AM, I fell, and I couldn't get up."

"Well, let's call Tim," Doris said.

"No, it's the middle of the night," Edmund replied.

"We waited on the floor because I didn't want to wake him up," he recalls. "The man works so hard. He had given us his cell, and I didn't want to use it."

They finally called Lepore at 6 AM, who, without even seeing Reggie, ordered a jet ambulance to ferry him to Boston from Nantucket's hospital. While awaiting the jet, Lepore ran a CAT scan and blood tests. The hospital's visiting MRI service wasn't there that day, and Reggie says he was later told by other doctors that "a person who needs to be more studious might wait longer and say, 'Stay overnight,' and wait till the MRI came."

But Lepore, who thought Reggie, then eighty-two, might have compression of the spinal cord, didn't want an MRI anyway. "You can't take someone who is not stable and put them in there." And with spinal cord compression, "you have a very finite period of time before you have permanent damage. If you put pressure on the cord, you damage the cord so you can't get electrical impulses across it."

Lepore "scooted me off the island," Reggie recalls. "The doctors in Boston told me, had he not called a jet so quickly, had Dr. Lepore delayed my situation, I wouldn't have been able to walk. My legs were dead. I couldn't move them at all."

Boston doctors performed surgery immediately, and with rehab, Reggie recovered. "Your rapid response is what saved my legs, and how can I thank you for that?" he wrote Lepore. "This grateful patient will always be in debt to you—always!"

A year later, after Reggie visited Lepore for leg pain and a hamstring tear, a package arrived at the Lepore house: peaches picked fresh in Louisiana and overnighted to Nantucket. "If Tim Lepore left this island, to replace him we would need four to six more doctors," Reggie mused in his light-filled living room one summer afternoon. "He does everything for Doris and me. Tim is my doctor."

Some doctors are more inclined to wait and see how a patient's condition evolves or deliberate with a team of physicians before recommending a treatment. But while Lepore regularly consults with mainland specialists, on Nantucket he is his own team. His nurse, Katie Pickman, says, "He will instantly pull things together, getting them to a specialist if necessary, in a ridiculously quick amount of time for being on an island." Ridiculously quick for anywhere actually. "If someone were in Boston, it would take them three months."

Lepore owes his confidence to the vast array of cases he's seen, to his voracious habit of reading about illnesses and treatments, and to his assertive, unequivocating personality. "It isn't always wonderful because sometimes he'll just throw the orders at you," admits Shelley Foulkes, a visiting nurse. "But I do admire that he is able to do that."

When a bartender came to him with inflammation of the penis, Lepore was concerned. One possibility was balanitis, in which the foreskin becomes red and inflamed. But "this was unlike any balanitis I'd ever seen. To me it was obvious it was cancer."

Lepore sent the bartender to a mainland urologist, but "the urologist thought it was just an infection, so he watched it for a while. It wasn't getting better." Finally, the urologist conceded it was cancer and removed affected areas of the penis, a potentially avoidable approach if he had confirmed Lepore's suspicions sooner and tried cancer treatment instead of surgery. The operation was unsuccessful because the tumor had already spread, so the urologist ultimately removed the entire organ. "The guy's alive, but he's gone through a lot of surgery, radiation. He's got some cancer in his lymph nodes," Lepore laments. "You can sit around and fool around," but "I just think you have to be aggressive and get after these things."

Nathaniel Philbrick, the best-selling author of *Mayflower* and *In the Heart of the Sea*, has been on the receiving end of his nimble diagnoses. "He is a man of action, and I think that's the only way you can survive and become the figure he is," says Philbrick, who lives on Nantucket year-round. "It's so easy to sort of ask for another test." But hesitating can be hazardous, "given the state of care here and the time-bound realities he, and everyone, is operating under. That puts a lot of pressure on him—to just sort of come up with that diagnosis and go with it. He has the courage to make those kinds of calls, to do something rather than waffle."

When Philbrick was bitten by a tick one Saturday, "I didn't want to go to the ER, so I just called Tim up, as do a lot of people. He just called an antibiotic into the drugstore, one big pill. It's almost prophylactic, if you don't know you have Lyme disease. I hadn't come down with the symptoms."

And when Philbrick's wife, Melissa, needed an emergency appendectomy, "that was traumatic. If Tim hadn't been there, I don't know what we would have done." In fact, "everyone on the island has a story that without Tim there, who knows what would have happened. Everyone thinks of Nantucket as this wealthy summer community where everybody's drinking gin and tonics all the time. It's not. It's an island where you can't get in a car and drive away."

Especially for a doctor, Philbrick reckons, "that's got to be extremely stressful. When you're trying to do everything, you always feel slightly incompetent. You always know there's someone else who could do it better. Out here, you just don't have that luxury."

Which helps explain Lepore's no-holds-barred brand of doctor-patient relationship. Philbrick's medical visits often blossom into discussions that help him with a project. For *Abram's Eyes*, about the history of Native Americans on Nantucket, Philbrick chatted with Lepore, whose passions include Indian bows and remains found at construction sites and burial grounds. Lepore had deduced, for example, by examining an unearthed partial jaw bone, that island Indians used shovel-shaped teeth to eat food mixed with sand. He'd spoken at a Nantucket Historical Association program on Indians, where Lepore, identified as "chief of medicine at Nantucket Cottage Hospital and enthusiastic amateur archaeologist," conferred excitedly with a panelist with an only slightly more exalted title: Slow Turtle, Supreme Medicine Man of the Wampanoag Indian Nation.

With Philbrick, Lepore discussed an illness that ravaged the Indian population in 1763. "Maybe they picked up yellow fever," Lepore speculated. "But none of the whites got sick. Hepatitis? Nah. Measles? No. And it couldn't have been anything carried by a flying insect because whites would have gotten it." Lepore finally concluded the mystery disease was louse-borne relapsing fever or louse-borne typhus.

When Philbrick was writing *In the Heart of the Sea*, about the sinking of the whaling ship *Essex*, he consulted with Lepore about dehydration. To help Philbrick understand how some marooned sailors survived by eating people, Lepore and Cathy's sister Beth Tornovish, who studied nutrition, estimated "the nutritional value of a human: how much protein, how much fat?"

And for *The Last Stand*, about Custer and the Battle of Little Bighorn, "I'm in my johnny, and Tim said, 'You got to see what I have here,'" Philbrick recalls. Lepore led Philbrick out of the exam room to the semipublic nursing station and showed him a topographical map of the Custer battlefield. Little did Philbrick know that Lepore was a card-carrying member of the Little Bighorn Society.

"There's these great unsolved mysteries where an entire unit was wiped out," Lepore mused. "Were the other officers all drunk? Did they hate Custer? Did Custer make a tactical mistake splitting up his troops? Was Custer betrayed?"

Lepore's enthusiasm didn't stop at maps. "Inevitably he'd show up to my physicals with a replica weapon for me to look at," Philbrick says. Lepore had replicas of every gun used in the battle, and he and Steve Tornovish, a detective, took Philbrick to the police shooting range, letting the author fire Lepore's Trapdoor Springfield rifle and 1873 Colt revolver. For extra verisimilitude, Philbrick recalls, amazed, "he actually made the gunpowder and put together cartridges of black powder for all these shots."

This is not the way other Nantucket doctors work. "I am not on call twenty-four hours, seven days a week, which he is, because I think that creates a lot of burnout and resentment," says Diane Pearl, a longtime Nantucketer and internist. "For most people it would not be healthy, and it can almost be pathological if taken to a certain degree. Unless you thrive on that, which Tim does."

When Margot Hartmann, now the hospital's chief executive officer, began working with Lepore a dozen years ago, she was shocked. She tries to draw the line because in a place where everyone sees everyone regularly, it's hard to carve out personal time when people are not asking for your medical opinion.

"You're sitting eating your oatmeal in a café, and someone pulls their hair back—'This thing is growing on my forehead. Could you take a look at it?'" Hartmann says. "You have to be able to say, in a way that doesn't prevent them from seeking care another time, 'I would so like to help out with that, but I'm just at breakfast.' It's not Boundaries 101 living in a small community—it's Advanced Placement Boundaries."

Lepore sees things differently. Patients, he says, "all have faces, and particularly on a small island like this, you see them again and again and again. In some places, you can call it a one night stand—you meet a patient, operate on them, discharge them, and they go back to their other doctor. I operate on somebody: I know their wife; I know their brother; I know their kids. Here, they don't go away, and you don't go away."

In most places, surgeons primarily perform surgery, often encountering patients after several other doctors treat them. "Once a patient's better, unless there's a complication, I never see them again," notes Richard H. Koehler, a Plymouth, Massachusetts, surgeon who covers for Lepore on the few occasions he leaves Nantucket. Lepore's protean perspective sets him apart.

"Unfortunately most stuff isn't stuff we can operate on," he knows. "Most stuff is a whole series of stuff that is nonsurgical, maybe even nonmedical. Even a guy with a hernia has a job, has a life, came from somewhere, is going somewhere. Unless you sort of understand that, I don't think you can provide good care. You probably can in Boston, where you're surrounded by residents. But here I'm the one taking care of that patient, and I want to understand that person and understand their life."

So Lepore typically follows his patients from start to finish, even after they have been treated, released, or transferred elsewhere. Sometimes he'll run to Boston to reassure a hospitalized patient. He always calls doctors at other hospitals to keep tabs. "Two reasons: I want to make sure my patients are getting good care, and I want to be ready for the next one. I want to know what they did in case I get another case like it."

At Nantucket's hospital, Lepore hounds other staff to move things along. Lab technicians at the hospital will inevitably see him at their door "'cause I want the damn lab tests done. I get itchy."

With radiology, he sticks his head in, asking to see the films. "Am I pain in the ass? Sure I'm a pain in the ass. But we get an answer right away. If I got a patient in the emergency room, I don't want to sit and wait for an hour for a goddamn X-ray report. I don't."

Once Lepore thought David Goodman, a patient and local columnist, needed an ultrasound, but the machine was booked all day. "Sorry, he's getting in there now," Lepore told the technicians. "He pushed them aside," recalls Goodman, who, as a thank you, installed tile in Lepore's house.

When the Lepores were scheduled to go to Ireland to visit their son T.J. in medical school, a breast cancer patient Lepore had operated on years earlier began experiencing a recurrence of cancer, in her lungs this time. "She was desperately ill, and there was nobody that could take care of her like I felt I could," Lepore believed. He told his wife he couldn't make the trip, and "Cathy went bat shit, but I was not going to go while this woman was dying." As it happened, bad weather made off-island travel impossible for several days. By the time the weather cleared, the woman had passed away.

Lepore doesn't make yacht calls, only because he fears he could miss an on-island emergency. While many of Nantucket's wealthy and prominent summer people never need pay him a visit—they have private physicians elsewhere—some are Lepore regulars even though they could see any doctor they wanted. John Chancellor, the television anchor, came to Lepore when he smacked his head into a door frame. Another patient, the author David Halberstam, liked to attend Nantucket high school football games, where he would chat with Lepore on the sidelines.

Gordon and Lulie Gund first heard "these outrageous Tim Lepore stories" from the caretaker of their Nantucket house, an old-timer named Gibby Burchell. When Gordon got the flu one summer, Burchell advised: "You gotta go see Tim." Gordon Gund is a venture capitalist and owner of sports franchises like the Cleveland Cavaliers. He is blind from retinitis pigmentosa, and the Gunds, who also have homes in Aspen, Cleveland, and Princeton, New Jersey, are philanthropists who cofounded the Foundation Fighting Blindness.

The Gunds' encounters with Lepore were pretty routine until August 2008, when Lulie, whom the hospital had diagnosed with Lyme disease and given amoxicillin, discovered that "my eyes had turned bright yellow." She also "lost any much desire to eat" and "felt so grumpy." She returned to the hospital for a blood smear, and Lepore was called. "You have babesiosis really badly," he told her. What's more, "because I didn't think it was important," Lulie, then sixty-seven, had not told anyone that she didn't have a spleen. Hers had been removed twenty years earlier, when she'd had Hodgkin's disease. Without a spleen, which collects damaged blood cells, a disease like babesiosis could spiral out of control.

Lepore gave her an antimalarial drug, Mepron, and an antibacterial medication, azithromycin. When she was ready to leave the island, he told her she could only go if she kept up the medication and got regular blood tests.

But soon after returning home to Princeton, Gund went to an infectious disease specialist who did a blood test that came back negative for babesia. "You're fine," the specialist told her. "Go off the medication." The doctor "wasn't familiar with babesia," Gund says. He didn't know that babesiosis can linger for months at levels a blood test can't always detect, and that for a Hodgkin's patient it may last longer. The doctor didn't know to give her a more definitive test, called polymerase chain reaction, or PCR.

"Four days later I was so sick I ended up in the hospital with congestive heart failure and a temperature of 103, 104," Gund recalls. "I was having trouble breathing. I had pulmonary edema," fluid in the lungs. "My husband called Tim."

Lepore insisted she resume taking Mepron and azithromycin immediately. He directed Gund's doctor to administer frequent PCR tests. He also did his own tests: the hamster protocol. He sent samples of Gund's blood to Sam Telford III at Tufts School of Veterinary Medicine. Telford injected the blood into hamsters. "If the hamster goes belly-up, then you know there are actually live organisms in there," Lepore said. As long as the disease was active in Gund, the hamsters died. They followed the hamsters' progress quietly, not wanting to alarm the patient. It took six months, until February, for babesia to completely quit her system. "My God," Gund realized recently, "I've never asked Dr. Lepore what happened to the hamster."

She was also impressed when Lepore referred her to Peter Krause, an epidemiologist at the Yale School of Public Health, who studies microbial diseases. "A lot of doctors are reticent to refer you and sort of share the limelight." Ultimately, the Gunds donated $1 million over three years to research Krause and Lepore are conducting on tick-borne diseases. Notes Lulie: "There are so many doctors who don't realize how sick you can get."

The Gunds know Lepore can lack the diplomatic demeanor common in their charitable and corporate circles. "I've heard him answer people very curtly at a public meeting if he really disagrees," Lulie acknowledges. "The flip side is he's so unbelievably humane when you're with him. And it doesn't matter if you're not there—he always has time for you. He has so many facets, he's like a diamond."

"Did you notice the new rug?" Lepore asks. It's a welcome mat in front of his office's reception desk. Under the word "Greetings" is a homespun, tapestry-like picture of a dog sniffing the ass of another dog with a raised tail.

"We haven't gotten any complaints—yet," remarks Lepore's long-time nurse, Diana Hull.

Lepore's sentimental side can be hard to decipher, encrusted as it often is in a gruff, unvarnished demeanor. It's certainly not apparent from his medical office, which has none of the soothing seascapes or pictures of cuddly babies that people might expect from their friendly family doc.

On one wall is another doggie tapestry picture showing dogs licking their testicles, with the caption: "Because they can." There's a taxidermied armadillo, lying on its back, holding a bottle of Lone Star beer. The most prominent chair in the waiting room is a huge, shaggy mountain goat–like animal with horns, black hooves, and a furry white chest, open-mouthed with a red tongue.

Yes, there are the framed degrees: eight, including his Harvard bachelor's. But those could be easily missed amid the gross-out and God-complex accoutrements:

TIMOTHY J. LEPORE, MD, WIZARD

TIMOTHY J. LEPORE, MASTER, TEMPLE OF DOOM

TIMOTHY J. LEPORE, BIG FISH—SMALL POND

TIMOTHY J. LEPORE, ANAL INSPECTOR, HEAD A.H.
(A.H. presumably stands for asshole.)

REMEMBER THERE HAVE BEEN MANY KINGS,
BUT THERE IS ONLY ONE CZAR (TIM 1–1)

There is a sign proclaiming the office a "House of Pain," and an uplifting Latin aphorism: "Cuius Testiculos Habeas, Habeas Cardia Et Cerebellum." When you have them by the balls, the heart and mind will follow.

"He has the most wonderfully politically incorrect facility there," Philbrick says. "I've heard earnest young mothers with their kids look around and say, 'This is inappropriate.'"

Philbrick thinks the office is a way for Lepore to indulge his independent streak. "It's hard to be a public person all the time. Some people, you just feel like they're posing. He's not—he's just having fun."

Nothing wrong with a little shock to the system, Lepore figures. At a town meeting, Lepore lobbied for broadening the law to require bicycle helmets for everyone, standing up so the light bounced off his bald head. "Feeling the wind in your hair is vastly overrated," he quipped, then wrote a poem about helmets, which he handed out on cards to patients.

It's the sort of thing that continues to make Lepore "a conundrum to people," Philbrick observes. "He comes off as an NRA, gun-toting yahoo, who is a Harvard degree medical guy, who is doing all these things that are causes that any liberal would embrace. I enjoy so much people who are outside of the stereotype. Irony is underrated in our society. I just sort of enjoy immensely Tim saying things that leave people gasping. He's always trying to needle someone. He's very mischievous."

Almost nothing is sacred. One summer, Lepore's friend Weinman was caring for an off-island friend's teenage daughter. The girl developed stomach pains, so Weinman called Lepore to meet her at the emergency room around 10 PM. For over an hour, the girl is "in with Tim, in with Tim, in with Tim," Weinman recalls. "He walks out without her, looks down, and says, 'I'm so sorry. I tried. I couldn't save her.'"

"What are you talking about?" Weinman panicked. "What do you mean you couldn't save her?"

"I'm just kidding," Lepore grinned. "She's fine."

Even though she knows Lepore better than almost anyone, Weinman was incensed. "It was a really mean thing to do." Lepore says if the situation were dire, he would never have joked about it. But he got a thirty-second charge out of throwing Weinman off balance. "It was interesting to watch all the color go out of her face."

Mary Monagle, a former nurse at the hospital, thinks Lepore plays up his eccentricities for effect but can also dial them back. "One minute you've got him labeled as the countrified quack doctor, and the next minute he's the Tufts grad, and you say, 'Where'd you pull that out of your pocket?' I have seen him be über-professional, and I've also seen him be, 'Yeehaw, I gotta go kill a deer.'"

The contrast between Lepore's practice and, say, Diane Pearl's, could not be more stark.

"My office is very quiet—his is like chaos," Pearl says. "I couldn't work in that situation."

Pearl has two employees. Lepore has at least ten, more in the summer. A typical Lepore staff consists of three registered nurses, a nurse practitioner, two physician assistants, a receptionist, a finance manager, and people who handle medical records and insurance referrals, plus a couple of people studying to be nurses or physician assistants.

Pearl will close her practice to new patients so as not to take on more than she wants to handle. Lepore's practice is elastic enough to accommodate the person who ran into the office and announced that a goat had gone on the lam. Lepore barreled out the back door to help search; the goat was found grazing among the Quaker cemetery's headstones.

He also makes room for people like Tony Yates, a welder who visits him once or twice a month. "Whether I need to or not, I just come to talk to him. I depend on him. He always has time to see me. I think he listens. Lots of people don't listen no more."

Lepore even had trouble turning away a woman who called and showed up at the house at all hours. True, she "could sometimes sneak out of the bushes," Lepore acknowledges, but the woman raised chickens, horses, and other fauna, and "people like that get a lot of latitude with me, frankly." The worst was when she would traipse into his office with a bag full of the snakes she kept as pets. "She just liked to share them with me. I am not fond of snakes. I liked her except for the damn snakes."

The woman's health issues were legitimate: pain, osteoarthritis, Lyme disease. It was just that she "occasionally had boundary issues," Lepore understates. "I don't have boundary issues."

For Lepore's wife, though, the line was crossed. "Cathy put a stop to that," her friend Michelsen remembers. She told the woman not to come around so much.

Cathy sometimes intercepts phone calls, lets the answering machine pick up, or gently discourages people from simply dropping by on a Saturday morning. She tells Lepore she is worried that people take advantage of him.

"I don't perceive it that way," he replied once.

"You," Cathy pointed out, "are not married to you."

But to Lepore, the people he treats, "they're like little piranhas. They take a little bit out of your heart."

CHAPTER 7

ARMS AGAINST
A SEA OF TROUBLES

The Lepore house was Lepore-less this particular April evening. Nantucket was Lepore-less too, something that happens once a year when the doctor runs (if one could call it that) the Boston Marathon. He leaves only a handful of other times, usually to attend off-island high school football games as the team physician. He worries that a medical crisis might erupt while he's gone or that he'll miss something interesting. Who knew his very absence this weekend would trigger just such an event?

It was during the dead of night that a woman the Lepores had asked to house-sit for their dogs thought she heard a noise. It seemed to be coming from the cellar, so the woman, who worked for the fire department, headed downstairs. She scanned what appeared to be an ordinary workroom of a home-repair hobbyist and, seeing nothing unusual there, cracked open a closet. A loud, rattlesnake-like hiss cut the air. Alarmed, the woman slammed the door and called her boss, the fire chief at the time, Bruce Watts.

Rushing to the house, Watts opened the closet too and was suddenly enveloped in a cloud of gas. Stinging, pinching, choke-inducing gas. Tear gas. The island doctor had teargassed the island fire chief.

Lepore was sorry to miss the commotion, but he was unperturbed by Watts's unfortunate escapade. "He opened up the wrong door. It's on a string, a trip wire, and if you open the door so far, then it goes off." Luckily, "it dissipates in a couple of hours. But he was uncomfortable for awhile."

The gassy booby trap protects Lepore's prized possessions: guns, scores of them, an extraordinary collection, all of them shootable and most of them shot, at least once, by the good doctor.

Chief Watts was lucky to get away with a relatively light gassing. The closet contains a safe with Lepore's rarest guns, protected by an additional trip switch that sets off "things that are sort of like little firecrackers." Another trip switch is attached to a twelve-gauge shotgun flare that, when fired, "shoots up like a roman candle." So far, though, that one is just for show—the rigging is there, but "I have never armed it. Thought about it, when I'm feeling particularly paranoid." Luckily for Lepore, his paranoia is usually under control because arming the shotgun flare would be "not quite legal," and "I would probably shoot myself and burn a hole in my chest, or burn the house down."

Once, Lepore accidentally tripped the tear-gas switch himself. He heard the misty hissing that preceded the full-fledged burst and hurled the door shut, high-tailing it upstairs. But once the gas dispersed, he ordered a replacement canister and, impressed with the efficacy of the deterrent, began thinking about putting another tear-gas trap at the top of the stairs. Some people never learn.

Lepore has some two hundred guns, stored in the safe, a vault near the basement boiler, and a locked cabinet in an upstairs closet. Occasionally, gun paraphernalia overflows to the main floor: a disabled rifle against the kitchen counter, a shotgun in the laundry room closet, a box of bullets by the phone.

Instruments of death prized by a man who saves lives. But Lepore is not bothered by any cognitive dissonance. "Guns: I never met one I didn't like. I like the history part of it. I like the shoot part of it."

Guns are not a common hobby on Nantucket. Despite its summer influx of corporate executives, the island is not a bastion of conservatism. It is notionally in Massachusetts, after all, and has its own long-standing liberal tradition, with roots that include abolitionist activism and Quaker fellowship. If someone were to poll people on favorite U.S. constitutional amendments, the Second would not likely top the list.

"Here is a person who is a pillar of the community, but he has all sorts of guns lying around, including a collection which he keeps under lock and key and tear gas," marvels Lepore's neighbor, Chris Fraker. Even his main floor powder room would be more accurately described as a gunpowder room—the toilet-side reading material includes *The Gun Digest Book of Firearms, Fakes and Reproductions*.

His collection is worth almost $200,000, by far his most valuable possession. There are guns from Russia, Finland, Germany, China, and America; rifles, pistols, shotguns, military guns, hunting guns. Some he buys at gun shows, but many are gifts or castoffs from patients or friends, "beaters" worth next to nothing. Lepore takes them all.

Even his medical office broadcasts his affinity for deadly weapons. A cap-and-ball pistol inside a shadow-box frame adorns the waiting room. The hall leading to the exam rooms exhibits photos of English and Spanish muskets, and Henry Deringer's single-shot pistol (the name is usually misspelled as "Derringer," but Lepore has it right). He has a Buffalo Bill poster and one for Peter's True Blue Smokeless Shot Shells.

The exam rooms are named Colt, Winchester, Smith & Wesson. The bathroom has a name too: P-Shooter. Inside are posters of Remington Cartridges, the Winchester Repeating Arms Company, and an Annie Oakley–like figure holding a revolver. A rack of arrows rests near the nurse's station.

"When I came into the office, there was a big fat jar with a deer fetus in it," recalls Martina Richards, who was one of Lepore's nurses. "I grew up in a household where everybody's a Democrat, and he's like, 'Can you order me six cases of bullets?'"

An arsenal of aphorisms is also scattered throughout the office: "Once more unto the breach, dear friends, . . . " "Sometimes you just have to come out shooting," and "This is the office of a dedicated hunter. Expect daydreaming, tall tales and sporadic attendance." Lepore's doctor's uniform has often been a hunting vest instead of a lab coat.

When Peter Swenson came to the island in 2006 to become executive director of Family and Children's Services of Nantucket, he was dumbstruck. Lepore is on the board of Swenson's agency, which provides mental health counseling, and Swenson's first impression of Lepore was: "This guy's weird. He has an old pair of khakis on. He has a shotgun vest on. He's got all these statements: 'You reel that in too fast, you're going to lose the fish.' I'm like, 'What does that mean?' In his office, there's stuffed animals everywhere, knives and guns. I really felt I'd been transferred to *Northern Exposure*."

In the courtroom farce *Boston Legal*, the leaders of Nantucket seek to sue in federal court for the right to construct a nuclear bomb.

"We want to build a weapon of mass destruction," the fictional head of the select board says earnestly. "We're a very small island, totally exposed. The homeowners are becoming increasingly concerned about security, and well, we're rich, we can afford it, we want one."

The lawyer they have asked to represent them asks the logical question: "What kind of drugs are we taking on the island these days?"

"Do you realize what a target Nantucket is?" the selectman continues. "When you think of the iconic staples of America that the world so hates: rich people, Wall Street gluttons, evil politicians,

Hollywood producers. They all have homes on Nantucket. It's one-stop shopping."

Plus, "if something ever happens, which the government says is inevitable, by the way, who's going to come rushing to protect us? The Vineyard?"

That kind of bunker mentality has some historical underpinnings. In 1961, a nuclear bomb shelter was built on Nantucket to provide a safe haven for President John F. Kennedy. It was never used, and to conceal its purpose the U.S. Navy described it as a "jet assist takeoff fuel bottle storage area."

Nantucket has so relished its independence that it has, in the not too distant past, threatened to secede from Massachusetts. And in 1977, after a change in the Massachusetts state constitution cut the number of state representatives, Nantucket and Martha's Vineyard launched an actual secession movement. The islands voted four to one to break off and form the fifty-first state, and there was even talk of forming their own country. But they needed approval from the state legislature, which, naturally, refused them.

For a visitor undulating to the island on the ferry, security doesn't seem like Nantucket's most pressing concern. Lots of year-rounders leave their doors unlocked. But antiterrorism agencies have their antennae on alert. One summer weekend in 2005, Nantucket's Hy-Line ferry got a call: "Don't let the ferry leave, or it will blow up." Before they figured out it was a teenage prank, a raft of state and federal agencies got involved, canceling ferry service and stranding hundreds of people on the island.

When a dignitary steps foot on the island, like Vice President Joseph Biden, who spends Thanksgiving on Nantucket, the Secret Service scours the hospital to make sure things are copacetic if the protectee should have a heart attack or a bad batch of clams. The hospital has to be well-secured enough to prevent prying eyes or psychopaths from getting near the patient. Lepore, who as the hospital's medical director is a designated emergency contact, says, "They get our names and phone numbers, talk about if the dignitary was injured, where would we go? What would we do? Where's the helipad? Can we lock off a section of the building?"

They probably don't think to ask if the medical director has brought any of his firearms to work that day. But it has happened more than once, because Lepore insists on being called for almost anything that comes into the ER, and sometimes when the phone rings, he's out in the field.

"Are they going to kvetch if I come in my duck-hunting clothes, or are they going to wait 'till I take a shower? They want me to go home and change, hey, I'll go home and change. But I'm not the one with the bad appendix."

Sometimes, if he's been out shooting, he has to bring his gun to the hospital. "It's illegal to leave a gun in a car," he explains. "I break it down and just put it somewhere in the back room."

Not long ago, Lepore came in on a day off to operate on a woman experiencing problems from a hernia repair performed in Boston. After Lepore's surgery, things looked fine, so he went hunting and "told everyone not to call him unless somebody was bleeding," recalls Mary Monagle, a nurse. The woman began bleeding.

"I'm in the deer stand," Lepore whispered into the phone (his cell phone ring is hard to miss in the field because it sounds like a dog bark). "I'll call you in ten minutes." He returned to the hospital in camouflage, no gun, but "he took out a knife," recounts Monagle. "Dr. L! We never know what he's packing."

Often in the hospital, he is packing several knives, part of an assortment he stores in the drawers of his bedroom dresser. "I see a knife, I like it. I could live to about five hundred before I run out of knives." Lepore doesn't use them to operate but whips them out when he wants to open a box of medical supplies, so "I can do it with panache."

The knives are also good for cutting up roadkill, something else Lepore collects. The dead animals are for Ajax, Lepore's red-tailed hawk, a sometime hunting buddy who lives in a large pen under trees in the backyard. In the early dawn light, Lepore cruises Nantucket's streets, looking for "bunnies that haven't looked both ways."

He usually puts them in his home freezer. But occasionally he'll leave them in the car, and Cathy will unknowingly drive them to her job as a counselor at Nantucket High School. "Mrs. Lepore," students have said, "somebody's trying to play a horrible trick on you."

Lepore's critters can pop up anywhere. In the sink might be pieces of frozen rabbit he has chopped up and left to thaw. By the mailbox or on the porch might be paper bags full of squished squirrels or crushed chipmunks, left by island residents helpfully supplementing Lepore's macabre menagerie. Nurses leave him a rabbit or two in the hospital freezer. The daughter of Lepore's friends Paul and Brenda Johnson began carrying a bag for potential roadkill with her when she was as young as thirteen.

"Oh, somebody brought me something," Lepore noticed one day. "For Ajax. Squirrel" was scrawled on the bag hanging from the gate post. "Yeah, it's been there a few days," Cathy said. "Why didn't you tell me?" he asked. "Let me put it in the freezer."

When some off-island friends of Lepore's daughter, Meredith, were visiting, the family was jolted awake by a screech. Racing to the kitchen, they found one of the girls standing stock still, holding an ice cube tray containing frozen mice. "Oh," shrugged Lepore to the traumatized girl. "Those are my mice-icles."

Lepore's friend Rhoda Weinman recalls that when he first got Ajax, he invited her over, telling her he had a surprise. Before she arrived, he left to attend a school committee meeting, so when Weinman walked in, "Cathy was sitting in the dining room with this hawk strapped to her arms. She couldn't even move. Tim didn't want the hawk to be left alone."

Some years later, David Goodman, a patient, walked into the Lepores' house to find the family unit in a not atypical tableau: "Cathy's stirring the soup, Tim's with the hawk on his arm, and the hawk is tearing a rabbit in the middle of the kitchen."

John Gardner, a friend of Lepore's son T.J., remembers that at high school graduation there is a tradition of giving the chairman of the school committee a gift. Gardner's year the chairman was Lepore, and although the students didn't follow through, "we talked about giving Tim dead mice in little plastic bags."

Lepore would have been at home in a world where hunting with hawks was an everyday activity. He makes his own stone arrowheads, using antlers from moose and deer to chip away at a piece of flint in a technique called flint knapping. He fashions his own bows.

He carves wooden duck decoys, although he has "this mental block against painting them," so "I got a box full of heads that I carved, but none of them are painted or have eyes put in them."

And he transports himself to the Stone Age by building atlatls, a prehistoric hunting weapon that resembles a spear-thrower—a long stick with a hook that can hurl a dart a hundred yards or more.

"We all have these mental pictures of Tim in a loincloth going out with an atlatl," says Jim Lentowski, who runs the Nantucket Conservation Foundation. It hasn't come to that yet, possibly because hunting with the Paleolithic weapons is illegal in Massachusetts. But at least Lepore can say, without much fear of a challenge, "I'm probably the best atlatl guy on the island. If we get an invasion of mammoths, just get behind me, and you're all set."

Lepore himself is baffled as to why he "emerged from the womb with a fascination with guns, knives, bows and arrows."

His father, John, despite serving with distinction as a World War II army surgeon, did not share his son's hobby. Only once did they ever fire weapons together, taking aim at clay pigeons at a skeet shoot. Lepore got his gun induction elsewhere, beginning in kindergarten at a Veterans Day commemoration at the cemetery in his hometown of

Marlborough, Massachusetts. When the soldiers fired their guns in salute, he scrambled to pick up the shells.

When he was a little older, Lepore took a Daisy Golden Eagle BB gun, which looks like a rifle, up to his attic. There he shot flies with the BBs. Flies. He spent hours doing that. "I used to get a lot of flies. I'm very good, really."

When flies got to be too easy, Lepore turned to pigeons, aiming his Golden Eagle at them from the roof of his house. His grandmother, sunning herself on the porch, "was not pleased to have a pigeon drop off the roof and land next to her."

Next he tried bow-and-arrow frog hunting with his friend Bob DiBuono. Zinging the arrows into the muck, the boys punctured a passel of frogs. "We'd spend hours in the swamp. We'd get the frogs, cut the frog legs off, skin them. Then Bob's mother would go and cook frog legs for us. She'd fry them. When you put salt on them, they'd twitch."

When he wasn't shooting small creatures, Lepore liked playing with knives. So much so that when he was about twelve, he sliced open the palm of his left hand while doing some random carving. "My father sutured it up. He was not overly sympathetic. I'm not sure he said anything. He may have reflected on the stupidity of it. It was a dangerous childhood."

Lepore joined the Marlborough Fish and Game gun club in his teens, thrilled that he "could walk out of my house with a gun, walk into the woods. If you walked around Marlborough town now with a gun, you'd have thirty-seven cops on you."

Lepore's mother hated his hobby, and "if I was out hunting and I shot something, my mother would not give me a ride home." But his father was "supportive in a benign neglect kind of way." He made Lepore a gun case and gave him his first gun when he was sixteen: a Marlin .22 lever action, model 39A, probably sixty or seventy years old. Later, after a neighborhood widow gave John Lepore a pistol that belonged to her husband, he passed that on to his son. It was "this Luger that a guy down the street had killed himself with."

As a kid, Lepore liked the adventure and technical challenge of shooting. As an adult, there is something else too. To Lepore, performing surgery to keep a patient alive has a lot in common with the act of shooting lethal weapons. Both "require a lot of concentration and a lot of effort," he believes. Shooting is "controlling where you want to hit, doing it right, and doing it repeatedly." Surgery is like that too. "If you're not in control, you have to figure out what's going on."

When Lepore is not performing surgery, he is almost always thinking about it. "Surgery should look easy. If I find I'm doing a case and I'm struggling, I try to remember why I was struggling. Did I ask the anesthetist, 'Was the patient relaxed?'? Did I set up the lights in the right way? Maybe you haven't made a big enough incision. What was I doing to make it look difficult?"

Shooting guns requires such intense focus that he considers it pretty much the only activity that forces his mind away from such detailed re-analysis. "It's very relaxing," Lepore insists. "If I'm operating, I'm not thinking about shooting. If I'm shooting, I'm not thinking about operating. Shooting, I'll tell you: it sort of wipes the slate clean for that period of time. The stress, when I'm shooting—that all falls away."

So much so that if Lepore can't get out to the police shooting range by the airport, he fires air rifles in his basement, where he has affixed a mattress to the wall.

Part of the joy for him is the history that comes with the guns. When someone gave him a couple of Ballard rifles, he boned up on their background as Civil War–era, single-shot-action guns. Same with pepper-box revolvers, which were shot from the hip in the California Gold Rush, and the M1 Garand, the first semiautomatic rifle to become regular army equipment. He owns a "Bolo" Mauser semiautomatic pistol made in Germany in the 1920s and several Russian Mosin-Nagant sniper rifles, including copies from China and Finland.

Lepore knows the 160 varieties of 1849 Colts, with their different barrel markings: "the one-line New York, the two-line New York, a Hartford, a London. You start comparing, contrasting; you start handling a piece of history."

Some of his guns are valuable, like a Browning Superposed shotgun, called an Over/Under, worth about $3,000. Others are "very, very nice guns that are flawed": a Winchester Model 70 carbine that somebody drilled into to mount a scope on it; a Colt pistol with ivory grips and decorative engraving but, alas, the wrong rammer. Still, they all work.

"His collection has a 'the Russians are coming, the Russians are coming,' feel about it," notes John Gardner, Lepore's son's friend. Nathaniel Philbrick thinks Lepore also likes the gun hobby because "it connects him with a segment of the population that I don't think most doctors would have interaction with." And guns, like island life itself, embody the frontier spirit: independence, contrariness, the ability to stand on one's own.

Lepore isn't reckless with guns, despite all his bluster. Occasionally, though, he has what might be described as a vigilante moment. One night, next door at Chris Fraker's, Fraker's daughter Jen came home with a date to find a man sitting on the kitchen floor. He was eating yogurt and seemed confused and on edge. Fraker was in the shower, and his daughter called out, "Dad, is this someone you know?" Fraker came out in a towel and yelled to his wife, "Debbie, call Tim Lepore and the police, in that order."

Lepore grabbed a gun, one of his Colt 1903s, and shoved it in his pocket, then headed to the Fraker house. He did not brandish the weapon, not wanting to provoke an already delicate situation, and once there he realized the man was drunk and nonthreatening. The police took him away. "It turned out to be a drug addict so high he didn't know where he was—he thought he was in a different house," Lepore recalls. But he was glad he brought the gun. "I didn't know what I was getting into."

Lepore also makes his own ammunition—out of fascination and because "I'm cheap as hell." At first, he just reloaded shotgun shells, picking them up from the ground and packing them with powder at home. He experimented with different techniques, switching from a "hot load," in which a large amount of powder creates pressure that spits bullets out faster, and instead putting "less powder in or a different powder so it doesn't kick as much."

He tried stuffing other types of bullet casings, collecting obscure calibers, which he stores in a rack of tiny plastic bins, the kind that might be expected to hold nails and screws. He has casings for 9 millimeters, .38 specials, .223s, .44 and .357 Magnums, the 7.65 Argentine, even the .303 Savage, a gun, he notes, that they stopped making seventy-five years ago.

When he needed a new challenge, he decided to make the bullets too. He'd send his sons, T.J. and Nick, to scavenge lead from the shooting range. He discovered that pure lead itself is too soft; it's better to have lead mixed with tin and antimony. So he sought out unusual sources: lead ingots people make fishing lures out of, linotype used in newspaper printing, and old wheel weights he'd ask for at gas stations. "I melt them all down, cast them into ingots, then melt them down again," pouring the liquefied lead into molds.

Lepore used to make bullets in his cellar, but the awful smell of the boiling pot of lead annoyed Cathy. He moved to the garage and then discovered a workshop next to the hospital's emergency room that was used by the maintenance crew. He carted in an electric pot, lead, and molds. As nurses did triage and swabbed wounds in the ER, Lepore played with molten metal to feed his guns. "I would go in there and cast bullets all day, waiting for patients." When the ER got reconfigured, though, Lepore's ammo lab was sacrificed, ostensibly for reasons of space, although, he admits "there's probably some health and safety concerns as well."

Lepore's ammunition work surprises even members of the gun crowd on the island, like Bruce Watts, the former fire chief Lepore teargassed. Although Watts is an avid hunter, he concedes, "I don't even load my own shells. I go to the store and buy them."

Meanwhile, Lepore sends his son Nick, a lawyer in Atlanta, "random text messages, asking me to get some reloading supplies for him," Nick says. "He wants some 1943 Japanese brass part of a bullet. I tell him, 'I can't buy these things and send them to you because that would violate federal law.'"

One Saturday, Lepore pulls on a hunter's orange vest and an orange wool cap and collects his Browning shotgun—square-back, auto five, twelve-gauge, circa 1935. "It's semiautomatic and goes bang five times for you," he says reverentially. He looks through his array of whistles that generate deer calls—Doe Bleat, Buck Grunt and Snort, Bleat-in-Heat—but opts not to take one with him. He only has a little time to hunt this afternoon.

Lepore drives to the moors, a stretch of heather, cranberry bogs, bayberry, huckleberry, and scrub oak. It is 35 degrees, but the island's ferocious winter wind makes it feel much colder.

Lepore couldn't care less. His boots crunching on frozen stalks and dried grasses, he points out branches where bucks have scraped their antlers. He spots a deer blind someone built, a ladder leaning up into a tree. He scans the brush for deer for an hour or so, but if any are around, they are waiting him out. Maybe they know they can. Lepore has no time to play the patient hunter, squatting silently until his quarry appears.

He can never be like his friend Ronnie Conway, an electrical lineman for National Grid, who hunts with a regular posse of buddies and has a living room festooned with the mounted heads of deer he has shot. Still at the taxidermists the day of Lepore's brief if-you-can-call-it-that hunt is a buck so impressive its antlers have twelve points, an animal Conway nabbed only after pursuing him for more than a year.

It's hard for Lepore to find time to hunt with Conway and his group, although "I like to get him out as much as possible," Conway says. During one such trip, Conway, in a deer stand, thought he heard a phone ring. "No, he can't have his cell phone out here," Conway thought. "But when I came out of my stand, he was gone. It turned out some guy had a heart attack."

Perhaps because of interruptions like that, Lepore says he has probably killed only eight deer over the decades, and none worthy of displaying. "I don't have any great racks—you can say it, I'm not ashamed. I've only shot does and a couple of small bucks. If I mounted any of them, it would be like stuffing a dog."

The antlers hanging in his office are "sheds" that he found on the ground after deer sloughed them off. Sometimes when Lepore is out in the moors looking for antlers, he wanders completely off the deer trails into thick, nearly impenetrable brush. As darkness falls, Lepore calls Cathy: "I'm lost—come find me. Go someplace high, and turn on the lights and honk the horn." Before her friend Pam Michelsen moved off-island, she and Cathy developed a system: Drive out to the middle of the moors and climb up Altar Rock, the island's second-highest point at all of 108 feet above sea level. Then blow a whistle. Keep on blowing until the doctor finds his way out of the woods.

Once, with forty-five minutes to spare before the wedding of one of his longtime nurses, Lepore decided to scout out a new hunting spot. He drove to Hidden Forest, bumping along dirt roads until the dirt became mud and the car got stuck. He called Cathy, who was livid and sent Chris Fraker to the rescue. But the car was so mired they had to wait for a professional tow. Lepore missed the wedding.

"Hunting—this is the best way I can put it—it's very different from going for a walk in the woods," Lepore muses. "You're more alive to everything around you, to the wind, to sounds, to looking to see things."

Besides, whatever gets injured on a hunt, it's a game animal, not a patient. "I haven't tried to fix anything I've shot," Lepore says, and maybe that's part of it. In hunting, it's okay to let things die.

CHAPTER 8

WE CAN
HANDLE WEIRD

Alexandra McLaughlin could see them and hear them: people buzzing around her, anxiously wondering what to do. She had just gone out for a walk with her dog. But suddenly she was sprawled on the ground, face down.

Passersby seeing her in the dirt panicked and called 911. Someone, perhaps thinking she was having a seizure and might bite her tongue, said, "Let's shove a wallet in her mouth." But McLaughlin wasn't having a seizure or a heart attack or a fainting spell. She wished she could explain what was going on, but, although fully conscious, she couldn't move or utter a sound. She could only lie there, humiliated.

"My face," she recalls, "was right next to a dog turd."

McLaughlin was the ultimate medical enigma. For more than two decades, since she was about ten, no one could determine what was wrong with her. Many doctors had tried. They suggested thyroid problems, renal problems, Lyme disease. One doctor proposed postural orthostatic tachycardia syndrome, POTS, in which the heart rate revs when people stand up. Brain cancer was tossed around. Depression? Bipolar?

"I kept getting misdiagnosed." And she kept getting worse. Falling down had been a rare symptom for most of her life, but since moving to Nantucket in 2009, she was collapsing constantly—face down on the street, on the beach, in stores. "People find me on the ground all the time. It looks like I'm dead." She's had surgery on her knee, wrist, ankle, and fingers, and "I had to give up horseback riding, which I love, because I would fall off."

McLaughlin's symptoms can be triggered when she's startled, even "when people honk to say hello to me" on the street. And "whenever I have a strong emotion, I can't move my arms," or her knees buckle, and she turns to Jell-O.

"When I'm really, really happy, I know it's going to happen. So I start thinking of something awful: dead puppies in a washing machine or something. When I get really angry, I can't move my head, and my jaw goes slack. I have to think of the funniest YouTube videos I've ever seen."

Once on the beach, McLaughlin saw a mother playfully chasing after her daughter with sunscreen, the girl squealing: "I'm a princess, and princesses don't get burned." It was so "funny and delightful" that "I was doomed," McLaughlin says. "I fell right down."

Glancing at photographs of close family or friends can make her "high five the table with my face" without warning. And watch out "if I'm talking to somebody I'm madly in love with. I don't look him in the eye."

McLaughlin's condition could cause her to hallucinate, seeing spiders where there were none, for instance. She was also experiencing sudden onsets of fatigue and "could nod off to sleep and not realize that I've slept. I was unable to get out of bed, unable to drive my car, can't work, can't do anything."

McLaughlin moved to Nantucket when she was thirty-one because the island, where her family had summered, seemed a good place to reboot after her marriage broke up. (She asked to be identified by her birth surname instead of her married surname.) Soon after arriving on-island, she began landing in the emergency room. She inquired about primary care physicians. "Dr. Lepore may be the only doctor taking new patients," she was told. "He doesn't turn anybody away." Lepore was not only available. He was fascinated.

"With him I could be more honest about what would happen to me. I had this huge history of symptoms that just never made sense. I couldn't tell that to anybody because it sounds crazy. He said, 'Oh that sounds really interesting.'"

McLaughlin, it turned out, had stumbled on a medical marriage made, if not in heaven, then on Nantucket. Lepore loves odd or inscrutable cases, and Nantucket has provided him with more than his share.

In the summer of 2006, Rob McMullen actually crawled into Lepore's office. It was an extraordinary predicament for McMullen, a ship's captain who has plied Nantucket's waters for almost two decades. He lives alone on his sailboat, *The Snowy Egret*, drives a small cruise boat taking tourists from town to an upscale inn on the island's northeast point, and was used to shrugging off ailments without any medical help.

But McMullen, then forty-four, was having strange symptoms. He got hot flashes and then chills so extreme that he was piling on sweaters and blankets in July. His legs began crumbling beneath him. "I really couldn't walk."

To get to his job, "I would crawl to the edge of the sailboat, pull myself up on the deck, pour myself into my dinghy, and then row it over to my work boat," the *Wauwinet Lady*. There McMullen would "kind of prop myself up" while steering and making safety announcements. When he got to the inn, The Wauwinet, where he usually ate meals, "I couldn't walk up to the hotel, so I would convince someone to buy me a turkey sandwich, and I would live on that for a few days. I was too proud, and I didn't want to stay in bed or go to the hospital. I think it was kind of messing with my head."

Finally, McMullen contacted Lepore, who zeroed in on what McMullen called "twin puncture wounds on my neck that looked like I'd been bitten by a vampire." Near the wounds was a raised lymph node that resembled skin cancer, but there was something atypical about it. "He wouldn't give up," McMullen recalls. "He wanted to figure out what it was."

Then one night, "it dawned on me," Lepore says. "Ulceroglandular tularemia. I'd read about it but never seen a case."

Only about a hundred to two hundred cases of tularemia are reported in the United States each year. It can cause skin ulcers, pneumonia, diarrhea, and swollen lymph glands, and can be fatal if untreated. "It's a great bio weapon," Lepore notes.

Sometimes called "rabbit fever" because it is carried by rabbits and rodents, tularemia can be transmitted to people if they handle infected animals, eat something contaminated with the bacteria, breathe it in, or are bitten by an infected insect, like a greenhead fly. On Nantucket, rabbits are nonnative animals, brought over from the Midwest in the 1930s so hunters had something for hounds to chase. But as rabbits do, their numbers have long since multiplied.

The greenhead flies that Lepore traps and sends to Sam Telford at Tufts for testing have never shown traces of tularemia, but Lepore knew that the nearby island of Martha's Vineyard had a small cluster of a different strain several years earlier. He called McMullen in, stuck a needle in the lymph node, sucked out fluid, and FedExed it to Telford. Sure enough, he told McMullen, it was "red hot for tularemia."

For a month, Lepore saw McMullen at least every other day, but since McMullen did not have insurance for such care, he says Lepore treated him "practically for free," charging only $440. Lepore tried three antibiotics before finding one that worked. "It was pretty powerful stuff," recalls McMullen. "It made my fingernails turn black."

Tularemia is the kind of obscure condition more likely to arise on Nantucket because the natural ingredients are there. But other characteristics contribute to a variety of medical problems. The population may be small, but it is hardly homogeneous.

As a summer resort community, Nantucket has visitors and natives who are highly traveled, sometimes to exotic places. A bride returned from her Caribbean honeymoon with a maggot wriggling out from between her shoulder blades. Another woman's vacation souvenir from Jamaica was a delightful hookworm called "creeping eruption."

And in a probable sushi-related incident, a lady from Greenwich, Connecticut, came in with a specimen: a fish tapeworm as long as a chinchilla—and the worm's other half still inside her. "I always say the only thing worse than finding a worm in your apple," Lepore told her, "is finding half a worm."

The population that supports Nantucket's summer community is increasingly diverse, with immigrants from Bulgaria, Cambodia, El Salvador, Haiti, Nepal, Latvia. Some immigrants visit the doctor only when their illnesses have become serious, like a man with "a canteloupe-sized scrotum with four to five feet of small bowel trapped in it." Some immigrants bring not only foreign maladies but foreign remedies—treatments like cupping, in which a hot cup is placed on the skin to suck blood to a certain spot, and medicines that have not been approved or studied in the United States.

"It's a very multicultural experience to practice medicine here," notes Margot Hartmann, the hospital's CEO. "You have to kind of understand from an infectious disease perspective what they might have been exposed to."

Other types of bizarre cases could happen anywhere, but Lepore believes he may see somewhat more of them because of the island's diversity and vacation atmosphere. There is, for instance, a subcategory, or perhaps a sub rosa category, of patient whose interests in unconventional erotica go comically, or tragically, awry.

One morning in August 2009, a twenty-eight-year-old tourist from Cambridge showed up at the hospital complaining of acute pain in his abdomen. He turned out to have a big tear in his rectum, a perforated colon, and a bad infection.

Lepore urged the man to explain, and he finally came out with the story. "He and his girlfriend were having some sex play, and he got a toilet plunger stuck up his butt. One could ask why, but I suppose there's no good answer."

The tourist told Lepore the injury had occurred around 4 or 5 AM, but Lepore thought it was "a lot older than he told me." Maybe he believed he could recover on his own, or embarrassment kept him from seeking help earlier. The damage was profound, and Lepore was concerned because the patient was developing sepsis, his bloodstream overwhelmed with bacteria. After all, of all the things one could insert in one's body, plungers are probably not the most sanitary.

Lepore pumped the man with intravenous fluids and antibiotics. The weather was bad, and the MedFlight helicopter was not planning to fly. But the man needed major care—the removal of a piece of large intestine and ultimately reconstruction of his bowel.

"I have done it," Lepore says. "But when you don't have the staffing and the other medical resources, and you start dealing with a patient that seriously ill, that's not a patient who should be on Nantucket." Fortunately, as Lepore was preparing to operate, MedFlight decided to fly.

The choice of a plunger might have been innovative, but, in Lepore's experience, the motivation for using it is not. One patient arrived with a cucumber in the same location. Another man had a vibrator there, insisting his wife was responsible, although she said she had nothing to do with it. Another man was vacuuming naked when his genitals got caught in the fan blades, suffering "a certain amount of destruction," as Lepore puts it.

One night in the fall of 2011, a Nantucketer in his twenties came into the ER with a predicament Lepore describes this way: "Picture a penis.

There's some loose skin by the corona at the head of the penis. The guy had put two very powerful magnets there on either side. They were pressing into the skin because they're attracted to each other. I wish I'd taken a picture. He was in a great deal of pain, and then he was in a great deal of embarrassment."

Nurses and a physician assistant were unable to pry the magnets off because "every time they pulled one, the other would pull it back." So Lepore anesthetized the area with lidocaine and used hemostatic forceps to dislodge them. "I really don't want to know what you were up to," Lepore told the man, sensing the moment was right for a proverb: "Idle hands are the devil's workshop."

Lepore was a little less diplomatic to the man who introduced himself by saying, "Doc, I think I have a ballpoint pen up my penis." How could Lepore not be charmed?

"You're a dumb bastard," Lepore told him.

"I didn't come here to be insulted," the man responded, doubly hurt.

"Look, you're forty years old and you *think* you have a ballpoint pen up your penis?" Lepore asked, amazed. "That's sort of black and white. There isn't a lot of gray in there."

Lepore had to operate to remove said pen by making an incision in the bladder so he could pull it out from below. The episode ended gentlemanly enough, however. "These cases," Lepore observes, "if you don't have testosterone, you don't understand it."

Lepore has seen a few cases involving the opposite sex, but most have been accidents, like the woman with a chunk of soap lost in her vagina, who had been trying to get clean, not trying to get off. Lepore removed the soap. On the patient discharge sheet he could not refrain from giving advice: "Soap on a rope could forestall this problem."

Lepore cannot fix some erotic experiments. "Death, rectal paintbrush, and penis ring" was the way Lepore characterized one case in an email. It occurred out on the water in the cabin of a small sailboat. The man, a summer restaurant worker, was found naked, kneeling, with a paintbrush stuck into his rear end and a noose around his neck connected to a penis ring. It was an arrangement the man had engineered himself, trying for "a little bit of strangulation because partial asphyxiation causes an erection," Lepore explained. A salacious video had been playing on his computer, and he had been smoking a small amount of marijuana.

"A friend of his discovered him, then called one of the restaurant owners, who then called the sheriff, who then called the police, who then called the Coast Guard, who then called me," Lepore said. Partial asphyxiation had turned into total asphyxiation, and Lepore went out to the boat to pronounce the man dead, see if an autopsy was required, and dispatch the body to the medical examiner's office in Boston.

"It wasn't," Lepore summed up, "a good picture."

While Lepore's black comic sensibility appreciates such gallows humor, it is the medical mysteries that really get his blood flowing. His diagnostic acumen is something of a legend among patients.

In 1994, Lepore knew John Gardner as a "tough-as-a-two-dollar-steak" defensive back on the football team, small in size but so determined that "if I said to John, 'I want you to run through the wall,' he would run through the wall."

So when Gardner at fourteen started losing coordination, speed, and strength, even though he was training five days a week, Lepore knew something was up. Gardner was having headaches and feeling dizzy but tried to shrug it off until simply hitting a tackling dummy caused an intense jolt of pain in his neck. Lepore sent him for an MRI, got the results on a Sunday morning, and immediately decided that "the kid's got to know what's going on."

Gardner was off-island, though, heading to the Patriots' opening game with his father and other relatives. They'd just stopped to eat breakfast at the Country Kitchen in Hyannis on Cape Cod when a police officer entered and called out the name Gardner. Lepore had tracked him down. From a pay phone, Gardner called Lepore, who told it to him straight: "John, looks like you have a brain tumor."

Lepore sent him immediately to Massachusetts General Hospital, where his tumor, which was not cancerous, was removed. But after the surgery, he experienced repeated puzzling setbacks, each of which Lepore helped diagnose: meningitis, a spinal tumor, leaking spinal fluid, and arachnoiditis—inflammation of a membrane that covers spinal nerves. "Doc was constantly trying to figure out what exactly was wrong," recalls Gardner, who had to have surgery three more times. "I always had the feeling that if I needed something, he was going to get it done."

Gardner could never play football again and for a while had to lie on the floor in class because he couldn't hold his head up and look at the blackboard. But Lepore pushed him to get back in shape, monitoring his exercise plan of walking to the end of first his driveway, then his street. "He was taking great care to make sure I was progressing. He was matter-of-fact. I asked him a question, and he didn't sugarcoat it. That, I appreciated."

Lepore considers his approach axiomatic. "You got to spend time. You can't be on a six-minute schedule. You got to ask the right questions."

Sometimes even before you actually see the patient. When Marilyn Bailey came from San Diego to visit her daughter, Carolyn Condon, who had just had a baby, Bailey's hip was in pain. As her son-in-law helped her upstairs, her hip "snapped in his arms," Condon recalls. In the emergency room, a visiting doctor who happened to be a bone specialist examined Bailey.

Bailey told the doctor she thought she had a groin pull, and without ordering an X-ray, he concurred, gave her painkillers, and sent her home. But Bailey's pain persisted, keeping the family up all night. Next morning, Condon, in tears, burst into the office of her own doctor.

"Dr. Lepore, what do I do?"

"How old is your mother?" Lepore asked.

"Sixty-nine."

"I'm calling 911; she's coming in. There's no way a sixty-nine-year-old pulled her groin muscle."

Lepore got Bailey to the hospital and sent Condon home to rest, calling her several hours later. "The pain that your mother has endured is amazing," Lepore told her. Her hip was completely broken, and Lepore had discovered that Bailey was having a recurrence of breast cancer she'd had years earlier. The cancer had metastasized to her hip and was spreading throughout her body. Lepore helicoptered her to Boston.

"Dr. Lepore just took the bull by the horns and said, 'This is what we're doing,'" says Condon, who runs a heating and cooling business with her husband. Later, the bone doctor called Condon, apologizing profusely. "He was beside himself. He was just blown out of the water."

Margot Hartmann thinks one key to Lepore's diagnostic success is that he is good at hearing what patients are saying and not saying. "People are self-selecting in the information they give you, out of their own effort to make sense of it and maybe because of where they want to lead you. You have to keep lots of differential diagnoses in play, while not assuming it is any one thing. You don't want to miss the subtle clue."

Clues like that are what Lepore lives for, Hartman says. "He loves to crack open those books" and read about cutting-edge treatments and oddball cases.

In 2010, when Eva Blathe was two months old, her mother, Michelle Whelan, changed the baby's diaper, dressed her in footie pajamas, and set her down for a nap. A couple of hours later, several of Eva's toes were turning purple, and one was bleeding.

"It was absolutely horrifying," Whelan recalls. "I was in hysterics. I knew the danger was that her toe would fall off."

Whelan rushed Eva to the hospital, and Lepore was called. He instantly recognized a problem many physicians would never have guessed:

toe-tourniquet syndrome. The syndrome happens when hair, often from the mother, gets wrapped around the baby's toes. A strand of hair is so thin it can slip onto a baby's foot unnoticed. A baby kicking and moving around inside pajamas can cause the hairs to pull tighter and tighter, cutting off circulation. The toes swell, often concealing the hair entirely.

Medical literature says that toe-tourniquet syndrome is not uncommon, especially because hormones cause women to lose more hair postpregnancy, but that many doctors don't know to look for it. Unable to see the hair, some misdiagnose the condition as accidental injury or, worse, as resulting from child abuse. The actual problem can take three or four days to diagnose, and by that time toes can develop gangrene or need to be amputated.

"I've read sixteen parenting books, and it's not in any of them," notes Whelan, who runs Sustainable Nantucket, an organization advocating locally grown food.

Lepore took the screaming infant and grabbed tweezers. He spent a long time teasing and pulling at the hairs, which were strangling the three middle toes. He thought he had gotten everything, but just to be sure, he told Whelan to bring Eva back in four hours. When they returned, he decided to perform surgery to make sure to catch every last strand.

Whelan, who had only known Lepore peripherally before, knew he could be "perceived as abrasive," so she was stunned by his commitment to her daughter's case. He performed the surgery on the delicate toes without leaving any scarring. He checked on Eva regularly in the days after the surgery but never charged Whelan for those sessions.

"Meet you outside my office—I'll just look at her toe," he'd say.

"He knew I was on maternity leave, and it was going to be hard for me to afford follow-up visits." And he knew "I was feeling like I was a bad mom."

Several esoteric Lepore discoveries have saved more than a toe or two. Foley Vaughan, a lawyer, went to the hospital with what he described as "the world's worst sore throat." Lepore was unavailable, performing surgery, so another doctor took a look and told Vaughan he had cold sores. "Go home," the doctor said. "There's nothing I can do for it."

An hour later, the pain was so intense, Vaughan returned and saw Lepore. By that time, he couldn't swallow. Within minutes, Lepore diagnosed Vaughan's ailment as adult epiglottitis, an infection behind the tonsils that can cause fever, painful swallowing, and can easily obstruct the airways. It may have been the disease that killed George Washington.

"It's almost impossible to diagnose," Vaughan notes. "But a swelled-up throat can kill you. He put me in intensive care for three days. I had to sleep sitting up."

In 2006, Elliot Norton, a fifty-six-year-old chef at the island's Rotary restaurant who had always been healthy, came to Lepore's office "just not feeling good," he says. The cause and even the symptoms were unclear. He made several appointments over six weeks, and finally, because he had pain in his jaw and a slightly drooping lip, Diana Hull, Lepore's longtime nurse, suggested Norton see a dentist. But Lepore sensed something more interesting, and threatening.

"Let's go get a CAT scan," he said. Hull teased him that he was going overboard, rolling her eyes and claiming that Lepore was on a wild goose chase. But Lepore had a hunch. "Something smells wrong."

After the scan, Lepore called Norton, who met him in the parking lot behind his office. Sunlight was glaring off the piece of paper in Lepore's hands: the scan readout, a piece of graph paper about twenty-five inches long and eight inches wide with "little lines on it," Norton recalls.

"I found out what's wrong," Lepore began.

"Oh good," Norton interjected. But Lepore looked concerned.

"You're standing there, . . . " he said. "You should be dead."

The scan showed Norton had an aneurysm on the right side of his brain that had ruptured, bled, and, at least temporarily, sealed itself off.

There was another aneurysm on the left side and another in the center; those hadn't ruptured yet but could at any moment. Aneurysms are ticking time bombs; if they rupture, they can cause strokes that are often fatal. Norton had none of the classic symptoms. "Even a blind pig finds an acorn now and then," Lepore shrugged.

Lepore rushed Norton to Boston for intracranial surgery. At the hospital, Norton overheard staff members discussing his case with tears in their eyes. He asked the neurosurgical staff "what my percentage was, and they said it was only 6 percent I was going to come out fine without brain damage." He landed in that 6 percent.

Still, Lepore's hunches aren't always foolproof. Sean Kehoe, who spent his teenage years on Nantucket, was sent to the hospital as a high school junior when his abdomen suddenly turned rigid. "I couldn't stand up or sit down," says Kehoe, now in his late twenties. "All I could do was lie on my back because it was so hard."

He was stretched out in the emergency room when Lepore came in and opined, "I think it's appendicitis. If this turns out to be what I think it is, we're not going to have time to fly you off-island. We're not going to have time to bring in a team. I'm here, and I'll do it myself. We'll have you prepped and ready in two hours."

Sean remembers quaking. "He had a look in his eye, like he wanted to see what I was made of. This made me really nervous. I think I lied about how I felt to avoid having him cut me open."

He told Lepore, "I want to wait till the last possible moment. I'm going to talk to my mom." Sean turned out not to have appendicitis, probably just really bad gas, so Lepore would not have operated anyway.

"Sometimes as a physician you program your thinking one way," Lepore acknowledges. "I try not to have tunnel vision. It's not always easy."

Lepore sometimes seems driven by the adrenalin of discovery and remedy; the more routine aspects of doctoring don't interest him as much. People who work with him say he can just wander out of the office in search of something more intriguing.

"He can be incredibly frustrating to work with," says Martina Richards, one of Lepore's former nurses and a close friend. "The guy's a surgeon, and primary care often is not that exciting. When somebody had a cold or a rash, he really didn't want to deal with it. It's boring."

Barbara Rives has experienced both his engaged and his disengaged sides.

In Rives, a fellow runner, Lepore has detected heel spurs and stress fractures, and at one point did an MRI because he thought, incorrectly as it turned out, that she might have a cracked pelvis. Another time, he sent her for tests, suspecting that her pain was caused by bone injury. He was right—it was a spiral fracture, and if she had run on it, more damage could have resulted.

"He hasn't always been right, but he has helped me a lot," Rives reflects. "I would never have gone to a doctor for the things I go to him for. Otherwise I would just be walking around in aches and pains."

But when Rives, who had experienced problems with the delivery of her first baby, wanted Lepore to deliver her second, he declined. "Please would you please do this for me?" she begged. But to Lepore, her pregnancy was simply not interesting enough.

"For a vaginal delivery, I do not have that degree of patience," he admits. "You have to be appropriately phlegmatic. I consider it mildly bovine, like cows sitting there and chewing their cud. When you're doing a vaginal delivery, it is set up to work, generally. There's a certain placidity, wandering in every couple of hours to see how things are going, that I find a little disconcerting."

He far prefers a case like that of the taxidermist who, in a manner of speaking, got stuffed himself when he slipped in the woods while rabbit hunting. "I got a stick up my ass," the taxidermist said when he came into the hospital. It was actually a potentially devastating injury. A branch had sliced through his urethra, the tube connecting his bladder to his genitals, and he needed surgery. "Everybody thought it was really funny—until I looked at it," Lepore recalls.

The case of Ruth Foulkes in January 2011 gave Lepore just the right mix of skill and shock value.

"Did I tell you about the hand I cut off?" he'll say, by way of introduction. It was only two fingers, but still: it was his first amputation of this kind, and he was proud enough of his handiwork to show off photographs he took. "Normally I may have sent this to a hand surgeon or plastic surgeon, but that was not really practical in this situation."

Foulkes was eighty-nine and had dementia. She had squamous cell skin cancer, and although Lepore had repeatedly removed the cancerous lesions on her left hand, they kept reappearing.

When Lepore, after consulting a plastic surgeon on the mainland, said that "amputation was the way to go," Foulkes's daughter-in-law, Shelley, a home health nurse, felt, "It did seem extreme." But the family had learned long ago to trust Lepore. A year earlier, during a routine physical, he had detected a heart murmur in Shelley's husband, Mark, that turned out to be a torn mitral valve requiring surgery. When it came to removing the ring finger and pinky on her mother-in-law's hand, Shelley knew it wasn't Lepore's area of expertise, but "I just figured: he knows his anatomy."

Having the operation on-island, with family close by, undoubtedly minimized the distress Foulkes might have experienced had she instead had to go to Boston. And Lepore was at his breezy best, assuring Shelley Foulkes that her mother-in-law wouldn't miss the two fingers because "she can throw a curveball without them."

Alexandra McLaughlin was still having a terrible time, falling asleep and collapsing even more than usual. Practically every time she ventured outside, she would end up crumpled on the ground, sidewalk, or sand.

People's reactions only made things worse. Rendered temporarily paralyzed and mute, McLaughlin could not tell a well-intentioned woman that she had not, in fact, gone into a diabetic coma or request that she stop trying to force a cookie down her throat. "You can tell them a hundred times, 'I'm not a diabetic,' but if they're a cookie shover, that's who they are."

Other people would pull on her tongue, in a misguided attempt to prevent her from choking. Some would begin CPR or call 911. "When people start touching me all over, I hate that," McLaughlin says. "I can hear people doing things to my body. I can't make them stop. Sometimes I can maybe move a finger, but nobody ever notices. I can't even change my breathing."

The unsolicited activity added to her stress, prolonging the time it took to snap out of the paralytic state. And sometimes the touching became sinister; more than one strange man has fondled her or worse while she has lain immobile on the ground. "I'm the litmus test for the gentlemanliness of the community," she observes.

Things got so bad that by 2010, "I couldn't leave the house at all." Trolling the Internet, she came across a condition called narcolepsy with cataplexy. Narcolepsy is a disorder causing people to sleep suddenly in short bursts, sometimes in the middle of driving, working, or talking. Cataplexy, which can accompany narcolepsy, causes sudden muscle weakness, sometimes triggered by intense emotions. Narcolepsy with cataplexy appears related to having too little of a brain neurotransmitter called hypocretin; its absence causes abnormal sleep cycles.

McLaughlin couldn't believe how uncannily her symptoms seemed to match. What she had more than anything, she realized, was "a sleep-wake cycle cluster fuck." She instantly called Lepore. "I am going to sound like a cuckoo," she thought. "But Dr. Lepore, he won't hold this against me."

When she told him, "this reads like my personal diary," Lepore replied, "Wow. I've only seen this once before."

He sent her to a neurologist at Massachusetts General, and she waited months for results of tests, only to be called back for more. Frustrated, she visited a doctor in Westport, Connecticut, where her parents live, who administered still more tests. Both doctors said she probably had narcolepsy with cataplexy, but they couldn't be 100 percent sure because "the test results were not textbook." For example, when she fell asleep, it took eight minutes to enter REM sleep. Textbook is under seven minutes.

The textbook definition mattered mostly because of money. The medication considered most effective for narcolepsy with cataplexy costs tens of thousands of dollars a year, a sum that insurance companies aren't willing to pay unless the diagnosis is ironclad. The medication is also controversial. The drug, Xyrem, is tightly regulated because its active ingredient, gamma-hydroxybutyric acid or GHB, has been used as a date rape drug.

GHB was originally developed as an anesthesia drug, and a few drops of the odorless, colorless liquid can be slipped into a drink, quickly causing someone to lose consciousness for hours and have no memory of events during that time. Although it became available as a dietary supplement, and was sold under street names including "blue nitro" and "liquid ecstasy," the government in the 1990s warned against its use and restricted its sale. GHB can cause coma, and the Drug Enforcement Agency has linked it to at least seventy-one deaths and 5,700 overdoses.

In 2002, though, Xyrem was approved for narcolepsy with cataplexy, the first FDA-approved treatment for cataplectic patients. Later it was approved for excessive daytime sleepiness in patients with narcolepsy.

A doctor prescribing Xyrem to McLaughlin would have to use a centralized pharmacy that tracks patients' drug use. McLaughlin would take it at bedtime, and it would knock her out cold for four hours, after which she would wake abruptly, take another dose, and sleep another four hours. There would be no possibility of waking her during those stretches, under the theory that uninterrupted sleep would make her less likely to need short, sudden naps during the day.

McLaughlin was convinced she should try Xyrem. For one thing, in early 2011, she found a fellow traveler with narcolepsy plus cataplexy, Justin Curry, who lives in Scituate, Massachusetts, southeast of Boston. He was taking Xyrem. McLaughlin invited Curry, who was twenty-five then, to Nantucket, relieved to have someone who shared her hair-raising, discombobulating symptoms. Curry, who'd been diagnosed as a teenager, knew the ignominy of it all: he had even survived passing out face-first in a bowl of chicken noodle soup in his high school cafeteria.

Curry's Nantucket cataplexies rivaled her own. Once, Curry recalls, he collapsed face down in front of the Ralph Lauren boutique, one of the only chains that has been allowed to set up shop on Nantucket. "Of all stores," Curry moans in recollection. "I just planked," part of him landing on the brick sidewalk, part on the island's quaint cobblestones. Good food, like a big plate of baby-back ribs, made him so happy that McLaughlin remembers it triggering a collapse, even if "I sat there talking about the Holocaust through the whole meal."

And while they love going to the beach because, with all the sunbathers, "everybody looks narcoleptic," they've found they have to be wary of other triggers: excessive heat and, especially for men, arousal. McLaughlin plays defense for Curry "when I see a really hot chick is coming his way," telling him, "Look at me, look at me, think of something awful." Once while they were eating on the pavilion at Jetties Beach, though, she stepped away briefly to return a tray and realized, "I just left Justin surrounded by hot women in bikinis. Sure enough, he went down." He landed under a table, and during the twenty minutes it took him to revive, McLaughlin had to calm down the "bikini girls" with a "stand-up comedy routine: 'Where are you folks from?'"

At Surfside Beach, he fell while waiting for McLaughlin outside the ladies room, and a police officer ran toward him, hands cupped, ready to do CPR. McLaughlin had to body block the cop because, for someone who doesn't need it, CPR can be painful and potentially harmful. "For men," she adds, "half the time when they collapse, they look like they're unconscious on the ground, with an erection. It's the most socially inappropriate illness."

One stormy night, McLaughlin and Curry were leaving the emergency room after McLaughlin had been taken there during an episode. McLaughlin was still in what she calls a hallucinatory "autonomic state," imagining that she was in Boston trying to hail a cab. Suddenly there was a big clap of thunder, and, right outside the hospital, they both went down. For a short time, hospital staff, perplexed about which medical personnel should bring patients back into the hospital after discharge, "left us in our little narcolepsy pile in the rain," McLaughlin recalls.

McLaughlin brought Curry to meet Lepore, "so if Justin went down," Lepore "would know what his face looked like." He sat in the waiting room during her appointment, unnerved at first by the large furry chair, the Picasso-esque hybrid of animal parts: black hooves, red tongue, goat-like horns. "What the fuck is this?" he asked. "Alexandra, do you see what I see? Am I having a hypnagogic hallucination?" Narcoleptics can have those before falling asleep.

"I swear to God, it's a real thing," McLaughlin told him. Curry couldn't avoid the psychedelic chair: "Even if I was looking in the glass cases with the bones and things in them, you can still see it in the reflection." And Lepore's office was full of Curry's triggers. "That door slams like the dickens every few seconds. Justin was bored, the room was cold—he didn't stand a chance."

Suddenly, Curry fell, "face down, straight as an arrow. You had the nurses freaking out, trying to figure out what is wrong." Other patients in the waiting room were perturbed. "I was just terrified," one told McLaughlin. "I really thought he was dead."

Before scooping Curry off the floor, Lepore, sensing a teachable moment, summoned the hospital's head of emergency nursing, telling her enthusiastically, "This is what it looks like!"

To try to acclimate Nantucket's emergency responders to their condition, Curry and McLaughlin printed a flyer with their smiling pictures and an explanation of their disorders. Rather than take her to the hospital, McLaughlin wanted emergency personnel to know, "it's much easier to drive me home and put me in bed."

They struck a deal: "If I cataplexy in front of a huge crowd, the EMTs have to bring me in to the ER because otherwise they look like incompetent jerks, and they can't just stay there until I wake up." But if she collapsed off the beaten path, they could leave her or drive her home. In return, when she and Curry wanted to attend an event, they would check with EMTs first.

Fourth of July fireworks were a challenge they wanted to tackle, even though the loud, startling booms would cause them to collapse, probably repeatedly. When McLaughlin asked Lepore about watching the display in their car with the windows rolled up, Lepore said, "Oh no. If somebody sees two unconscious people in a car with the windows rolled up, they're going to think it's a suicide pact." People invited them to fireworks-watching parties, then disinvited them when they realized they might make a scene. "How do you find a spot where two people can be unconscious-looking on Nantucket and nobody's going to notice it?" McLaughlin puzzled. Finally, they snuck into a yacht club, plunked down on the beach, and told EMTs where they were.

Another time, they wanted to attend the annual demolition derby, although "watching cars crash together is going to stress me out," McLaughlin knew. To be safe, she and Curry sat near the EMTs, where "I cataplexied nine times in front of everyone. I was part of the show."

Despite these accommodations, McLaughlin continued to have episodes that unnerved her. After her collapse while walking her dog, she called Lepore distraught, desperate to try Xyrem: "I know that this diagnosis is me. This is fitting the things that are just so private I never told anybody. Please, Dr. Lepore, let's try this new medicine. I'll pay for it out of pocket—I don't care."

While Lepore began researching Xyrem, McLaughlin had another episode on her doorstep and was taken to the ER. Lepore swung by and said: "Absolutely, I'll write the prescription."

McLaughlin felt a swell of gratitude. "He didn't care about the perfect diagnostic criteria. It looks like this. It fits me perfectly. Wait-and-see is what's been the nightmare of my life. He's just saved my life for me."

In August 2011, she began taking Xyrem, a foul-tasting liquid she mixes with water. McLaughlin expected to pay for the Xyrem herself, but somehow Lepore's office persuaded her insurance carrier to cover it.

So far, McLaughlin is napping less and "having fewer cataplexies." During a two-hour visit with McLaughlin in January 2012, for example, she knocked out only once, after being startled by the ring of her mother calling her on her cell phone. But only a few minutes after her head dropped to the table, she awoke. (Curry, who was with her, cataplexied briefly soon afterward, during a discussion of a fatal accident that he found too distressing.)

McLaughlin finds she can drive if she hasn't eaten recently, if there's no chance of thunder, if she isn't tired, and if she sings along with the radio. She is aware that for brief moments after taking Xyrem, her brain thinks "whatever I'm doing is fascinating," prompting her to order ridiculous merchandise like a dog wig from late-night TV. And she has taken precautions, telling the fire department, for example, that in the event of a nighttime fire, she won't be rousable. She is getting a service dog that will be trained to catch her when she falls.

She even got a job: office manager for a theater company. "Who would want to hire this?" she'd thought. And it was a close call. During her interview, the interviewer, upset about the recent drowning death of a child at a Nantucket summer camp beach program, cried and hugged McLaughlin. McLaughlin couldn't allow herself to feel sadness; already her arms felt paralyzed. "I knew I had twenty seconds before I was going to collapse. I was trying to think of something humorous."

But when McLaughlin explained why she could not return the hug, the woman was very understanding. The job was short-lived, as it turned out. Still, McLaughlin considered it progress. Lepore is trying to find her another job or some volunteer work, and has jotted a note on his prescription pad, saying that she has narcolepsy and that concerned parties should call him. She carries it in her pocket, but it doesn't work all the time.

People still misunderstand and overreact, or they think her symptoms are figments of her imagination. But the message Lepore hopes to convey is clear, McLaughlin says: "It's Nantucket—we can handle weird."

CHAPTER 9

FAMILY PRACTICE

Lepore and his neighbor, Chris Fraker, were outside in the small compound that contains their houses when they noticed something glinting in a patch of woods. Moving closer, they saw a bottle of yellowish liquid: Captain Morgan rum.

They realized the bottle must belong to Lepore's son Nick and Fraker's son Porter, who were both sixteen and fast friends. Other parents might confront the kids with the seriousness of their behavior or let it slide, thinking that confrontation would make things worse. Most would confiscate the bottle, to at least temporarily deprive the boys of booze and let them know they'd been caught.

Not Lepore. He poured out some rum, unzipped his fly, and without ceremony pissed into the bottle, refilling it with his urine. Then he put it back in the bushes.

Soon after, Nick, Porter, and another friend grabbed for the bottle and drank. Lepore waited a few months before telling them what they had swallowed, impishly asking them "if it tasted a little salty."

Nick, who swears he was drinking only beers that night, was mortified. "My friends said that didn't happen, and then they never talked about it again."

But Lepore savored his victory. How many parents, especially how many parents who are doctors, would divest of their own bodily fluids in the distinct hope that their children would drink the waste, be disgusted, and sober up?

"He's insane" is Nick's verdict. "If he was living on the street, they'd call him crazy. But because he has a house and family, he's eccentric."

Growing up as one of Lepore's children was always an adventure. He could be unpredictable, given to unusual hobbies, competitive flights of fancy, and off-the-cuff comments steeped in shock value. But he was also a strong, dependable presence, someone they could see was vital to their island. It's probably no accident that all three Lepore children's jobs relate to health care, but also no accident that they are not trying to do the work their father does.

"My father's a big personality—he casts a very large kind of shadow," says T.J., the middle child. "He and Nantucket have been a little like Kurtz up the river," he adds, referring to Joseph Conrad's *Heart of Darkness*.

Meredith, the oldest, often called Meri, did not realize until she attended nursing school how "different he was from your typical physician. He goes above and beyond. And he gave up a lot to move to Nantucket. I was like, 'Why did you move here? You could have been a big-time surgeon. You picked up and moved to this teeny little island?'"

The Lepores had been on Nantucket only a few years when they came face to face with the island's medical limitations. It was shortly before Christmas, and Lepore was working the emergency room. Suddenly, Cathy called to say that something was wrong with T.J., who was seven. He had been sitting on a couch complaining of a headache, and when he stood up, he went limp on his left side. "I crashed to the floor," T.J. recalls.

Lepore bolted home, but when he arrived, "I had everything back," T.J. remembers. "He didn't know what to think. He walked me around in circles, and he left. And I went limp and crashed to the floor again."

Lepore rushed back, scooped up his son, and headed to the hospital. T.J. had had a stroke, and his left side was paralyzed.

Lepore felt T.J. should get to a bigger hospital where state-of-the-art diagnostics could determine exactly what damage occurred. But the weather was dicey, and boats had not been running regularly for days. "The hell with it," Lepore decided. "We're going to Boston."

After three hours of wrangling, Lepore got T.J. on a small plane, so tiny he had to fly with only a nurse. He remembers being wrapped "like a potato in this tinfoil warming blanket." A brain scan showed an infarction, an area of dead tissue, in his right parietal lobe, which helps coordinate spatial and mapping abilities.

Even for Lepore, the experience at Children's Hospital Boston was frightening. "No terror like a sick kid," as he puts it. "Your kid is totally paralyzed on his left side, yet he's the best kid on the floor, because all these other kids got tumors."

Despite an intensive diagnostic workup, the stroke's cause remained a mystery. Lepore, the master diagnostician, couldn't solve the riddle of his own child's condition. His impulse to fix things took hold: he planned a ramp to their house and obsessed about helping T.J. learn to walk again.

Late Christmas Day, the hospital discharged T.J., and for months he underwent physical therapy. That summer, Lepore devised an additional workout regimen, taking T.J. to Mount Katahdin, Maine's highest peak, where Lepore and his limping son hiked the Knife Edge trail, a narrow ridge with a dauntingly shear drop-off. "I was terrified," T.J. recalls. "It was not the best parenting decision. But he got me out there."

T.J. now exhibits only "a small amount of motor dysfunction," is "very right handed," and has "a little bit of atrophy on his left leg," Lepore says. "If he gets tired, he sort of contorts his left hand." When T.J.

wanted to be a doctor, some medical schools were concerned. "People wanted to know whether or not he was going to have a repeat of it."

But he has become an obstetrician-gynecologist in Springfield, Massachusetts, able to perform surgery, even though "I hold my forceps a little funny" and "my grip for my left hand is just a little bit impaired." He sees these simply as "areas where I'm a little weak and I have to compensate."

Lepore tried to model the need to compensate for deficiencies and take initiative to fix problems. No one else would do it for you—or should—was his belief.

When T.J. struck Nick with a hockey stick above his eyelid, causing a deep gash, it was Lepore who stitched his face. Doctors are generally advised against treating family members, but Lepore never considered asking anyone else. "That's easy, of course," he says. "No surgeon thinks he is second best."

Sometimes, though, his pragmatism verged on boot-camp toughness.

One late fall day when Cathy was off-island shopping, her friend Pam Michelsen got a call from Meredith, who was about nine. "Her daddy had locked them out of the house because he was reading, and they were fighting. He was mad at them, and he just threw them out. And it was bitter, bitter cold."

Michelsen called Lepore. "Tim, you can't lock the kids out of the house. It's freezing."

Lepore, from an upstairs window, tossed coats outside. Soon Meredith called again. "We're still freezing to death!" Michelsen jumped in her car. It took a while to reach the Lepores' because she lived far northwest of downtown, "which is the other side of the world because, you know, ten feet is ten miles" on Nantucket. She grabbed the children, who were huddled on the porch, and took them until Cathy got home.

It wasn't the first Lepore lockout. When the children argued, he'd send them outside, then race downstairs to lock the bulkhead from the inside and block other means of reentry. "I don't think any other parents have been locking their kids out," he acknowledges, and "I don't think Cathy endorsed it. But I'm trying to keep things comfortable, and the kids are fighting and raising hell."

It wasn't just self-interest, he asserts. "It was a way to catch their attention. They stopped fighting, and they had to work together. It united them against a common enemy: me." Besides, contends Lepore, it was more humane than a spanking. "No blood, no foul."

It worked, at least temporarily. "They were a good deal more contrite. You just keep them a little bit uneasy, and they have to deal with an irrational parent." They never knew what to expect. Once, after he had locked them out, "I caught Meredith sneaking in the house. I had fallen asleep on the couch downstairs, and she came in through the window. She wasn't quite prepared to see dear old Dad sitting there."

The Ajax episode demonstrated another side of dear old Dad. Nick was about twelve, and Lepore took him hunting for rabbits for Ajax, his red-tailed hawk. As Lepore recalls, "Nick wasn't working particularly hard. He was lollygagging instead of beating the brush trying to get rabbits moving."

Suddenly, Nick recalls, he heard a "Whoof!" and whipped around. "There was Ajax, with its wings fully spread out and its talons and feet pointed. I ducked as quickly as I could, and it went whap on the top of my head." Grappling for a secure hold, the bird "started refooting and plucking out tufts of hair."

"The bird is on my head!" Nick screamed, immobilized with terror.

"My dad said, 'I'll be right there.' So nonchalant." A friend of Lepore's displayed more urgency, "charging through the brush" and ordering Nick not to move. "He reached down, gets the bird off my head. It felt like a half hour, but I'm sure it was about five seconds."

The hawk punctured holes in Nick's scalp. Blood cascaded down. But Lepore did not react the way Nick expected. "Nick, go sit in the car—there's about twenty minutes of light left," he said. "I just want to hunt a little bit longer."

Nick gaped at his father, thinking, "Are you serious? I have blood streaming down my head!" Hiking through the brush to the road, he approached the only house. An old couple answered. "My dad's bird attacked me," Nick panted. They were patients of Lepore's, naturally. They brought Nick inside, where he got cleaned up and drank orange juice. As Nick left the house, his father, having finished hunting, approached, notably unruffled.

"He looked like a waif in this bloody T-shirt, like something out of a horror movie," Lepore recalls. "They were just little puncture wounds, but on the scalp they really bleed."

Nick realized later that his father "knew it was nothing serious. He just didn't take into account how I didn't know that. I was never angry at him about it, to be honest. I was fine, and he was right. He has made a lot of sacrifices as far as his time, and this day was his chance to do something fun. I should have blamed him somewhat, but I just blamed the bird. I told him to never let me watch that bird if he's out of town because when he comes back, it's going to be stuffed."

The incident "made its way around the island pretty quick," Nick recalls. After all, "I had a tuft of hair missing." He'd expected people would be shocked. But Nantucketers knew their doctor. "Of course," people said. "Of course, he told him to just go wait in the car."

Lepore's children were immersed in the medical ins and outs of a small, self-contained community, not only because of his job, but because Cathy was a school nurse before becoming a school counselor.

"In a lot of ways I grew up at the hospital," notes T.J., who, with his siblings, would hang out at the nurse's station while Lepore did rounds. Once, Lepore dissected a heart in Meredith's third-grade class. She recalls that "about three-quarters of my class left the room and wanted to throw up."

At home, "the phone rang a thousand times a day," T.J. remembers, and patients constantly dropped by. One Sunday morning, T.J. opened the door to see Steve Tornovish, then an acquaintance of Lepore's (later, he would marry Cathy's sister Beth). Blood covered Tornovish's face; he was injured playing flag football. "Dad, it's for you," T.J. called. Tornovish never considered going to the hospital. "That kind of shit happens at the Lepores all the time."

Many people assumed the children knew their personal business, making it a mixed blessing to be Dr. Lepore's kids. "It seemed like you always had to be very careful what you did in public," Nick remembers. Other times, "people would just come up and say, 'Oh, I want to thank your dad for so and so,' and I had no idea who they were."

Still, Lepore "always tried to shield us" from the pressures he felt, T.J. recalls. "Things were playing on his mind, but he lacks a certain ability to share, which is normal in his age group. He also bottles a lot up. I can remember as a kid he would get grumpy with us. That's usually a good sign that something bad was going down or something that he hadn't expected."

By all accounts, Cathy is a vital stabilizer. "The woman's a saint," is the way Rhoda Weinman, Tim Lepore's close friend, describes it. "She is right to heaven, I keep telling her. Just his craziness alone. She's very, very kind; she's very sensitive; she's very intuitive. She, of course, absolutely adores him. And you could tell from the things he said that he adores her."

To Michelsen, Cathy "is the glue that keeps him together. He would be that crazy person who goes out in the moors and never returns if it weren't for her."

Michelsen says, "if there's a problem in the office, Tim won't deal with it—he hates confrontation, so Cathy has to go in and break up the fights and the issues that arise." Cathy tolerates not only Lepore's clutter, impulsiveness, and unpredictability but also the most frustrating thing for her, having to "play the role of the Tim wife," when people, usually summer visitors, don't recognize Cathy's own importance to the island.

"She really does love him—God knows why. She told me everything he does and talks about is just so interesting. I don't know anybody else who would be that patient."

There is more than enough to be patient with.

Sometimes Lepore seems to blow off steam with macabre practical jokes. When Meredith's best friend called one day, she hung up in tears because Lepore told her Meredith had been in "a horrible accident— she's dead."

When a girl Nick had begun dating in sixth grade phoned, Lepore said, "No, I'm sorry, he's not available. He's upstairs growing a penis." The girl dumped Nick at a school dance soon after.

Paul Johnson, a friend, compares it to the antics of Hawkeye Pierce and the other army doctors on the TV show *M*A*S*H*. "I think some of these little eccentric things are there for that reason—you throw in a little bit of insanity to get some relief because there's a huge amount of stress." In Lepore's job, "you're it, and if you can't fix it, that person dies or gets maimed for life."

Lepore's hobbies are his principal outlet. Some are short-lived flashes of passion, like when he suddenly decided "he wanted the entire family to just eat polenta," Nick recalls. "He said eventually we'll start growing our own corn. We would go buy the corn meal, and every meal was polenta. He had cookbooks, everything you could imagine— until my mother said, 'Okay, that's it.'"

He asked his office manager to order flax, planning to make linen. And he scooped clay from spots on the island, scheming to make pottery the way Indians did. Buckets of clay filled his car, which on a normal day is often littered with animal bones, old socks, and other detritus.

Once, says Martina Richards, a former nurse, Lepore "got all excited about something called *Back Tuva Future*," a CD blending Nashville country music with the throat singing of the Tuvan people of Siberia. "He'd come into the office and try to do the Tuvan throat sound."

And Nick, when he grew up and moved off-island, "got a random phone call telling me he needs a couple of pounds of acorn flour. It's some kind of Korean flour; its main virtue is that it fills you up quickly. He wanted me to get it for him, but I know where it's going. I'm not going to subject my mother to weeks of eating acorn flour."

After all, Lepore had already subjected Cathy to his stone circle fetish. When he glimpsed a boulder he liked while running somewhere on the island, he would return to the spot with one of his lovingly-rehabilitated vehicles—military Land Rovers like the 1967 *Chocolate Thunder* or the 1973 *Runaway American Dream*. He hauled the stones home and arranged them in a circle on the lawn. "In the event that we lose calendars, these stones mark the winter and summer solstice," he explains.

And what could be better to keep all those oversized rocks company? A Neolithic above-ground tomb called a dolmen. You build one of those and "you're prepared," says Lepore, who decided to improvise a version of these ancient structures using huge curb stones he scavenged from construction sites. He hasn't quite collected enough of them yet. "Need a legion of serfs, perhaps."

His plan to knit dog hair sweaters lasted for years. Lepore began saving shed fur from the family's dogs—they've had up to five at once, three Nova Scotia duck-tolling retrievers, a Jack Russell, and a "Mississippi mutt," one of the puppies regularly sent to Nantucket from an overflowing animal shelter in Mississippi. Lepore stashed the fur in plastic bags tucked in corners around the house.

It was a new one for their house cleaner, Mariellen Scannell, who thought she had "seen everything from A to Z." Encountering a bag of hair, "I was like, 'What the hell is this?'" Of course, "there's a lot of stuff throughout the house that I ask myself that question: What the hell is this?"

Cathy began trashing the bags of fur, but Lepore never quite abandoned the notion. "He had a bag of dog hair that he kept in the car for the better part of five years 'cause he knew my mother would throw it away if it was in the house," T.J. recalls.

Once something becomes a Lepore collectible, it's almost impossible to discard. Cleaning is not his top priority. "Cathy has to do it all, including flush the toilet," says Michelsen. "One night the furnace blew, and there's water flooding the basement. Tim says, 'I'm reading my book.' Cathy and I are down there with mops and everything. We're in the furnace room with all these boxes. I picked one off the floor, and the bottom falls out, and a real human skull and a bunch of bones roll out. I said, 'Oh my God, Cathy. Who is this?' She said, 'Who knows?'"

Once Michelsen asked Lepore, "What's the grossest thing you've ever seen?" thinking "it would be a one-sentence reply."

"Hold on a minute," Lepore answered, his eyes dancing. He dashed from the kitchen, returning with slides he had taken of horrific trauma cases he had treated years earlier in Rhode Island. He had Michelsen hold them up to the lamp light, one by one. "Here's a guy who got shot, and his guts are lying over here. That's his kidney. This one came in one night with no clothes on, and look what I found. Look at these things I pulled out of this guy."

When Cathy asked Scannell to clean for them about eight years ago, Scannell was unprepared for what awaited her. She is not easily surprised because her clients run the gamut. At the top end, she cleans and cooks for Edmund and Doris Reggie, the in-laws of Senator Edward M. Kennedy, and Louis Susman, the American ambassador to the United Kingdom. Often, guests she is cooking for include Senator John Kerry and media personalities like Chris Matthews and Maureen Orth.

But with Lepore, while "I had an inkling because I had been to his office" as a patient, she had never been to their house. The first day, the Lepores happened to be off-island, and someone was house-sitting for the dogs. "Well, here goes nothing," Scannell thought. "I'm going along the counters and kind of organizing stuff, and then I get over by the sink, and I wasn't really paying attention. I'm just spraying the Windex, and oh my God, there's a rat thawing out on the counter here!"

The house-sitter came running, explaining that Lepore "has a bird of prey and that's his lunch," Scannell recalls. "I was slightly disturbed for a short period of time."

Scannell hung in there. When people ask, with astonishment and sympathy, "Are you the lady that cleans Tim's house?" she replies, "Well, I make an attempt to." She figures Lepore embodies the expression "a clean house is a sign of a wasted life."

Scannell considers "the whole house somewhat of a Tim man cave," especially with "all this hunting stuff." Does she clean the gun areas in the basement? "No, no, no. Cathy knows where I draw the line." But once, Scannell found herself struggling to pull the vacuum cleaner from its closet. "What the hell?" she grumbled. She switched on a light and immediately asked Lepore for help. "What's the problem, Mariellen?" he asked. "Well, the vacuum cleaner seems to be wedged between a shotgun and a chain saw, and I'm a little concerned about having my head blown off."

Still, Scannell can relate a little to Lepore's sensibility. She did, after all, furnish a new home almost entirely from the take-it-or-leave-it pile at the town dump, a feat that landed her on the Nate Berkus interior design TV talk show. And she occasionally matches wits with the doctor. When she realized that Lepore leaves the radio on to keep the dogs company, the dial set to Rush Limbaugh, Scannell began changing it to a liberal political station and leaving a note: "Stop torturing the dogs. This is animal abuse, making dogs listen to Rush Limbaugh."

Discovering an old prescription pad, she scribbled a prescription for Lepore: "Your book levels were very high in books so please watch your intake of books." She signed it "Dr. Scannell."

Lepore's leaning towers of books cover sizable sections of the floor. Scannell is convinced "he is probably ordering ten, twenty books a day." That doesn't include the magazines: *Bowhunter*, *Primitive Archer*, *Traditional Archery*, *American Rifleman*, *American Falconry*, *Guns &*

Ammo, American Handgunner, Handloader, Rifle, Gun Digest, Shotgun News, Man at Arms, Bulletin of Primitive Technology. And those are just the weapons periodicals. There's also *Trail Runner, UltraRunning, Marathon & Beyond, Archives of Surgery, Journal of the History of Medicine and Allied Sciences, Annals of Internal Medicine, The Medical Letter, Emerging Infectious Diseases, The New England Journal of Medicine, Journal of the American College of Surgeons, Current Problems in Surgery, Selected Readings in General Surgery*, and *Morbidity and Mortality Weekly Report*.

This seemingly unscaleable mountain of reading material fuels another Lepore collection: an arcade of arcane facts he stores in his sand trap of a mind. Once Weinman, who raises championship dachshunds, got a license plate in their honor: Doxie4. Lepore took one look and smirked. "Do you know what a doxie is?" he asked. (It's a word for prostitute.) Weinman had no idea. But since no one else did either, she decided to keep the plate.

Dr. Scannell's prescription also noted that "due to high sneaker count I'm putting you on a sneaker-free diet." Tough medicine for a man who has saved every pair he has worn in the Boston Marathon, which he has completed each year since 1968. He also insists he needs different shoes for running on different surfaces. One pair came in handy, for example, when Lepore boasted to Richards that he had found "the only waterfall on Nantucket" and took her running out to the middle of the moors. "We came across a trickle of water, and he was like, 'Look, there it is!'"

Cathy has tried to jettison some of Lepore's sneakers, which are in various stages of disrepute. Lepore dug them out of the trash. Cathy bought a large shoe tree, which Scannell describes as "a teeny-weeny Band-Aid. Now we've got shoes all over the floor and a shoe tree in the middle of the room."

That sneaker addiction might suggest a die-hard runner, but Lepore's training and preparation is hardly rigorous. Sometimes he has time to run; sometimes he doesn't. He doesn't work out like an athlete or eat like one. "He's a doctor, but he doesn't take optimal or even average care of his health," Nick says. "He'll come home, grab a bowl full of tortilla chips, and spray mustard on it, and that's his dinner."

Weinman has run twenty marathons with Lepore in a head-to-head rivalry that became island lore. "My goal this year? To humble Rhoda Weinman, to have her eat my dust," was Lepore's boast to the Nantucket *Inquirer and Mirror*. He almost always lost; Weinman says she's beaten him eighteen times. Although Lepore got her into marathon running and they ran together for years, Weinman says his training regimen is so laughable that one of his best friends, a doctor, wrote her: "If you want to run a successful marathon, get rid of him. Don't even think about training with him."

In April 2008, Lepore entered the marathon after having major knee surgery. He was in such pain that he took Percocet and prednisone, and injected himself with "some long-acting local anesthetic" before the race, he says. "Alas and alack, not quite long-enough acting." By seven miles, Lepore was "in some serious hurt, limp and gimp." It took seven hours, so long that the official time clocks had been taken down, but he hobbled across the finish line.

"He's turning in times that are right before the meat wagon," Nick says. "He's never in good shape for it. I've been trying to get him to stop for years."

But Lepore's not about to stop. Instead, he makes accommodations. His toenails, for instance. Sometimes running makes his toes blister under the nails, "get fluid underneath and hurt like hell." So "I take a scalpel and take the nails off. It hurts for a couple of hours, but it's better than hurting for a couple of days." Sure, it's unattractive—"my wife thinks I have the ugliest feet in the world"—but Lepore even offers to share his remedy, telling fellow runner Barbara Rives that "he could pull out all my toenails." She demurred.

"For the smartest guy I've ever met, he does some of the craziest things I've ever seen," Tornovish says. But Tornovish, a recovering alcoholic, has to hand it to Lepore. At least they are "healthy outlets" that "help him deal with terrible stress."

Lepore's self-invented contests are occasionally self-delusional. When his sons played high school football, Lepore showed up at a practice and approached the coach, who ordered the Lepore boys to the goal line. There, in front of the whole team, Lepore challenged his sons to a hundred-yard dash. The boys were not shocked. He had threatened to "come down and humiliate us" in a race, Nick recalls. "He said it was going to be ugly. He was always all worked up, saying, 'I'm faster than you. I'm stronger than you. You'll never be able to beat me.'" But it didn't go exactly as Lepore had planned. "He swears he slipped because he wasn't wearing the right shoes," Nick says. "It turned out for him it was only a sixty-yard race." And an ignominious defeat. "I was so chagrined," Lepore recalls. "It's nighttime. The lights are on. All the kids are there watching. And this old fart just doesn't do it. I couldn't believe it. My boys were faster than I was."

When not challenging his sons to feats of strength in a homemade strongman competition with concrete balls, Lepore engineered trivia contests. On a trip to a Boy Scout ranch, he'd give extra food to the son who answered detailed questions about World War II aircraft. When another boy joined in and knew obscure answers, like the arrangement of pockets on the pants soldiers wore during the D-Day invasion, Lepore's inability to stump the kid "just drove him nuts," T.J. says.

He had better luck at the Boy Scouts' Pinewood Derby races, where boys race cars they build from small blocks of wood. But the path to success was bumpy. When T.J. was about eleven, he and Lepore won the Nantucket derby, but at the district level on Martha's Vineyard, "we got our doors blown off," T.J. says.

When Lepore asked to see the winning vehicle, its owner wouldn't let him, making Lepore suspicious. "Okay, good enough. I'm coming back, and I'm hungry."

Lepore pored over books and interrogated Pinewood insiders, learning tips that weren't exactly "kosher." He polished the wheels and axels with a tool he used on his guns. He added weights in strategic places. He gutted out the wood and poured in lead that he melted the way he liquefied lead for bullets. And he shaved the plastic tires so that only a ridge would touch the track, reducing resistance so the car would go faster.

Lepore even built backup cars in case something went wrong or judges disqualified one of his vehicles. "Nobody was going to beat my car—nobody."

In the Nantucket competition, "my car was three feet ahead of the next one. The only way you could be faster than my car is if it had a jet on it."

At the district competition, though, T.J. recalls, "there was kind of an awkward moment" when the judge examined entrants' cars. "He knew that people had been finagling," Lepore says. "I said, 'Let's race.' I am in competition with a lot of guys that are carpenters, woodworkers. Everybody had a little fudge. It's just, I did it better than anybody, because I'm shameless."

Lepore's car did so well, Nick remembers, that it "was one of the reasons that the Boy Scouts had to change the rules. Word had gotten around."

Lepore's other competitive outlet was boxing, a dead-of-winter activity the island organized so people wouldn't go stir crazy. "He was always going on about how good he was—bring the thunder and the pain," Nick recalls. "He would have testosterone patches on, and he came out snorting like a bull."

Anyone watching Lepore's pugilistic exploits could see what the doctor apparently couldn't. "He was an insult to boxers everywhere," says Steve Tornovish, who met Lepore boxing at the Boys and Girls Club. "He couldn't break an egg."

Once, as T.J. held a sign that said, "Doctor Death, Doctor Death, Doctor Death," Lepore fought Nick's twelfth-grade government teacher. "Everybody who came to my house for decades saw that video," Nick says. "He's talking about how he's pulled his double jabs, and it's the slowest thing you've ever seen. He says, 'This is the punch that put him down.' There's no punch. The guy must have tripped or something."

Lepore does point out that when he retired from boxing in his late fifties, the head of the Boys and Girls Club, a former pro boxer himself, pronounced Lepore the senior heavyweight champion. "I'd conquered everyone in my age class," he says. "I'm like Rocky Marciano. I fought everybody that wasn't in a wheelchair and then a few that came close. I was looking at the nursing home for other contenders."

Even when T.J. got married, Lepore could not suppress his competitive streak. At the rehearsal dinner, during a sentimental slide show about the bride and groom, a burst of sound erupted, and T.J. heard, "Yeah, yeah, do it. Go, go, go!" It was his father, and "he's got just about every guy between the ages of fifteen and sixty in a group, and he's got these nails." Lepore had cut the heads off the nails and was challenging men to bend them with their bare hands, including T.J., who had to "bend the nail in front of my wife's father." More than a few wedding guests cut their hands.

Meredith began working at her father's medical practice in middle school, "organizing all the dead people's files," she recalls. She returned to work for him in high school after her inability to operate a cash register got her fired from a job selling T-shirts. Later, she tried different careers—teaching, lab work—but eventually decided "I wanted to be like my dad."

After becoming a nurse practitioner, she had trouble finding a job, so Lepore said, "Why don't you come down and work for me?" He immediately threw responsibilities at her, having her perform a spinal tap, although she'd never done one. She watched him break bad news to patients, always no-nonsense: "This is what's going to happen; this is what we're going to do; here's my cell phone number."

And she admired how in situations where "other doctors would probably say, 'Well, let's wait and see,' he'll say, 'If you're sick, you're sick. I'm going to give you something.'"

Meredith also learned that although "you go into this field sort of wanting to save everyone," often "there's only so much you can do. You can make yourself crazy trying to do everything to fix them." Her father, she believes, is "the smartest person I know, hands down," But while, "sometimes I was so impressed, other times I was so frustrated."

After three years, Meredith moved to Seattle, because "otherwise, I'm going to end up alone and bitter with nobody to talk to because there's nobody to go out with" on Nantucket. "The few people I went out with were all patients in the office." And she knew a little too much about some. "One guy had a history of genital warts, and I was like, 'Oh!' Another patient who was hitting on me, I knew he had herpes, and I'm not really game with all that."

T.J., who became a doctor, had less direct exposure to Lepore's practice. In fact, "I always felt that he shielded me. I've actually probably only seen him in a patient care situation a dozen times. I've been in four appendectomies and a bowel resection with him, but just observing, never in a clinical capacity. He's always been very cagey about having me see him in that environment."

Still, T.J. recalls that watching his father skin deer that had been hit by cars, "seeing him find tissue planes in a deer, actually really helped me in gross anatomy and surgery. I still remember the smells and the sights. And we had an entire freezer of dead things. Once, someone left the door open overnight, and in the morning it looked like something Jeffrey Dahmer had collected, a quarter inch of blood on the floor, really a horror show of dead things that he picked up on the road for the hawk."

Lepore did offer some advice, telling T.J. he was "too nice to be a surgeon" because a surgeon "needs to be a little compartmentalized. I always joke that you have to have a certain loathing of patients. You need to be able to reach in and say, 'I can solve this problem.'"

T.J. thinks his dad's judgment also reflected a lack of social confidence. "He always saw that people liked me. He doesn't see immediately that people like him. He gets uncomfortable when people say nice things about him. He has a lot of self-doubt about what he does and whether or not he's doing the right thing."

Now that T.J. is an obstetrician, people often ask if he wants to practice on Nantucket. He's concluded that being the island's second Dr. Lepore "would be a very hard thing to do while he's still working. And he's the one person who hasn't asked me to come back."

Lepore has told T.J., "You don't see me working in Marlborough," his hometown. He knows the perils of being in someone's shadow. "That's why I didn't go into practice with my father," Lepore says. "He was the big guy. I covered for him one weekend, and they kept asking for the real Dr. Lepore."

Nick's path was much rockier. "With T.J. and Meri it was very easy, out of a textbook on parenting," Lepore recalls. "Nick was difficult, 180 degrees from how I was. I worked hard. I was four square. We'd go to a teacher's meeting with Nick, and he'd be sullen and angry and hostile and a pain in the ass. All of a sudden I was faced with the fact that a child of mine would not necessarily view life as I did."

It's not that they weren't close. They had the same sardonic humor, and Nick was interested in guns. But "I was much more impulsive," Nick admits. "I would be sitting there baiting him and baiting him. And oh God yes, I got in trouble a lot."

Nick had skipped fifth grade and found it tough to make friends the following year. In junior high, he got suspended for a day. In high school, "I didn't apply myself. I was just really trying to get through the day and hang out with my friends and my girlfriend."

Nick got caught up with alcohol and marijuana. He cut his hair into a Mohawk. While his brother and sister were National Honor Society members, Nick's graduating rank was forty-four out of sixty-six students, which, he acknowledges, "especially coming from a small public school, is not exactly what college recruiters are looking for."

After high school, Nick did an extra year at a private school on Cape Cod, where things seemed to be going well. Then a few days after New Year's, at 2 AM, Nick and a friend stumbled drunk onto the village green in Falmouth, with its giant Christmas display that included thirty life-sized Styrofoam carolers and a huge Santa. "We started laying waste to the place, punching these Styrofoam figures in the face," Nick remembers. If only he'd stopped there. But he happened to notice an adorable Styrofoam baby Jesus, and "I went over there and grabbed him."

They fled, but the police pulled them over. In the car, "we have the baby Jesus, the three wise men, and a goat," recounts Nick, who covered the Christ child with his feet to hide it from the cops. "They said, 'We know you did it.' We said, 'Okay, we did it,' and they said, 'We'll come get you tomorrow,' and they let us go."

Instead of going home, the boys decided to get rid of the evidence: "We went down to the ocean and dumped everything, being really smart criminals." When the police came the next day, they offered to drop one charge "if we could bring back the baby Jesus. We ran out to where we had dumped the stuff. Out on the horizon, we could just see Joseph's head bobbing. We would have gone for it, but really we needed the baby Jesus, and he was gone."

They were charged with malicious destruction of public property, vandalism, disorderly conduct, and larceny—misdemeanors, but still. The crime was splashed on the front page of the local paper. "A woman wrote in saying we should all go to jail for ten years," Nick says. The case was continued without a verdict on the condition that the boys paid the cost of replacing everything: $4,100. The Lepores paid the fine but ordered Nick to repay them by working summer jobs. He was sentenced to community service—vacuuming, mopping, and changing light bulbs in a church.

Nick says his father "got mad at me for that, but he didn't really get mad." In a way, Lepore could relate. In high school, Lepore totaled three cars, including "my mother's beautiful sky-blue Skylark convertible that she loved" and a car the nuns at his high school let him borrow. "I did a number of stupid things, and I got away with it. Nick did some stupid things and got caught."

Those stupid things were not yet behind him. Enrolled at Wheaton College in Norton, Massachusetts, Nick was placed on academic and housing probation in his sophomore year. He attended classes sporadically and, says his father, "made an honest attempt to sleep with every woman at Wheaton." He was using and selling pot.

One day, as public safety officers approached, Nick ran. He tossed his backpack into some trees near the soccer field, not wanting the cops to find the ounce of marijuana he'd been carrying. But he slipped on wet grass and fell. "And in a decision that will live in infamy, I decided to play dead." When the police rousted him, he lied about where his backpack was. "I was an idiot." Told he would face criminal charges unless he left Wheaton and didn't show his face for a year, Nick returned to Nantucket.

His parents were less forgiving this time. "I remember my mom crying, 'What were you doing? If you wanted money, you could ask for it.' I just remember my dad repeatedly saying how stupid it was—stupid to use it, stupid to sell it."

Nick went to counseling, where he realized "I was kind of angry at the world for no good reason" and "felt powerless to change what I was doing with my life. Maybe it was because I was always Tim Lepore's son."

Lepore, who attended some sessions with Nick, understood. "It was a little intimidating to be my son on Nantucket."

Nick had been counting on a summer police officer job, a position he'd held before, but Nantucket police heard about his problems at Wheaton and rescinded the offer. When the Lepores called Wheaton to complain that its security chief violated a promise not to tell anyone about the incident, the college agreed to allow Nick to take finals and get credit for work he'd completed. That jump-started Nick's turnaround. "The Wheaton episode caught his attention," Lepore notes. "He was really, really upset about that."

Nick got into Suffolk University in Boston, graduated, and worked in San Diego doing construction. He had one more run-in with the law when, traveling in Texas, he and a friend got pulled over with pot in their car. Told charges would be dropped if they pleaded guilty and paid $500, "I said, 'Hey, no problem,' called my mom, she sent the check out, and two days later the charges were dropped."

After that, though, Nick improved. He applied to law school, getting a recommendation from the dean of Wheaton College, who "said I was a young kid with a lot of problems, but I got myself together."

He became a lawyer, first in Seattle, then Atlanta. "I always wanted to be away from the island. I love Nantucket, but I have a hard time being there for more than a week."

Nick works for a personal injury law firm that, among other things, sues doctors for medical malpractice. To that, Lepore's reaction is: "I prefer that he play piano in a whorehouse."

But Lepore is happy that Nick has made good and is "getting a unique perspective from the other side of the handcuffs."

Nick doesn't take it for granted. Life, he reflects, can be "really tough for people coming from Nantucket" because "you're in a really small, inclusive, supportive environment and all of a sudden you're just kind of thrown out into a bigger environment. It was difficult sometimes. But I was very lucky to even have a father, let alone someone who gave a damn."

CHAPTER 10

UNMOORED OFFSHORE

Sean Kehoe had hit a wall. A high school senior, he missed days of school because "I was drinking cough syrup" to get high. He developed what he called "a reputation for outlandish behavior" that often got him reprimanded. "I didn't want to go to class; I didn't want to do homework; I always showed up late. I was just a pain in the ass."

Then he got suspended after joking that he was going to "do something during the graduation," something disruptive like wearing a blood-soaked T-shirt. Although he wasn't expelled, he was banned from attending graduation. "The principal didn't want to risk anything," Kehoe says.

Feeling "just out of my mind with rage and anger," Kehoe went to see Lepore. He wasn't his regular doctor, but Cathy Lepore, then the school nurse, suggested that her husband could help.

"I'm going crazy," Kehoe told Lepore. "I'm punching holes in the wall. I can't control myself. I want to hurt myself."

Lepore didn't coddle Kehoe or psychoanalyze him. He didn't pepper him with questions. "It's just high school," Lepore responded. "It's bullshit. You're going to forget about it. It's not going to matter in ten years."

Disarmed but not quite buying it, Kehoe asked Lepore for Valium, although, as he recalls, "if you saw what I looked like in high school, there was no way that anyone with a conscience could give me Valium" because he'd either abuse it or sell it.

"Don't be a baby," Lepore retorted. "Be a man. Don't knock yourself out 'cause you can't deal with it. Just rise above."

Then he told Kehoe how. "Go and distract yourself," Lepore prescribed, telling Kehoe to spend a couple of days on Cape Cod. "Go buy shit you don't want and don't need. Go see a terrible movie you don't want to go to. Get out and clear your head."

Which is exactly what Kehoe did. Lepore wanted to make sure "I didn't go and get arrested, or start a fight with the principal at graduation." So Kehoe stayed away. "I didn't do vandalism. I didn't do anything stupid. I went to Hyannis for the weekend. I saw *Pearl Harbor*. I bought some weird crap. I did all he told me to do." And, Kehoe says now, "he was right."

Surgeons, and even many family doctors, wouldn't get involved in a case like Kehoe's. They would refer him to a mental health professional, something Lepore sometimes does as well. But some people find his type of counseling especially effective, and some will only come to him.

He acted as therapist for a man who, while out scalloping on the island, had a vision and began quoting the Bible. Later, he ran into Lepore's house and announced that the light on his phone meant that there was a nuclear weapon in Nantucket Harbor.

He also intervened when a woman took another islander's dog and dyed its light-colored fur black. The woman's logic was simple: she figured nobody would suspect she was a dognapper if the pet she so suddenly acquired was a dog of a different color.

But Lepore knew his patient and recognized this was more than a bizarre crime. She was a troubled soul needing help. He'd operated on her when she was injured in a case of apparent domestic violence. He'd helped her cope when her daughter gave birth twice while in high school. He'd worked with her when she went off her medication and began hearing voices. So, in the dog case, he counseled her too.

"I've taken care of her a long time," Lepore notes. "She's a person who was rode hard and put away wet."

Lepore's informal therapy, and his ability to prescribe psychiatric medication, fill an important need on Nantucket. While mental health and substance abuse issues occur everywhere, of course, certain attributes of island life can exacerbate those issues, and a limited supply of therapists doesn't help.

"The depression numbers out here—nowhere else I've been even compares," says Peter Swenson, executive director of Family and Children's Services of Nantucket, who estimated that more than 1,500 people a year get help from his agency, a significant percentage of the 10,000 people who live on the island year-round. Those numbers are particularly notable, Swenson says, because of the transparent and tight-knit nature of island life. It's hard to hide that you're going to a mental health counselor or a therapist, and "it's more intense of a stigma than other places. People know where you are. Why else would you be parked here? You're on stage all the time."

There are, notes Jim Lentowski, executive director of the Nantucket Conservation Foundation, "very few secrets on Nantucket. You can run, but you can't hide. If you've got a problem and you don't want everybody to know about it, you internalize it."

Swenson often tries to work around that by scheduling sessions in unconventional places—at church, or on the beach so it looks just like a chance encounter. The fishbowl feeling goes both ways and can make it hard to attract and keep therapists on the island. People can easily bump into their counselors at the grocery store, restaurants, and community events.

"You're trying to figure out what tomatoes you're buying, and there's your client asking, 'What are you having for dinner?'" Swenson says. "I've been out fishing, and someone walks up and starts talking about their kid. I have to say, 'You know what, I'm really trying to get a bass here.' This is a very open environment. You have to be okay with that."

One of Swenson's counselors moved off-island after encountering a patient at a party where the therapist had been hoping to relax and drink. He realized he could not separate his personal and professional lives on the island. "I can't deal with it," he told Swenson.

Other people are driven off-island by a winter that seems to stretch endlessly. "People think of Nantucket as having tourists and lots of people, and the weather is beautiful, and it's just flowers and gorgeous," Swenson notes. "Really, from November through the middle of April, there's not a lot of people here, there's not that much to do, the weather's not great, and finding work is very, very difficult. People's lives get condensed to about a three-mile circle—you're at work; you're at home; you're at Stop & Shop. People off-island who come here in the summer, they have no concept of what that's like." And staff members who have moved to the island in the summer "invariably come in in February and say, 'I think I'm losing my mind.'"

And March, affectionately called the "Hate Month," can seem sixty days long, Lepore says, and sometimes, "you just want to kill everybody."

When Swenson arrived in 2006, the agency was fielding ten or fifteen requests for help per month. These days, there are about thirty requests each week. "There are no full-time, year-round psychiatrists," Swenson says. Two psychiatrists who live on the island give the agency about one day each week, and one who lives off-island comes out twice a month. Until recently the agency had to rely solely on off-island psychiatrists. Still, the need is great enough that patients usually have to book appointments eight weeks in advance. Lepore, on the other hand, squeezes them in more or less immediately.

"In a lot of ways, being a mental health facility here, it's almost missionary work," Swenson asserts. "We deal with it all. We're it; we're all it is. And Tim."

Coping with stress and depression on the island can be aggravated by the inability to always get to someplace else, by the quiet sparseness of the off-season compared with the thrum of vacationers in the summer, by the cost of living in a place where even the basics are strikingly more expensive than the mainland, and by the economic disparities between summer visitors and year-rounders.

"It's hugely significant, the vast differences in wealth," Swenson says. "The money is outrageous. I think that does have a huge impact on people. It's hard to understand that disparity, particularly for people living here. People try to tell you that restaurants are affordable, and you know you could never eat there. We're here nine months of the year, and there are these people three months of the year giving you the finger and screaming at you. We are living where they are coming. People can't stand them, but we can't live without them, and that has a huge effect on people's self-esteem."

More and more people find that the economy is pushing them off the island, especially during the recession, when a slowdown in building and renovating houses has meant that contractors, landscapers, and caretakers have trouble finding work, and people with other jobs also suffer. "Some people who have lived here all their life can't afford to live here anymore," Swenson laments.

People who stay have to be able to handle the seasonal economic changes, the move from a summer tourist economy filled with jobs in restaurants, shops, and the waterfront to a doldrum economy in which many jobs involve taking care of summer people's houses or scalloping. "People make a lot of money in the summer and have too little to do in the winter," Lepore says. "Psychosocial issues end up as the biggest thing here. If I'm not empathetic, if I don't listen, if I don't ask the right questions, I'm not taking care of that patient, any more than if I did half an appendectomy. Whether it's disease or dis-ease, there's something going on."

The wrenching case of Nicole Garcia Tejada called upon both Lepore's medical skills and his psychological radar. Three-year-old Nicole landed on Lepore's hospital gurney on March 14, 2011. Her limp body had been found lying on a table in her home, but there was a delay in getting her help. Whoever discovered that she wasn't breathing was apparently more comfortable calling a Spanish-speaking friend instead of police. That friend called 911, but the call was first routed to the state police on the mainland, an extra step before getting to the Nantucket police. The friend had also given the dispatcher the wrong address: Pine Street instead of Pine Tree Road. It took a second call from someone at the house to inform police of the correct address.

By the time Lepore saw Nicole, she was still warm, but barely. "I worked for about half an hour trying to get the baby back," he recalls. "She was just blue and dead dead."

Then, Nicole's mother, twenty-six-year-old Dora Alicia Tejada Pleitez, came into the emergency room extremely agitated and confused, Lepore says. She was given some Ativan, an antianxiety medication. Then he watched in chilling amazement as a police officer entered the hospital room and charged Tejada with the murder of her own child. It was only the island's fourth killing since Lepore had arrived.

Tejada, a house cleaner from El Salvador who had lived on Nantucket for about five years, had according to local newspapers reportedly hallucinated while napping on the couch with Nicole, imagining that Nicole was possessed by the devil, that demons were inside her. She told a pastor that she believed that God wanted her to force a rose down Nicole's throat to exorcise the demons, and so, police said, she complied.

Lepore had questions about Tejada's mental state in the hospital and concluded that her behavior was "disorganized enough that at that point it wasn't appropriate to send her to jail." He filled out a form so she could be involuntarily committed to a psychiatric institution, but the weather was too thick to fly, and she stayed at the hospital overnight, murder charge notwithstanding. She was eventually found competent to stand trial and her case is pending.

One of Lepore's many hats involves serving on the board of Family and Children's Services, and he and Swenson have bumped heads at times: "I think we need to do more fundraising, and Tim hates it: 'Well, I'm not doing that crap.' At least you know where he stands. But when we've had people in trouble, he's there—boom. Doesn't matter whether it's 2 o'clock in the morning, 'cause that's what he does care about."

When a kid with bipolar disorder bolted from the emergency room and began running around town, for example, Lepore ran after him. He couldn't keep up but alerted police, who found the teenager at the home of a man Lepore had previously treated for bipolar disorder but who had stopped taking medication and seeing doctors. (With the latter patient, Lepore notes, "I wasn't that successful. I did such a good job he shaved all the hair off his body.") Police brought them both to the hospital.

Lepore will also give patients cover, helping arrange a smokescreen to shield their problems from public view as a way to encourage them to get help. When teenagers come to see him, he'll often "take some blood just for kicks, just so the parents think we did something medical."

Alexandra McLaughlin, whom Lepore is treating for narcolepsy, knows several people with addictions to drugs or alcohol who "keep his number on file" in case they slip out of sobriety. They feel safe coming to his office, she says, because "Dr. Lepore's the one you can actually talk to, and he's not going to ruin their medical file for life."

Still, sometimes Lepore's counseling attempts fall on deaf ears. After a sixteen-year-old boy who was on probation for drugs failed a drug test, Lepore arranged for a bogus medical follow-up appointment for him just to get him to come into the office. He sat down with the teenager for forty-five minutes.

"You're hanging around with stupid people," Lepore told the boy. "You're doing stupid things. You just got out of rehab, and you tell me you're cranking oxys, drinking, smoking dope."

The boy listened but was not terribly swayed. "At the end of the ser-monette," Lepore recalls, "he told me to go shit in my house, essentially."

About 60 percent of the people who seek counseling at Family and Children's Services come in at least in part for drinking, Swenson says. "People on-island don't like to talk about it because we're a tourist community, but alcohol is the biggest problem we have on-island. It's connected to anything and everything. You spend time downtown in the summer, you see people walking around just blotto."

Peter MacKay, the social services manager for the hospital, is seeing more alcoholics, and "the time to treat them is longer."

Lepore sees a slew of intoxication injuries. The cobbled downtown streets are "hard to walk on when you're drunk," he notes. "People think it's Disneyworld and that you can't get hurt at Disneyworld."

One drunk driver struck a deer and flipped his car over, killing a man and a deer. Lepore drew a chalk outline around the deer. Another man, with an off-the-charts blood-alcohol level of .300, stumbled into another person's driveway and lay down. The homeowner didn't see the man and drove into him, causing severe injuries.

In 2009, after two house painters, Scott Bernard and Thomas Ryan, went drinking, Ryan stabbed Bernard, whose body was found alongside a road.

The summer before, at the Bamboo Supper Club, in an attack stemming from an apparent love triangle, a woman smashed a coworker in the face with a pint glass and a high-heeled shoe. The victim, Erica Sparks, a Canadian working as a summer waitress, was left with a permanent scar from a six-inch gash from her left eye to her mouth. The attacker, Laurie Ray, was convicted of mayhem. Both women appeared to have had a substantial amount to drink. Lepore, who treated Sparks in the emergency room, said her blood-alcohol level was .249, just over three times the legal limit.

"If I became king of the island, I'd close all the bars at 9 PM," Lepore proclaims. "I think it's a horrible problem. It breaks up families, kills people—get rid of it. Half the island goes to AA, and the other half should. It isn't a surprise who you're going to see at AA. The only surprise is that more people don't go."

Lepore has seen people "come in three days in a row drunk to the emergency room." Occasionally, when he needs to suture up an especially surly drunk, he will be a little less generous with the Lidocaine that he gives to numb the site of the wound. "Some people I put in more, some people I put in less. At 3 o'clock in the morning, dealing with drunks who are spitting up on you and cursing at you—sometimes you're allowed to return the favor."

One man was such a problem drinker he got into three moped accidents in a single day. Not long after that, he came into the hospital with a sword. Lepore wrote out a Section 35, an official request to a court to have him involuntarily committed to a rehab facility, where he would be evaluated by a court-appointed forensic psychologist and could be institutionalized for up to thirty days. It was the fourth time he had given the man a Section 35.

Lepore frequently encounters teenagers with alcohol problems. He says "there has historically been this acceptance of underage drinking" on the island. "It used to be the cops showed up at a party, and the kids dropped the beer, and the cops went away. Now the cops show up, the kids don't drop the beer."

Swenson reports that a 2009 survey found that Nantucket's youth drinking rate was about 50 percent, outpacing the rate for Massachusetts and the rest of the country. He thinks new programs his agency has put in place are "starting to move this in the right direction," but "I still think we're a little bit higher than the state and national average."

Swenson and Lepore say that some parents, with the goal of preventing their teenagers from driving drunk, allow parties where kids can drink, but take away all car keys. "It's pretty common," Swenson says. "But if a child begins to drink before the age of sixteen, he is four times more likely to have problems with addictive disorders late in life. Doesn't it make sense that we should not let them have alcohol when they're sixteen? Some people say, 'Wow, I didn't know that.' Other people don't care. My response is you're playing Russian roulette."

Cathy Lepore, a counselor at the high school, tried to stop one boy, who kept getting into fights, from drinking. She told him he shouldn't go to any more football parties. The boy's father, enraged that she had the temerity to speak to his son, showed up at Tim Lepore's office, yelling at him for suggesting his son had a drinking problem.

"You know, it's not coming out of the blue," Lepore told him. "There's a pattern here, and you can look at it and think about it, or you can just deny it."

For years, Cathy invited teenagers to the Lepores' house for evening group sessions that allowed them to share feelings and concerns. They often revealed they were involved with alcohol or drugs. Some were robbing their friends' parents' medicine cabinets for prescription medication. Some kids drink out of boredom. Others, she says, "move here from other countries, get depressed, and turn to drugs and alcohol. The kids, they're sort of stuck here. I always tell kids: the lucky ones get caught."

Many kids who drink excessively eventually stop, Lepore says, but before they do, it can tarnish bright potential. "You know these kids; you've seen their pictures in the paper; you've seen them in the science fair. You almost feel responsible for these kids."

So Lepore will try everything, sometimes asking his brother-in-law, Steve Tornovish, a recovering alcoholic, to talk to teenagers with drinking problems. Tornovish is happy to oblige because during the two and a half decades he has been sober, "if I felt squirrelly, Tim has never failed to support me." Once, Tornovish felt so depressed he couldn't get out of bed. He attributed the depression to a kidney stone, but Lepore "took me aside and said, 'Look, you've got a problem, but it's from the neck up.'"

Lepore has taken it upon himself to compensate for what he considered to be a hole in the network of addiction services on the island. He was particularly concerned about heroin addicts and tried to arrange for methadone treatment to be available on Nantucket. People have had to travel to Cape Cod, which is time-consuming and expensive. That can discourage them from regularly adhering to a methadone regimen or, if they do, can make it challenging for them to get their lives together because "it's a little hard to hold down a job when you're spending two hours on the ferry" to get your methadone dose.

Lepore's first plan was to procure methadone from an off-island clinic and get an island pharmacist to distribute it in doses that Lepore would keep in his office for patients to sign out. He ran into resistance from the hospital, though: "Someone higher up than me didn't want to do it."

Then, a methadone alternative, Suboxone, became available, instantly popular with addicts and treatment professionals because it is less addictive and less likely to be abused than methadone. As a result, it can be taken home and used there, rather than having to be dispensed at a clinic. "We would have sixty people waiting to take the boat off-island to get Suboxone," Lepore says. Ultimately, Family and Children's Services, looking for someone to prescribe it on-island, "asked me if I could get involved. I volunteered."

Cathy disapproved, calling it "a bad idea. I didn't feel like it should be passed out in our office. Addicts take anything that's not tied down."

Lepore went ahead anyway. "It's one of the nondiscussable items. I don't bring it up, and she doesn't ask me." He made time to take an eight-hour course required to become legally authorized to dispense Suboxone, and is already prescribing it. He is allowed by law to take on up to thirty patients at one time.

"For someone who has a narcotic addiction, if you get them on something legal, you have removed the criminality associated with it, and the financial detriments, so that you give them a chance. This is a very edgy subject area but is needed by our addicted population. It's something I think is worth trying."

Of course, he says, "if Cathy gets wind of this, I may be sleeping in the car."

Not long after Lepore arrived on Nantucket, he was at a friend's house one night having a gin and tonic. "The sun was over the yardarm": it was cocktail time. Lepore had one drink. Nothing to write home about. Then he got a call.

Fourteen-year-old Jamie Legg had fallen off his moped. He had a head injury and a ruptured spleen. He came into the hospital with no vital signs, in full cardiac arrest.

Lepore raced to the hospital. He was sober, his abilities and thinking were intact, but, he wondered, what if that weren't the case? "I had one gin and tonic. What if I had had two?"

There was no time for speculation like that. Lepore opened up Jamie's heart. He massaged the boy's chest, and he got a heartbeat back. Jamie's belly was blowing up. Lepore took him to the operating room and removed his torn spleen.

By 3 AM, Lepore realized Nantucket did not have the wherewithal to save Jamie. He worried that the boy was severely brain-injured, but since the hospital didn't have the ability to do a CAT scan then, he couldn't tell for sure. "I had his vital signs stable; I had him great below the chin. I didn't know if what was going on inside of his head was fixable, and I wanted a neurosurgeon to evaluate him."

A horrible thunderstorm was raging, and it was not the night to be trying to get off-island. Lepore called a doctor at Tufts Medical Center, his former teacher, who ran the pediatric trauma program. "We're coming up," Lepore said. The doctor told Lepore he was crazy. There was nothing that could be done for Jamie. He was going to die.

Lepore refused to accept it. "If you got a fourteen-year-old kid, you want to take your absolute best shot. He is going to get the benefit of everything that can be done in Boston," he thought to himself.

He began to fight with his one-time teacher. "I know he's going to die," Lepore barked. "But he's not going to die here. He's not going to die on Nantucket."

Finally, Lepore convinced the Coast Guard, which summoned a helicopter. Lepore, a nurse, and a nurse anesthetist climbed in alongside Jamie. Thunder and lightning whiplashed them in the air. They made it to Boston, but by morning Jamie was dead.

Lepore never regretted the decision to send the boy to Tufts against the advice of its pediatric surgeon. "I really felt that the kid needed whatever chance he could get," he says. "If people want to yell at me— I'm thirty miles out to sea—go ahead."

But Lepore did make a promise he has never broken since. He decided never to drink while on Nantucket: "It's not that I'm against drinking— I'm not a member of the Women's Christian Temperance Union. But I would not feel right about myself. Things don't always turn out right, but if they don't, it's not for want of being clear-minded."

Despite Lepore's disciplined teetotaling since the Jamie Legg case, he seems to have a special rapport with the alcoholics he counsels. He connects with them in part because of a tough experience, trying in vain to stop the drinking of a close friend from high school and college, who ultimately died of alcoholism. People on Nantucket also know that Lepore's son Nick indulged in the party scene and that it was only after several hiccups that he made good.

Moreover Lepore's round-the-clock work habits and unusual hobbies strike some people as being as obsessive as an addiction, albeit a healthier one. "Tim's going to knit with dog hair—anywhere else you would think he's crazy," Swenson says. "But if you can lose yourself in that kind of stuff, you don't get caught up in the other stuff. I think that's one of the things that Tim has."

It's also something that can help him connect with patients. "His issues are a lot like mine," notes a woman Lepore has repeatedly counseled for alcoholism. "They're just work-related, being on all the committees. When you think about his life, he is on call 24/7. He said to me, 'We all have our issues. Trust me, I have mine—I work too much.'"

The woman, afraid to be identified because she doesn't want the island to know her secret, is not a daily drinker but has had at least two recent episodes in which she drank so much she passed out at home and had to be taken to Nantucket's emergency room and then helicoptered to a Boston hospital.

"I don't know what the heck snapped," says the woman, who has a daughter and works in a family business. "It was a lot of anger," plus feeling trapped, "growing old in a place that you didn't grow up in. I've chosen to live on an island, and there's a lot of baggage with it. The other thing I can't take is the extremes, and that's what this place is. Extreme extremes. The weather, the people—the population goes from 10,000 to 60,000 from winter to summer."

Lepore says the woman had some underlying psychiatric issues, including hebrephenia, characterized by disorganized behavior and thinking and by acting inappropriately silly at odd times. "It was not her first rodeo. She's been hospitalized before; just something triggers, and she's off. I've been involved with her and her husband, in the hospital, off to rehab, and back to rehab. When she goes off on a toot, she goes off on a toot big time."

After the most recent episode, Lepore visited the woman in the hospital, sat with her, and urged her to see him when she was discharged, which she did. "You know what, Dr. Lepore, this is crazy," she admitted. He prescribed some medication to help reduce alcohol cravings, but mostly he just asked questions and listened without "that look" of pity or wariness. "There's a lot of shame involved, but with Dr. Lepore it's more like, 'You know better. What are you doing?' If

I was feeling funky, I would call and get in to see him because he's so real."

Drinking problems take many forms, and Lepore sees them all. He often refers to patients he is counseling as ETOH, using medical and rehab lingo. ETOH is the chemical term for ethanol, the primary ingredient in alcohol.

"People come in, and they feel disgusted with themselves," Lepore says. "My feeling about it is nobody made them drink, nobody is going to make them stop. Sometimes you can be the person that crystallizes an idea for them to get them to stop. When people start putting up hurdles to their sobriety, they're not going to get sober and clean. But if somebody comes to me with a substance abuse issue and they are honest and forthright, if they hit bottom before they die, I sit down, and I spend a lot of time."

One patient had been sober for seven years before he started drinking again. He was very ashamed. "If you want to stop enough, if it's the most important thing in your life, you'll stop," Lepore told him. "If not, you'll be back here next week. If you unload that fear and shame, you don't have to drink." The man listened, visited Lepore repeatedly, and sobered up.

Morgan Browne and Alison Stark were being pushed to the brink by alcohol and wanted help quitting. Since the time he became mired in a brutal divorce in about 2007, Browne started drinking more and more. "In the end I found myself drinking all the time. I even played hockey on Nantucket after drinking."

Stark, a graphic designer and photographer whom Browne began dating and later married, was more of an evening drinker. A cocktail at 5 PM. Half a fifth to a fifth of vodka at night until she fell asleep. Stark had grown up in a family with alcohol problems. At ages seven and eight she called the police frequently because her drunken stepfather was beating her mother—breaking her arm or leg, throwing her down a staircase. Her mother eventually divorced the man, but continued drinking and rarely got out of bed, forcing Stark to steal money from her mother's purse to take a cab to third grade.

"Those experiences were very formative, and I remember them clearly," says Stark, who ultimately moved in with her father. Alcoholism caused her mother to fall and die from a hemorrhage when Stark was fifteen.

In 2009, Stark, also having experienced an ugly divorce and having been laid off from her job, started drinking to self-medicate, she says. Eventually though, Stark realized she was mirroring some of her mother's behaviors, and she did not want to put her then ten-year-old son through anything like what she had been through.

Stark and Browne knew Lepore as a regular doctor who'd helped them manage various medical situations, but nothing psychological. He had stepped in to deliver Stark's son, when her obstetrician neglected to tell his patients he was going away and Stark's water broke and she needed an emergency C-section. She took note of his no-nonsense approach even then: For two days after the birth, he "wouldn't let me eat until I farted."

Lepore helped Browne after an ear, nose, and throat specialist had removed a cyst on Browne's neck, leaving a wound that became infected, oozing, and excruciatingly painful. A "fancy, fancy specialist in Boston was going to take out my whole salivary gland," Browne says. But the surgery got delayed, and Browne was feeling so sick he consulted Lepore, whose first reaction was, "That is definitely not a chick magnet."

Lepore put Browne in the hospital and gave him intravenous antibiotics. And when the surgery in Boston continued to be postponed, Lepore announced, "This has gone on long enough." He told a nurse: "Get the green box." Before Browne knew it, he was getting an anesthetic—"I think it was liquid cocaine, but it could have been crème de menthe." Instead of taking out the gland, Lepore simply removed a stone the size of a tooth. "Can I keep this?" Lepore asked excitedly, running down the hall to show other doctors. "Look what I've got!"

But drinking was something else altogether. At one point, Stark asked Lepore for a drug called naltrexone, sometimes prescribed to help diminish cravings. Lepore gave her a prescription, but naltrexone was ineffective, and Stark continued to drink.

"For me alcohol really was a numbing thing, not wanting to deal with certain problems," she says. "But I could feel how it was affecting my health."

Both Browne and Stark felt Nantucket was something of an enabler. "The island, because it's at the end of the world here, people come to Nantucket to escape," says Browne, who arrived in 1982 after dropping out of college and reading an article about scallop fishing. "It's not a big jump from coming here to escape to escaping in other ways, like with alcohol."

Stark, whose family moved to the island when she was a teenager after her father left Wall Street and became an artist, finds the winters "extremely isolating. On a February night you can go to a bar or an AA meeting."

But "we were both a little resistant to going to AA. And on Nantucket, there's really no anonymous."

Browne and Stark considered a thirty-day residential rehab program like Hazelden, but it was expensive, and they balked at separating themselves from Stark's son and other aspects of their life for an entire month. Stark feared that the detoxification process "can be very dangerous, and some people die from that." And they were afraid of failing, of finding out they wouldn't be able to manage life without alcohol.

"I wanted to stop drinking but I knew I needed help with the physical dependence," Browne says.

No one seemed to have the answer, "except Dr. Lepore on a Wednesday." The Wednesday in question was December 8, 2010, when Browne and Stark walked into Lepore's office.

"You're going to have to do a lot of it yourself, but I can help you, and let's do it now," Lepore told them. He prescribed Librium, a drug that can alleviate anxiety and agitation caused by alcohol withdrawal.

"Take these whenever you feel like it—it's hard to OD on this stuff. Come see us Friday."

"You're not open on Friday," Browne pointed out.

"I'll be open for you."

By Friday, Browne's cravings had quieted so much that he didn't even take the Librium. "I felt like stopping drinking would be this great big deal. Dr. Lepore just met me where I was—and he saved my life."

Lepore also encouraged Browne to change his medication, and treated Browne for his ADHD.

Stark had a bumpier path. After her visit to Lepore, her hopes of staying sober were stymied by the force of her habit. Five days later at about three in the morning, she drank from a case of Prosecco they had in the house, drinking one to two bottles in one sitting. A week later, she did the same thing. Around Christmas, she had a Bloody Mary (her mother's name was Mary) at her father's house. "It made me feel physically ill," she recalls.

Stark returned to Lepore and confessed what had happened. He listened and urged her to keep trying. "I didn't ever feel ashamed or embarrassed," she says. In December 2011, both she and Browne celebrated a year of not drinking a drop. "I went and got my one year chip," Stark says. "I brought my son. It felt really good." They now keep their Polpis Road home stocked with a wide assortment of teas, not alcohol.

They still consult Lepore. "I even love going to his office, where there's all these weird knick-knacks," Stark says. "It's more like a gun shop than a doctor's office with all those stuffed creatures. I don't think he dusts. You really get a good feeling in there."

Browne says that "everyone I know who drinks way too much, which is a lot of people on Nantucket, I want to tell them to go see Dr. Lepore."

They believe they could never have broken their addiction under other circumstances.

"There's something really lost in modern medicine—it's so removed and impersonal now, waiting and going back to get tested, you just feel so worked over," Stark says. "It can be so demoralizing and exhausting. The whole medical system is a form of mafia; doctors are afraid to do anything. That's what the beauty of Dr. Lepore is. He's a maverick. He's excited to figure things out. He's not afraid to do things."

CHAPTER II

THE FOURTH DIMENSION

Down a dusty lane near the village of Siasconset, universally called 'Sconset, sits a tidy cottage tucked behind a wooden fence. Inside are cheerful aqua-colored curtains, seaside decorating touches, and a ceiling fan whirring amiably overhead. A visitor to this charming home is more than likely to be invited in for tea and cookies.

The cookies look like Grandma's—round, about two inches in diameter, with a little rise in the center and a tinge of golden brown on the bottom. But Henry, who lives here, makes them in his own special way. He starts with basic oatmeal, chocolate chip, or sugar cookie recipes and then adds his secret ingredient: pot.

"You ever get high, good girl?" he asks a visitor, setting out cookies on homey china plates. "With these, you're not thinking suicidal thoughts; you're not retaining fluid; you're not having nose bleeds. You have to decide in your heart that you want to know what the fuck is going on. You will be rocketed into the fourth dimension."

Some cookie. Henry—who asked that only his middle name be used because otherwise "they would put me in jail," and "if I get popped over this shit, a lot of people are going to suffer"—started baking his cookies at Lepore's request and has become Lepore's supplier. The confections are not for the doctor himself but for patients, especially cancer patients who can't handle nausea from chemotherapy or have trouble eating enough to maintain strength.

"The hospital doesn't know—this is just something I do," Lepore confesses. "If I feel a patient needs it, I'll ask, and he will make me some cookies or brownies."

Medical marijuana is not legal in Massachusetts. The closest the state has come is a bill introduced in the legislature that would protect patients, doctors, and caregivers from getting prosecuted for using medical marijuana. Possession of more than an ounce of marijuana is a criminal offense in Massachusetts; less than an ounce is subject to civil penalties like fines. (Henry doesn't reveal how much pot he puts in a batch.) But Lepore is not fazed that he might be going outside current law in these circumstances. If he believes it is right for a patient, he believes he should take the risk.

It isn't the only way Lepore moves beyond what many doctors would do. Some of his methods are impish—pants stealing, for instance. If he thinks someone should stay in the hospital longer than that patient wants to, "I just take their pants away. They have no choice but to run out in a johnny."

And part of the portfolio he assigns himself is driven by curiosity about how far he can stretch his skills. Can he treat an altogether different species? A horse with Lyme disease? A sheep with pregnancy complications?

But Lepore will also undertake practices that clash with his own political or philosophical beliefs. He'll dole out Henry's cookies even though he is against legalizing marijuana because "people don't handle it right in this culture."

And although he is not in favor of abortion, he has recently become one of a very few doctors this side of Boston (he thinks he may be the only one) who will perform abortions. In doing so, he has had to confront not only his own moral discomfort but the resistance of members of his staff, as well as threats from anti-abortion advocates.

"It is not considered a practice builder," Lepore admits. "I do not advertise it, but people understand what's going on."

Lepore met Henry nearly two decades ago, not long after Henry arrived, a complete Nantucket neophyte ("I didn't even know Nantucket was an island 'till I got up to the boat," he says). One day, Henry got hit in the eye, and Lepore was the doctor stitching him up.

"Can you do something about my wrinkles?" Henry asked Lepore in the hospital.

"No, but I can give you tits," Lepore replied.

"I've got to know this guy," Henry thought to himself. "I asked him one day if he went to the Joseph Mengele school of medicine."

Lepore credits Henry with introducing him to falconry, something Henry got in trouble doing back in Florida when the authorities "got pissed at him because he was drinking," Lepore says. "He had a real alcohol problem." By the time Lepore met him, though, he had sobered up. "We have had long talks about substance abuse, primarily alcohol. Now he's a staunch AA guy." But he hasn't tried to kick his marijuana habit or his habit of disseminating dope to others.

Talking to Henry, now white-haired and in his late sixties, can be a bemusing exercise in patience and redirection, especially if he has indulged in his own tea or cookies, as he does frequently these days. The day he spoke about Lepore, he had eaten a cookie at 8 AM and sipped tea at 9 AM ("Or a cookie at 8, tea at 10—I don't know. I'm getting immune to it now. I can eat five cookies or ten cookies").

Every few minutes, he drifted to his experience in Jamaica, where he got involved with marijuana about a dozen years ago: "In Jamaica they told me the weed cakes put men in the nut house—I had to try it. What I saw in Jamaica is what you'll see on your deathbed. You'll see life itself. Infinite oneness."

Henry is given to coining new elisions of words that he unspools with great profundity. "Mystic words," he calls them. Instead of heaven, he talks of "heav-in." He says "people look up to the sky for heaven," but "heav-in" signifies something like a soul. If you've got a problem, "in order to get it out, you gotta go to heav-in."

There is "overstanding," kind of a "whoa dude" version of understanding: "When I eat the cookies or drink from the chalice, every time I go to a place of overstanding knowledge. I don't know where I'm going to go, I don't know if it's going to be fun, I don't know if I'm going to have the shit scared out of me, but I go there anyway."

And when his thoughts turn political, he might use a word like "civili-nation." Where does he come up with these? "In that place far, far away."

Asked what kind of marijuana he uses, he is vague: "It doesn't have a name because it doesn't have that kind of consciousness." But he says it is "bubble hash, a real pure form of hash."

Henry's bubble-hash bakery is a relatively new innovation, begun in 2010, when Lepore, aware that Henry was making tea, asked if he could make marijuana desserts too. "Sometimes it's better to have nice brownies or cookies or muffins," Lepore reasons.

As a special treat, Henry even infuses Jell-O Pudding Pops with pot; he particularly likes working with pistachio flavor because the marijuana makes it "kind of chunky." The cookies are made with "hand-chopped weed," and although their high lasts ten to twelve hours, "they aren't that strong," Henry claims. He recommends refrigerating them ("if they get too hard, you warm them up in the nuke"). They can also be frozen "if you put 'em in a Tupperware so they don't get freezer burn. They'll last forever, man."

Henry has also devised a coffee drink Starbucks probably doesn't offer. Take some pot and "boil it on the stove for a long time, then add half and half. The half and half will absorb the cannaboids, pull stuff out of the weed, and it sticks to the cream molecules. You strain it, and you can add chocolate milk to it." Henry stores his cream concoction in what was once a bottle of Ocean Spray blueberry juice. "If you put that in your coffee at 8 AM, you'll be stoned until noon," he confirms with gentle satisfaction. Order it half-caff, no-foam macchiato, if you like.

But for the full-throttle experience, go for the tea. "You ever smoke a joint and get high and smoke another, and you don't get any higher, and smoke another, and you don't get any higher?" he asks. "The tea doesn't do that. Oh Jesus, yes man, I drank it three times, and I kept getting put in a higher plane. I have to escape to a different level, and you can't follow me there because if you do, I'll escape to another level."

Caution, though. When Henry's sister drank the tea, he had to "put her in a tub of ice water because she was burning up in her mind. She thought she was having a heart attack, or about a hundred of them. She wouldn't speak to me for a year." This tea would give Earl Grey an embolism.

"I had to tone it down because people were losing their fucking minds. Some people that drink it, you never see them again, and some people that drink it, they know a little more than they did before. You drink the tea, and what you have in that near-death experience is a judgment of your life, a trillion seconds, 31,000 years. And there's not even half that many stars in the Milky Way."

Through trial and terror, Henry has learned to titrate his tea so it meets medicinal specifications of a sort. In one case, "a friend of mine turned me on to a dude" who was bedridden at home, so sick he needed both a heart and a liver transplant. Henry whipped up tea mixed with vanilla-flavored Odwalla protein drink. "I kept him in tea, strong-ass tea, and ran it through the feeding tube."

Still, Dr. Henry will occasionally decide not to treat. "I've got a buddy who's dying. I ain't giving him no cookies. Aw, he ain't that much of a buddy. I think he's got Karma to deal with. He's a state cop. He was a prick and misery to a lot of people. He ain't getting shit from me."

One day, a card arrived at Lepore's office. On it was a picture of a new-born baby, and the message "Don't Do It." If he didn't already have one, indeed scores of them, "it would give me a reason to go buy a gun," Lepore says. "It's not something I want to get shot over." But it isn't enough to compel Lepore to stop performing abortions. Nor is his Catholic background, his often-conservative political views, or his personal distress about terminating a fetus.

Robin Rowland, program director for Nantucket Family Planning, first discovered that Lepore was willing to perform abortions about five years ago. She was on the school committee with Lepore and mentioned in passing that it was difficult for women seeking abortions on Nantucket. She had a patient who wanted one and could not get off-island.

"He said that he would do the termination," she recalls. "And I was shocked because I didn't think he would do that. Politically, he would appear to be very conservative."

Even in the liberal northeastern United States, many surgeons won't perform abortions. It can be a lightning rod for controversy. And with most doctors working in group practices these days, "the partners are going to say, 'That's wonderful that you're all full of piss and vinegar, but we don't want you to do it,'" Lepore says. "It's legal, but radioactive."

Perhaps even more radioactive in these parts since a doctor on Cape Cod, Rapin Osathanondh, was convicted of involuntary manslaughter when a woman he performed an abortion on in 2007 died. Prosecutors and the state medical board said Osathanondh did not adequately monitor the woman, twenty-two-year-old Laura Hope Smith, who was thirteen weeks pregnant, while she was under anesthesia, and did not have oxygen ready if she needed to be revived. They said he delayed calling for an ambulance when Smith's heart stopped and tried to cover up his actions. He was sentenced to six months in jail and lost his medical license.

Lepore says the Osathanondh case has pretty much left him the only doctor between Nantucket and Boston who regularly performs abortions. "He went to a meeting on the Vineyard with all the local docs," Rowland recalls, "and he asked them, Do any of them do abortions? And none of them did. He was willing to stick his neck out, saying, 'I do it.' He had one of his usual quips that he was the only Dark Lord."

Lepore says he probably does about two abortions a month. Some are considered "medical abortions," which don't involved surgery and can be done until about seven weeks into a pregnancy. He gives an injection of methotrexate, which stops the embryo's development. Then, about eight days later, he administers misoprostol, a pill placed in the vagina that forces the uterus to contract and expel the dead embryo.

When drugs are not appropriate, Lepore performs surgery. "I don't want to make a career out of it, but I'll do them." He doesn't abort pregnancies beyond the first trimester because he feels "it gets a little iffy." The procedure can be technically trickier, and "that is starting to get fairly deep into some ethical issues, as opposed to first trimester, which is less objectionable, albeit still a termination."

Lepore's actions have been controversial even among some Nantucket medical personnel. In 2010, an ultrasound technician at the hospital showed up to assist, not knowing the procedure would be an abortion. "She didn't understand what I was doing. She left crying after the procedure," Lepore recalls. "I got called by the head tech in radiology. I went and apologized."

Now, Lepore tells hospital staff beforehand: "We're going to do a termination. I want you to understand it. If you don't want to do it, that's okay." He understands "it is fraught with some overtones that are uncomfortable for people, and I don't think people should be forced to do things they're uncomfortable with."

Resistance from Lepore's own staff has been a little more challenging for him. Some of them have ethical, moral, or practical concerns. Diana Hull, his longtime nurse, says: "I'm all for pro-choice—I just don't want to be the one to do it. My personal opinion is they should definitely take this to the mainland."

Other staff members are concerned about whether women having abortions on the island have access to appropriate counseling.

When Lepore's daughter, Meredith, was a nurse in his office, from 2007 to 2010, she handled most abortion counseling and pills for medical abortions. Even she was ambivalent. "When I started out, it was like, what's the big deal? Who cares? Somebody needs to do it," Meredith recalls. "Then I started doing them, and it's a big deal. I was just giving them the medicine, but you're still giving them what they need to make whatever's there die."

Still, "when Meredith was here, I had someone who could arrange things," Lepore says. "Now I have to arrange things. My nurses want nothing to do with it."

In January 2011, Lepore, concerned about his staff's reactions, asked Rowland from Nantucket Family Planning to meet with him and his staff. Rowland thought she was simply going to educate them about the procedure. But, she says, "really, I ended up sitting back and watching them all have this discussion. They were all saying they didn't want to do it—they didn't want anything to do with it."

Most raised moral objections, and some worried about their safety if opponents made threats. The meeting, recalls one staff member, "didn't go well. He seems to think it's happening less often than we do. We feel if somebody wants to do it, that's okay, but it's the personal involvement that we object to."

Lepore, Rowland says, "shrugged a lot. And he kept saying, 'Look, we've got to provide it. Somebody has to do it.' Without saying it, he was really saying, 'Look, I really don't care what you think. We're going to do it.'"

Rowland was so appreciative that she wrote Lepore, thanking him "for sticking to his guns on that and not letting his staff sway him."

Lepore did have "a long conversation" with a young woman who was twenty-eight weeks pregnant and her mother about how "the knee-jerk reaction is to have an abortion. I thought it was reasonable to have the baby and give it up" for adoption. That's what she did.

But in a case that particularly upset his staff, he agreed to perform an abortion on an older woman with three kids who'd had two previous abortions. His nurses believed the woman was being reckless by not taking steps to prevent pregnancy and then aborting the unwanted fetus. Lepore replied: "I don't think she is."

Mary Monagle, a former nurse at the hospital, says, "A lot of us were kind of shocked" about Lepore performing abortions. "But that's Dr. Lepore's moral decision. I'm sure he's not going around saying, 'Woohoo, come in, gift with purchase!' I'm sure he struggles with it in his own way. It's another part of him being an enigma wrapped in a riddle wrapped in a question mark."

Rowland had certainly considered Lepore an enigma. When she first got on the school committee (on which Lepore has served, Rowland says, "for 1,000 years—he can't lose an election"), "I had anticipated that I wasn't going to like him at all. I came away really, really admiring this guy. He's so much more sensitive and giving than you would know. He has a generous, generous heart."

Rowland says many women seeking abortions are low-income immigrants with limited English, daunted by the American medical system. Many would also find it difficult to travel off-island. "I just look aghast at the idea of sending them to Boston." Plus, Lepore provides most abortion services for free if needed. He cannot waive hospital operating room charges, but "he's always willing to see people for less or no payment."

Since the meeting with his staff, Rowland says she tries to refer women to Lepore sparingly because "I don't want to overdo it with his staff. I don't want to burden him with this."

And it is a burden, morally, for Lepore, says his son, T.J., an obstetrician-gynecologist who also performs abortions. "We see a lot of the same stuff, but I see more of it, really bad cases," says T.J., who practices in Springfield, Massachusetts. "In my field, we do them farther along. These are very delicate situations. It's not a happy story. Nobody goes into an abortion thinking this is a great thing. Even the people who have had five, six abortions, you can see they leave something" behind, emotionally, after it's over.

Lepore make it clear he believes an abortion after the first trimester is "wrong and it's killing," T.J. says. And although he performs earlier terminations, he doesn't want "to be known as the guy who does abortions." But "if a patient decides that this is their choice, someone shouldn't be made to feel degraded. If you're a physician, the most important thing is, especially in a small town, you can't lay judgments on people because everybody's coming at you with their own baggage and their own history."

Margot Hartmann, CEO of Nantucket's hospital, says Lepore's willingness to perform abortions is a sign of being "emotionally brave, willing to hold conflicting and sometimes confusing positions in trying to do the right thing and probably err on the side of commission rather than omission. He's really quite unsentimental in the most beautiful sense about the life cycle, accepting of mortality, and that there's living and dying all the time."

T.J. says the reactions of Lepore's nurses "bothers him because he sees that he shells out every day for his patients, and I think it disappoints him in some way when he doesn't see that in other providers. And his office staff is all people that he has strong feelings for and he protects them a great deal."

But while abortion is fraught with personal and moral challenges for Lepore, his handling of it is typical of his approach to other controversial subjects. "He does not shy away from getting in the line of fire," Rowland says. "He shoots his mouth off without thinking quite often, but it's total gut response, and oftentimes it's totally right on, even though you're saying, 'I can't believe you said that in public.' There are those that love him and those that hate him. He's the only surgeon on the island, so we need him, and we got to take him with whatever he comes with."

But "the thing about him is every issue is kind of a separate issue. You don't have to have fisticuffs with him. You can have your differences and walk away from it, and he's okay."

The marijuana cookie idea first occurred to Lepore when he began treating Louise Hourihan, a fifth-generation Nantucketer diagnosed with breast cancer in December 2009. Hourihan, who with her husband, a bank executive, is deeply involved in island community programs, did not know Lepore well.

"For years I went to a different doctor. Dr. Lepore, he says and does things other people think are crazy." Some people who "see him only on school committee, they say, 'I wouldn't let that guy touch me with a ten-foot pole.' I mean, you walk into that office, and he has an armadillo"—dead, stuffed, lying on its back—"chugging a beer, when we're trying to stop the whole youth drinking problem . . . " Her voice tails off in wonderment.

The first time she went to Lepore, she was accompanied by her then-teenage son Evan, whose reaction to the office was, "Oh my God, where are we?" Evan, who needed treatment for warts, was convinced "he's going to use one of those knives to remove them."

But Hourihan's regular physician, David Voorhees, had died, and she decided to give Lepore a try.

When a tumor was discovered in Hourihan's right breast, she found Lepore's initial reaction somewhat disconcerting. "He started telling me about the history of breast cancer and how they used to have to open them up," she recalls. But she discovered he could be sensitive and generous with his time. Lepore reassured her the tumor wasn't too large and recommended a specialist in Boston, who performed a partial lumpectomy. She returned to Nantucket with a tube implanted in her breast to drain excess fluid, and Lepore came in on a Saturday to remove the tube.

Hourihan had four weeks of chemotherapy, twelve weeks of Taxol and Herceptin (two breast cancer drugs), and then radiation—flying to Cape Cod Hospital daily for two weeks. That was followed by more Herceptin every three weeks for a year.

After the chemo, Hourihan started wanting something to ameliorate the side effects, to help her sleep, quell nausea, restore her appetite, and improve her mood.

"Friends said, 'You need to get some pot. You need to smoke,'" remembers Hourihan, who was in her mid-fifties and had not smoked marijuana for two decades. A friend's husband gave her some joints. But "when, all of a sudden, you're smoking pot, that's weird. I didn't do well with it. It was strong. I wasn't enjoying it."

Hourihan started experiencing anxiety and went to Lepore's office, where Meredith gave her Ativan, an antianxiety drug. It didn't help much. When she next saw Lepore, he declared that the dose was so low "it's not worth opening the bottle."

She asked Lepore about marijuana pills, made of synthetic tetrahydrocannabinol or THC, the main psychoactive compound in marijuana. But Lepore knew that THC pills, though legal, are difficult to get and insurance companies won't pay for them.

"I'll get you some cookies," he told Hourihan. "I have a guy who makes them."

Lepore actually didn't know for sure that he could get cookies. But he visited Henry, and in June 2010 Lepore told Hourihan he had some for her. She stopped by his office, but they weren't there. "I went to his house and knocked," she recalls. Lepore came to the door and said, "I can't have them in the house. I have them out here in the car."

As soon as Hourihan started eating the cookies, she began feeling relaxed. They helped her sleep, eased her nausea, and put her in a better frame of mind: "It definitely helped you think about something else besides how sick you are." And a little bit of cookie went a long way. "The pot today is much stronger than we were smoking. I can remember one summer day going to the beach and eating one and then starting talking, and I couldn't stop."

Plus, "they were delicious. They were like a sugar cookie, and they were amazing." She allowed her son to try one but had to keep them hidden so her granddaughter wouldn't get them. The only problem was "I only got the one batch." As soon as they were gone, she thought, "I'd like to get my hands on more."

But right at that time, Lepore was preoccupied with the death of Tony One-Eye. Tony—real name Anthony Viera, who had long ago lost an eye—was a well-liked islander who ran a junk yard and frequented the town dump to pick through stuff other people discarded. He was also known for digging up a continual bounty of sea creatures— mussels, littleneck clams, and quahogs—from spots whose locations he kept top secret.

That June, Viera brought the landfill crew some quahogs and was carding through piles of construction debris, searching for scrap metal, when a trash truck accidentally crushed him. Lepore, as medical examiner, had to pronounce him dead, and since "Dr. Lepore was involved in that, I felt weird asking for cookies," Hourihan says. She stopped by the hospital and approached a nurse. "She goes, 'Cookies, what cookies?'" Hourihan recalls. "So I didn't feel comfortable asking for cookies."

The marijuana didn't erase Hourihan's every symptom, but it helped ease the numbness under her arm, the slight mental fogginess from chemotherapy, and the embarrassment of losing her eyebrows and lashes. "It's a lot for women to go through," she says. "Cancer—it's a big deal."

One August night in 2011, Lepore's voice when he answered his cell phone was short and breathless. "Dealing with a horse with cyanide poisoning right now," he growled. "Gotta go."

Lepore was in the middle of a field and his patient was an eight-year-old half-Percheron, half–quarter horse named Grace. Around 7:30 AM that morning, Grace had started trembling and acting strange, and her owner, Suzanne Duncan, made a beeline for Lepore's office. She visited him repeatedly during the day, consulting about what to do. But by early evening, when things had not improved, Lepore headed to Duncan's, where he would devote hours to a desperate attempt to save the animal—pumping her stomach, administering intravenous fluids, and even, to protect the horse from injuring herself, ripping fence posts out of the ground.

It's not unusual for people to ask Lepore to treat their animals. Veterinarians can be in short supply on-island or lack certain medical equipment. Veterinary bills can be expensive, while Lepore usually isn't. And for some, Lepore is just always the person they call. "He's my main point person," as Duncan put it. "He's always open to things."

Lepore has great respect for veterinary medicine because "an animal can't talk to you" to explain the problem. But the patients can be easier. "The animal isn't drugged or drunk or embarrassed." Plus, "they don't have lawyers, and they heal well."

He also turns to butter around animals. On his iPhone he keeps a list of every dog he has ever had—Prince, Lucky, Chico, Norman, Odie, Rosie, Hobbs, Betty, Macy, Monique, to name a few. "I think about them. I can picture each one of them. I can't even watch *Old Yeller*, which is a little-known secret. I can't even read about it; it's horrible. Even cats. I remember driving and seeing this cat get hit by a car—that was thirty years ago, and I still remember it."

Lepore tried to pitch in by officially offering occasional animal medical care, but "the hospital has refused to help," he says. "They've got CAT scans and X-rays, but they have forbidden me from bringing animals in, even though a lot of times these animals are cleaner than some of the patients."

Still, he has managed, usually when the senior X-ray technician is not around. He X-rayed a goat with a funny-looking foot and dead birds of prey that he found, looking for bird shot in their bodies to see if they had been killed or died of natural causes. "That's what they make nights for," he insists.

In the hospital, Lepore worked on a deer hit by a car. The driver had put the animal, unconscious, in the back seat, but the deer revived on the way, and "raised a lot of hell," Lepore recalls.

In his office, he sutured up an injured mutt cut on its head and back. On his zoological patient roster, "sea gulls are big items." And he tried in vain to help a sheep that had just given birth and had a prolapsed uterus, in which the womb collapses into the vaginal canal. "I kept trying to push it back, but I couldn't get it to stay. So I popped the sheep. There was nothing you could do."

He had greater success with Sula, a golden shepherd with two broken bones in her leg. Her owner, Beth Peterson, a home health nurse, first took her to an island veterinarian, who "put a splint on it and said the dog would have a limp," Peterson recalls. Then the splint came off. Peterson asked Lepore for help.

"I met him over there on a Saturday morning," Peterson says. "He scooted the dog in the back door, did an X-ray on Sula's leg. It was so sweet and so natural and so fine to put her there in the back room. He resplinted her leg like three or four times."

Once, someone called Lepore's house to say "they had an eagle who was hurt and they were bringing him by," Cathy Lepore remembers.

"Don't bring him by," she told the caller. "I've got people here visiting. He's not a veterinarian." They brought him by. "Get—Get out of here," Cathy sputtered. "The nerve!"

The island also has a large population of feral cats that, Lepore says, are a threat to songbirds, pheasants, quail, and other fowl. He thinks many of the cats should be trapped and euthanized, but knows that would not be popular. An animal rights advocate, with whom Lepore had butted heads over his conviction that more deer should be killed to reduce tick diseases, was also concerned about the cats. She wanted them spayed or neutered so they wouldn't overpopulate the island and endanger their own survival.

Lepore offered to provide that service, figuring it would help solve the problem and earn him some goodwill from a deer hunting foe.

"I've read enough books about spaying and neutering," he told Cathy. "I have an anesthesia machine around. I can do it."

"Where would you do that?" Cathy asked, incredulous.

"In the back room."

"I think you've gone too far now, Tim. What patient is going to want to be in the room after a cat's been in there?"

"They wouldn't know," he assured her. So far he hasn't catered to the feral cat trade. But if it ever becomes necessary, "I'm poised."

The case of Grace the horse was an unfamiliar challenge. Lepore had had only minimal experience treating horses. He had treated one with Lyme disease, administering IV antibiotics, but the horse bled out and died. He had sutured up the nose of a horse that cantered into a wire.

But Grace was in distress, and it wasn't clear exactly why. She had been "perfectly healthy" until that morning, says Duncan, a physiatrist, who bought her from Amish farmers in Ohio and would ride her downtown to pick up the mail and to the nursing home where she works weekly with elderly residents.

When Duncan came to see him about Grace, Lepore mined his brain for possibilities. Duncan said she had gone out to feed Grace and found her standing there shaking, her gums white. Then she mentioned a berry stain on her mane and said Grace might have been munching on a nearby chokecherry tree. Lepore happened to know that the seeds of chokecherry fruit can contain large amounts of hydrogen cyanide. So while Lepore was seeing patients in his office, Duncan brought over samples of the plant, and Lepore studied toxicology reports. He gave her a big batch of vitamin B_{12}, used to treat cyanide poisoning.

It helped, but not enough. Duncan got assistance from a veterinarian and a veterinary technician, who gave the horse enemas and walked her around. But not long after Lepore drove to Duncan's early that evening, the horse sank to the ground. Lepore went to the hospital and his office to cadge some supplies: more B_{12} and some Ringer's lactate, a saline solution to restore lost fluid. Besides the vet and the vet tech, Lepore was joined by Wayne Wilbur, a nurse anesthetist from the hospital. With no large-animal veterinarian on Nantucket, they called some on Cape Cod for advice.

"It was a real in-field kind of warlike situation," Duncan recalls. "Dr. Lepore was in his element."

They inserted an intravenous tube in the horse's neck—not easy with a 1,400-pound, thrashing animal. The horse kept dislodging the tube, and Lepore repeatedly helped sew it back in. They arranged three sticks like a teepee to hold the IV bag in place, so gravity would help propel the fluid, and they eventually pumped in thirty-six liters. "That's what kept her alive for so long," Duncan says. "I have this image of Dr. Lepore squeezing the IV bags so the fluid would run faster."

Although "we thought it was cyanide," Duncan says, there were other possibilities. Hoping to pinpoint the diagnosis, Lepore recalls, "I even got the hospital to run some blood work for me in the middle of the night. Sometimes they can get a twist in their bowel," or "they can get a fecal impaction."

The team in Duncan's field commandeered a bilge pump, using it to flush out the stomach by pumping water through a tube Lepore inserted in the horse's nose. To clean stool out of the horse's rectum, "one guy was going in up to his elbow without a glove," Lepore says. "That was not me. I chew my fingernails."

Grace kept "struggling and struggling to get up, and falling," Duncan remembers, and as she moved, she was getting too close to fence posts in the field. Finally, Lepore and Wilbur pried the posts up so Grace wouldn't get hurt knocking into them. They gave the horse pain medication to ease her discomfort. As the night stretched on, they worked by the beam of one of Lepore's $200 flashlights. "It's a pain in the ass to see the goddamn horse trying to get up," he recalls. "It's a bitch to have it down like that because they really don't tolerate being down that much. It's just so frustrating because it was a nice horse."

At one point, Duncan got the fire department to come, and using a front loader a construction company had left nearby, firefighters tried hoisting Grace to her feet. "But there wasn't an ounce of strength in her to stand up," Duncan says.

Still, when Lepore left around midnight, "I thought we were going to make it," he says. Duncan says the B_{12} seemed to give her more energy, and "she was doing some hopping around, so we thought she might get better."

Lepore got home to find that "Cathy was pissed off at me" for having stayed there so long. "She'd had dinner ready. She thought I should have been home. But what are you gonna do? If somebody has a sick horse, I'm going to try and help them. Even people I don't like I try and help. And sometimes dealing with other species is interesting— you learn things."

Around 6 AM the next day, Lepore dropped by to check on Grace, but "the horse was down, and there was nobody there. It was just awful."

Duncan had called a veterinarian to put Grace to sleep at 4 AM, having run out of medication for her pain and realizing that nothing could save her. Later, Duncan and Wilbur performed two autopsies, concluding that it was not poisoning but a twisted gut that blocked Grace's abdomen, ruptured a blood vessel, and caused her to bleed out.

The case was over, but Lepore's interest in it was not. You never know when another horse would have a kinked bowel or would eat the poisonous parts of a chokecherry tree.

"I had somebody get me all the stuff on cyanide poisoning," he said that day. "I'll be ready to go tomorrow."

Henry has thought a lot about why he is involved with marijuana and offers a mélange of religious and spiritual references, some more intelligible than others.

He says, for instance, that God, in Leviticus, said "he wants you to eat from the fullness of the earth," and that "God hid man's divinity right inside of him, the last place you'll ever look. Every time you have a cookie you stay in that consciousness, you learn to stay in creation, you learn to overstand the condition of man."

Henry also has political arguments of a sort, saying that John Hancock "and those guys all got high" and that "Mahatma Gandhi said that only an unjust man obeys an unjust law." To Henry, of course, that law is the one making marijuana illegal, which he thinks is absurd. "The same people who want to lock you up—when their relatives get sick, they're the ones who want the cookies from you."

He says marijuana makes as much medical sense as taking legitimate drugs. "You watch a drug ad on TV, and they list side effects, and you're like, holy shit—people are buying this?"

And he cites compassion. "I'm so sorry that by the time these people get the cookies most of them are on their way out." But, "if you're dying, sweetie, or if you're sick or just fucked up, and you do some weed, and it makes you feel better and have consciousness, there should be no law against it. If you're going to die, you might as well have fun."

In 2010, Henry felt sick and visited Lepore, who discovered that he had anemia and suspected he might have cancer. It turned out that Henry had multiple myeloma, cancer of white blood cells in the bone marrow. Lepore arranged for him to see a specialist in Boston, and he began receiving weekly blood transfusions. Henry was also prescribed steroids, which he continues to take, but the side effects have been unpleasant.

"These steroids turn me into a total asshole," Henry claims. "I told a nurse to get a job at a gas station so she won't be around sick people."

He has to take the steroids, sometimes ten a day, in a regimen of three weeks on, one week off.

So Henry turned to his own remedies to offset the steroids' impact. He couldn't smoke a joint or use a bong because his immune system is compromised, and "if I smoked, it could fuck up my blood and my system. That's when I thought of cookies. There's no downside or side effects that make you want to go to the bell tower with a gun or start a war. The cookies take away the hostility and aggression."

Henry's condition has been touch and go. About six months after getting diagnosed, he was so short of breath that "I couldn't walk from this chair to the couch, and I would get up to go pee and have to brace myself on the window because I couldn't just stand there unsupported."

But then, perched before tea and cookies at his sun-dabbled kitchen table, Henry brightens. "I truly believe," he murmurs, "I'll beat this thing."

CHAPTER 12

THE LOST

One winter night in 2007, Tim and Cathy Lepore drove to a house on Cow Pond Lane. It belonged to a family Lepore had treated for years, and he and Cathy, a counselor at the high school who was widely trusted by students, were concerned about one member in particular: Vaughn, fifteen, a freshman. Cathy knew that an older girl had recently broken up with him and that some of his friends were worried about how he might react.

"I figured the best way to do it is to go over there, just to check on him," recalls Cathy, who chatted with Vaughn for a while that night. "He didn't say he was depressed. He said, 'I'm fine—don't worry. I'm not going to do anything.'"

Cathy was somewhat reassured, but she advised his mother, Linda, to keep an eye on him. Linda had been trying to do just that.

Linda, a down-to-earth woman who wears her hair in a single long gray braid, grew up on Nantucket, left when she was twenty, and returned in 1990. She raised three daughters and Vaughn, the youngest, who never knew his father, a different man from the father of his sisters.

When Vaughn was young, Linda married a man on Nantucket, a coworker in the high school's food service program, but they went through a bitter divorce in 2005.

Vaughn, whose blond hair almost touched his shoulders, was popular and athletic. He played football, golfed, surfed, and snowboarded. But by the age of fourteen, he was smoking cigarettes, using marijuana and alcohol. Linda struggled with how to handle it.

"I never yelled at him, never swore at him, never raised my hand," she says. "I just talked to him calmly. Vaughn would smoke and drink and misbehave, and as a mom I would take care of the situation, get him to bed, and if he was too heavy on the floor, I'd leave him there and talk about it in the morning." The biggest punishment she levied was taking his cell phone away when he was drunk.

Vaughn was getting counseling on-island, but things did not improve, and in the fall of 2005 Linda told the counselor, "I need help. What are my options? What can I do?" The counselor recommended sending Vaughn to a therapeutic school in Utah. So Linda arranged it, without telling Vaughn, who found out when he was picked up one morning by a service that escorted him on the plane to Utah. "I thought if he stayed here, he would get arrested and have a rap sheet," his mother worried.

In phone calls and letters home, Vaughn would say "how sorry he was," urging his mother to "come pick me up." Linda told him he wasn't ready and kept him there nine months, until she ran out of money to pay for the program.

In July 2006, Vaughn returned to Nantucket and seemed okay for a while, getting slightly better grades than before and staying out of the hair of a school official he had tangled with. Although his previous counselor was unavailable, Linda found him other counselors. But eventually he drifted back toward a group of kids who were doing drugs, stealing cars, and breaking into houses, recalls Steve Tornovish, a police detective.

One January night, one of Vaughn's sisters, who was working undercover for the Nantucket police, busted some drug dealers. Vaughn had nothing to do with the arrests, but Linda says he was taunted about it at school: "Oh, your sister's a snitch."

Then, soon after the Lepores' visit, Vaughn took his mother's car in the middle of the night and was pulled over by a trooper. At the police station, an officer told Vaughn he would now be denied a driver's license until he turned eighteen.

"Why are you so rebellious?" Linda asked Vaughn at the police station. "Who has a hold on you more than me? Do you realize what you have done? It will be put in the paper. You will be back on probation. And my insurance just doubled moneywise because you took the car for a spin. Am I right, Mr. Officer?"

"Mom, I'm sorry," Vaughn said.

Vaughn missed school for several days after that, but by Saturday, February 3, Linda thought he was improving. He was up early and ate breakfast with her. He asked her for a printer and some paper, discussed cleaning his room, and inquired about her plans for the day.

"I have to go into school to call parents," replied Linda, whose job included balancing accounts and making sure parents paid for school lunches. "Why don't we go out to lunch today, that place where you like the steak sandwich, and I'll have a hamburger? You call me, or I'll call you. When you're hungry, call me."

Linda was so busy at work that by the time she caught her breath it was 2 PM. She called home, and when Vaughn didn't answer, she left a message: "I guess our lunch turned into dinner."

Not long afterward, she arrived home, called out to Vaughn, and began walking upstairs toward his room. Hearing his cell phone ring on the main floor, she paused. No one answered it.

"Why would his phone be on the kitchen level?" she wondered, and headed back downstairs. She saw the phone. And then she saw the note. She began to cry.

"I went to his room, couldn't find him. I went all around the house, couldn't find him." She finally tried the basement: "I found him there."

Linda opened her mouth to scream, but nothing came out. Her fifteen-year-old son had stood on a chair and hanged himself with his own belt. She bolted upstairs, grabbed a knife, and cut him down. But it was too late.

She called 911, she called one of her daughters, and she called the Lepores, who raced over. Vaughn was still in the basement. Lepore had to pronounce him dead.

Linda never showed anyone the note Vaughn wrote, not even the police. It mentioned two other teenagers, and "I don't believe in an eye for an eye," she says. "I'm not one to accuse someone that what their child did was wrong. I called the two mothers, and I told them I have to talk to you. Your child was mentioned, and that's all I'm going to tell you. If your child says, 'Oh, did he write about me?' say, 'Yeah, he'll miss you.'"

The note did say that Vaughn was "really sorry for all the pain he caused me and he loved me very much, and his sisters too," Linda says. "He was so depressed; he was so sad. They talk about the dark hole. They don't see light at the end of the rainbow."

What Vaughn's mother couldn't know, what the island didn't know, was that Vaughn would not be the only one to look at a rainbow and see darkness. In the months that followed, several other young people on Nantucket, most of them teenagers, would die. Others would attempt suicide or talk about wanting to. "At one time we had about six kids in a week with suicidal ideation," recalls Peter MacKay, the social services manager for the hospital.

Even the day after Vaughn's death, a boy who knew Vaughn tried to kill himself. "I put a message out to the kids: bring that kid to me," Linda says. "I took him to my bedroom. I said, 'I know you miss him, but you can't do this.' He was so sad and so upset that he lost a very good friend, and he wanted to go see him right away. But I said, 'I can't worry about you and Vaughn.'"

Linda realized then that she could not hibernate in grief over her son's death. It would have broken her, for one thing. And she felt a responsibility to try to keep others from following Vaughn's path. She couldn't sleep. The day after he took his life, a Sunday, she was up at 3 AM, writing a message for Vaughn's friends and classmates. She called a friend and asked her to make sure it was read at a school assembly the next day. The gist was, "If you're depressed or angry, you should talk to somebody, go to counseling. If you don't like that counselor, find another one. This is not a movie that you can flick off."

People, Linda reasoned, "have to know about the aftermath. The pain, the what-ifs, the crying, the sadness, the never-recover-from." They have to know that life is full of "wondering what the person would look like, if they would have got married, what kind of career would that person have."

Linda went to work that Monday but showed up only at the beginning and end of the day, 5:30 AM and 3 PM, because she didn't want children to see her. She worried about falling apart in front of them. "If I had said something wrong, parents would have been mad at me." Her house was swarmed by Vaughn's friends and classmates—cheerleaders, football players, strangers. The Lepores were there too, trying to help her cope. After a week, Lepore insisted she put a note on the door and take a sleeping pill so she could get some rest.

But while the community pulled together in support and shock, it could not manage to predict or prevent what would come next. Eight months later, in October 2007, a seventeen-year-old girl took her own life. Four months after that, a sixteen-year-old boy was found unconscious at home and later died at Nantucket's hospital. Some, including his family, believe it was an accidental death, that he might have been playing a choking game.

Eight months after that, in August 2008, an eighteen-year-old hanged himself from a tree in the state forest off Rugged Road. And in July 2009, a twenty-year-old killed himself in the garage while members of his family were home.

"It's an awful lot of kids committing suicide," Lepore agonized. "It's our kids that are killing themselves."

The deaths wrenched the island. Nationally, the suicide rate for young people ages ten to twenty-four is about 7 per 100,000. In two and a half years, Nantucket, which has one high school with about four hundred students, had lost far more than its share. And six days before one of the on-island suicides, a young man who had grown up on Nantucket killed himself off-island. All these young people were known in the small year-round community. All had friends, were liked, were accomplished.

"Jesus, what do we do?" wondered Jim Lentowski, a longtime islander who runs the Nantucket Conservation Foundation, after the death of the sixteen-year-old, a talented athlete and good student. "It feels almost like living in an urban area and having drive-by shootings. And the kids who are getting killed are people who you wouldn't have any idea that they would get killed. The kids keep asking themselves as we have more of these things, What is going on here? How do you identify this, and how do you respond to it?"

Even mental health professionals on the island were stunned. Peter Swenson, executive director of Family and Children's Services of Nantucket, recalls that when he moved to the island in 2006, a friend of his was starting a job in New Hampshire's remote north country to work in addiction and suicide. Swenson told him, "That's the last thing in the world I want to do." A year after his arrival came Vaughn's death, the first suicide of a Nantucket High School student in decades.

While Lepore, like others, suspected that "the initial suicide probably in a way lowered the threshold" for others considering taking their own lives, the deaths were still shocking. "We're talking about high-performance kids from two-parent families."

Teachers were especially stricken. "They were really wounded, collateral damage," says Lepore, who is also a member of the school committee. Some teachers questioned the role of academic pressure. Others feared they had missed warning signs or somehow failed to take a step that could have prevented a death.

"In the beginning people thought it was the school's problem," Swenson says. "It's really the community's problem."

The community mobilized as best it could. It brought in specialists from the mainland. State Department of Public Health counselors spoke to teachers and students. A trauma specialist and Harvard psychiatry researcher, Robert Macy, ran training programs and helped set up suicide prevention protocols, including a program to educate students about suicidal tendencies and a drop-in center supervised by a substance abuse counselor. A licensed clinical social worker from Family and Children's Services helped out in the schools. And Cathy Lepore was asked to become a full-time adjustment counselor to work with fragile and at-risk high school students.

A posttraumatic stress management team was activated with about twenty members from various agencies. The community tried to find the right balance.

"I don't think a kid gets through these years without having crazy thoughts, but they need someone they can talk to," Lepore says. "We had all of these people come and volunteer, but the kids didn't know them."

Mental health professionals and school officials wanted to sound enough of an alarm so that struggling teenagers would know they had someone to turn to and adults and peers would be aware of warning signs. But some were concerned that memorials and tributes to the teenagers were giving the suicides too much attention and might encourage others to think they would be celebrated if they died.

A grief counselor from Children's Hospital Boston urged parents not to treat the suicides as a contagion but to describe them as isolated incidents involving young people who could not handle their problems well. That made sense to some Nantucketers.

"You couldn't go to a game anywhere on the island where there wasn't a recognition" of the life that had been lost, Lentowski said. "Students are not persuaded from glamorizing it. You just put thoughts in kids' minds, 'Well, if I do the same thing, at least I'm going to be recognized.' We have to tell them, 'No, it's bad.'"

Since then, Swenson says, "We've learned a tremendous amount, how to respond to things, how to do it appropriately. It's been very difficult for the island and for the community. People are scared."

For Lepore, the deaths took an emotional toll, even as he kept up his raft of professional roles. He knew the families as patients or through his various medical positions, and Cathy knew them through her school responsibilities. As medical examiner, Lepore pronounced each one dead. He was named to a newly-formed disaster response task force. And as a school committee member, he was involved in helping the schools respond.

"Could we have prevented one of these kids from killing themselves? I don't know," he kept asking himself. "I've been on school committee for years, and kids were not killing themselves. What has changed? What's led to this loss of hope?"

Lepore's son T.J. recalls how trying the experience was. "My parents were involved in every single one of those in a very personal way. I remember him talking about one of them, where he had gone to the funeral and said it was really bad. When it's a kid, it just doesn't make sense. It's not something you can really wrap your head around."

Richard Ray, director of Nantucket's health department, observed it too. "That's when you see emotion come out in Tim, when kids are at risk. I've only seen him cry once. That was with a suicide. For a brief couple of moments, he just fell apart."

The teenager in that case was the seventeen-year-old girl, Kate. Her death was what Detective Tornovish called "heartbreaking to one of the inner circles of hell." Lepore knew her parents. "The family was very high-achieving. This is a kid that you'd be so proud of. This was a star athlete, very, very bright kid, very, very driven kid. She had lots of friends."

Her death occurred on an afternoon when Lepore was seeing patients in his office. "They called me and said a seventeen-year-old is coming in, not breathing. The emergency room was a very chaotic scene with high emotions and anxiety. We attempted to resuscitate her for over half an hour. There was just no way we could get her back. It was gut-wrenching for her parents, the staff, and everyone involved."

Lepore found the last suicide, of the twenty-year-old, Dean, especially devastating as well. He and members of his family were patients of Lepore's. He had just graduated from culinary school, landed a job, and was known as a talented chef who had worked at many of the island's finest restaurants. That night, he had been playing video games at a neighbor's house, giving no hint of what was to come.

"He was a nice kid, a quiet kid," Lepore says.

The method of death, cutting his neck with a band saw, was also highly disturbing. Detective Tornovish said the young man's sister was in the next room and "heard the band saw turn on." She asked what he was doing, but her brother told her not to worry.

It was, Lepore laments, "just a particularly violent way of doing it. This was violence beyond a certain dimension."

Since that death, there have been no other youth suicides. Family and Children's Services and the Nantucket Suicide Prevention Coalition have taken numerous steps, including screening programs for middle school and high school students, and training for adults who come in contact with young people: clergy, police, EMTs, workers at pizza places and taco shops.

"We've even done some outreach into the bars to educate people who work there," Swenson says. The message was: "'We just want you to know what it looks like if you're seeing something.' We've tried to capitalize on the fact that, look, Nantucket went through a pretty horrible time, and everybody wanted it to stop."

The efforts have led to improvements. "We don't like to say it out here on the island, but on the mainland they say we've stopped it in its tracks," Swenson says. "We like to say we're doing really well."

Lepore still gets reports of young people with suicidal ideation, and both he and Cathy encounter teenagers who cut themselves and engage in other self-destructive behaviors. And "we have a number of adult suicides," he says. "Nantucket is different. If you can't make it here, it sort of pushes you over the edge. The social isolation, the drug and alcohol issues, the socioeconomic disparities, I think that pushes people."

For Ben, the summer of 2008 should have been a time of optimism and excitement. He was about to head off to Pratt Institute to study architecture, something he had been interested in for years. He had been accepted to all but one of the schools he had applied to. And Pratt was giving him a $25,000 scholarship, on top of $6,500 he received from the town of Nantucket. He had a summer job plastering and painting, and he had friends.

"Everything was right there for him always," says Ben's mother, Barbara, one of Lepore's longtime patients and running partners. "Dr. Lepore said Ben's the last kid we would have expected . . ."

Lepore knew the family well. He had been Barbara's doctor for years. Barbara considered Ben, brown-haired and soft-eyed, her easygoing child. His brother was somewhat more emotional, she says. When Barbara and the boys' father divorced after more than two decades together, Ben's brother, then fourteen, was more obviously upset. Ben, then eleven, was calmer. He was also an honor student. "He didn't have issues in school. He didn't have a ton of pizzazz. He was a second kid. Ben was a pretty even-keel person with fewer ups and downs. I trusted him. He always seemed really intelligent, and he had that measured response."

Not that Ben never experienced upheaval. In eleventh grade, Ben's parents sent him to a private school, Cushing Academy, west of Boston, a school they had planned to send him the previous year until housing arrangements fell through. By eleventh grade, when he arrived, he felt out of place as the new kid, and he bridled at the rules. "He was there for a week and was miserable," Barbara recalls. "He came home, and we didn't make him go back. It was a mistake because in the long, long run, it would have been better for him. I don't think he would have been as worried about going away to college. Maybe he was afraid of failure because in the back of his mind he had that Cushing experience. Getting him away from here would have helped. He didn't have that wider perspective."

Nor was Ben entirely free from trouble. At fifteen, he was arrested for possessing marijuana when he was caught rolling a joint with an eighteen-year-old. He was placed in a juvenile diversion program and given community service. About a year later, police stopped Ben and other teenagers in a car, searched and found some pot, as well as a pipe in Ben's pocket. Barbara says she considered that latter arrest "actually harassment—why are you following around my kid? Clearly there are dealers on the island, and why don't you just leave Ben alone?" But overall, the arrests "weren't huge things to me. They were annoyances."

After the suicides began and the school arranged for more counseling and discussion groups, Barbara asked that Ben be included. His brother was in college by then. An uncle had killed himself several years earlier, and around the time of the first Nantucket teen deaths, a cousin of Ben's had killed herself too. That girl's sisters had come to live with Ben's family, so unspoken reminders were close at hand.

"Ben has had two relatives who committed suicide in the recent past, and it's looming there," Barbara told school staff.

Ben had also known the two teenagers who died in 2007. In fact, he and a friend had been walking by Vaughn's house around the time his body was found in the basement. Ben's friend was also close to another teenager who lived on the mainland but had visited in the summer and who had recently taken his life.

"One of the things that's shocking is you don't know everything about your kid," Barbara reflects.

Then, in January 2008, the sixteen-year-old, Will, died. Ben knew one of Will's sisters, and the family was familiar to many. After that, a group of kids gathered in Ben's living room. "This house has always been central for them," Barbara recalls.

Barbara still didn't really think Ben was at risk himself. She was sure she would know if he were. She remembers that, at one of the funerals, "I said to Ben, 'If you ever feel like committing suicide, promise me you won't ever do that, that you'll talk to me.' He said, 'I would never do that.'"

But with the turmoil on the island, and the family history of suicide, Barbara thought Ben could use some comforting and a sense of stability. "He's not going to step up and say he needs it, but I think he does," she told the school.

A counselor the school brought in, Jeffrey Bright, met occasionally with Ben and other students during lunch. After Ben's second marijuana arrest, he began meeting with Bright more often because Ben's community service sentence was to paint the walls of Family and Children's Services, where Bright worked. Bright, a British-born counselor with decades of experience, would conduct Ben's required drug-testing. One of Ben's test results was invalid because he had drunk cranberry juice, a tactic employed by users to try to clean out their systems before a test. According to Ben's mother, "Jeff handled it in a way that Ben saw him as an ally, but was legally appropriate. Ben trusted him."

Cathy Lepore, in her role as high school counselor, also noticed that "Ben and Jeff really connected. He wouldn't talk to anybody else."

Then Bright was abruptly forced out after a judgment call he made while chaperoning a trip for high school seniors to Washington, DC. Another chaperone fell ill in DC, ending up in the hospital, and Bright decided to stay with her and send the seniors home on the plane by themselves. Some parents complained, and Bright was barred from future work in the schools, says Swenson, who strongly objected to the school's decision. Bright found that "the pressure was just overwhelming," and he quit his island counseling jobs, Swenson says.

Soon afterward, Ben told his mother, "Jeff's just gone. He's not there anymore."

Barbara believes that "for Ben, it was a huge thing. Here was this person Ben could look for at any time. The fact that he just kind of disappeared off the planet was, I think, a difficult thing for a kid like Ben. But I didn't connect the dots."

When Ben's senior year ended, Barbara did not think the issue of teen suicides "would still be in the air." Ben seemed to be having an enjoyable summer, putting together rave dance parties with friends. She was aware that "he was experimenting with drinking, a fact of life around here."

But not long before he was supposed to leave for college in New York City, things began happening that his mother only learned about later. In early August, Ben was arrested again. He was downtown when he and an older boy came across each other. Both of them had been drinking and the other boy called him a fag, and they fought. This was surprising, says Detective Tornovish, because Ben "was not known to be violent." Because Ben was eighteen, the police could not call his parents, and he spent four hours in jail, bailing himself out for $40 at 5 AM on Thursday morning. He was scheduled for court the following Monday. Ben didn't breathe a word about the arrest to his mother, who was asleep when he came home.

Later, Barbara, reflecting on the street fight, considered whether Ben was gay, but dismissed that idea because no one who knew him thought so. Ben had had girlfriends, Barbara knew, "but nothing serious. I had a sense he was in love with a girl who didn't return it, but I didn't get the sense it was a big deal." Although Ben didn't seem to be struggling with his sexual identity, she thought someone who was might have encountered challenges because "islands are different than small towns.

There's no town over. There's no place to drive to. There's no anonymity. If a kid is gay, there's no big city where you can meet up at a gay bar."

That Thursday morning, August 7, Barbara was surprised that when she woke up, Ben was already awake. "He seemed kind of cheerful and lighthearted. I thought maybe he had met a girl."

She went to yoga and an off-island doctor's appointment, and when she returned at 5 PM, Ben and his brother were watching TV. Later, Ben was getting cleaned up and dressed to go into town. He seemed happy.

"I had no awareness of him being depressed, but I had the sense that that upbeat light feeling came with him having made a decision," Barbara recalls.

By that evening, when Ben went with some friends to the creeks, his happy mood was gone. The young people were lying around, looking at the moon. Ben was carrying around a large rock, then threw it, and it landed on someone's porch. "Fuck promises," Ben said. Nobody knew what it meant at the time. When Barbara heard about that later, she thought he might have been talking about breaking his promise to tell her if he ever felt suicidal.

Later that night, after attending a party, Ben had some friends drop him off downtown. And strangely, Barbara notes, "with all the busyness of summer, nobody saw him."

When Barbara didn't see Ben the next day, Friday, August 8, she began calling his friends and had Ben's brother text-message them. Then she went to Ben's bedroom and found paperwork about his arrest. They looked for Ben for hours. Around 11 PM, she called police and filled out a missing person's report.

Around 1 AM, Barbara's older son remembered that when he was using Ben's computer the previous day, he noticed that Ben had looked up safe methods of suicide. Then he told Barbara about a place in the woods where some of Ben's friends had been building a fort. She and her older son got on their bikes and rode to the state forest.

"And," recalls Barbara, "we literally walked straight to him. It was pitch dark. We were walking to the fort calling his name." Ben's brother "started looking in the fort, and I started looking around, and that's when I found him. There was a rope hanging from a tree."

Barbara and her older son called the police and stayed in the forest for hours. She wanted to "go back and see Ben," but police had blocked off the fort as a crime scene. Lepore was called to examine the body. An autopsy conducted in Boston showed Ben was sober and had had nothing to eat or drink for twenty-four hours. There was a trace amount of pot in his system, but that could have been weeks old.

"This is a kid, little bit of a goth, dabbled in some drugs and alcohol but a good kid, very, very bright kid," Lepore says. "There are a lot of people very surprised by it."

Barbara pored over the coroner's report with Lepore, but it contained no revealing clues. "Here's this perfect boy," she says. "There's nothing wrong with him. He's intact. Except there was blood on both his hands and blood on his neck. Dr. Lepore thinks the rope cut his neck, and I think he may have reached up at the last minute."

Ben left no note. He had brought nothing with him except a backpack that police found high up in the tree. It contained a stuffed monkey Ben had had since he was three years old. "I still have it," his mother says. "Now, Monkey is a kind of talisman."

Barbara partly blames the police for the way they handled the fight two nights earlier. "Here's a kid who'd grown up on-island, he's going off to college—putting him in jail doesn't seem like a good idea when he's part of this class that just lost so many people," she says. "Whatever made him decide to do it, I think it was highly affected by the fact that other people had done it."

Barbara also thinks that in retrospect Ben "was really scared to go to college. My children were simply not prepared to live off-island." Others who have grown up on Nantucket have felt the off-island challenge too. Lepore's son Nick says, "Some kids would go to college and then come right back to the island. You're in kindergarten with the same kids, in middle school, in high school—it's almost like it kind of stunts your ability to meet people in a way, because you don't have this shared history."

Whether that was Ben's real fear, his mother will never know. "Where a person goes when they decide to commit suicide isn't the same place that you live in when you're with the rest of the family," she has realized. "Your kids try to protect you too. They don't want to tell you things that will make you mad. You wish you could just hold them all the time and never let them get hurt."

CHAPTER 13

WAIFS AND STRAYS

After school one afternoon, a twelve-year-old girl named Julie was lounging around the house like she always did. She usually lied to her mother and said she had already done her sixth-grade homework, or that she had none to do. Then she would submerge herself in video games, often bloody and violent ones like Diablo, which she was playing that day.

Julie was surprised when her mother, Patricia, sidled over and handed her a cup of hot chocolate. "Well this is strange," she thought. "She never does that unless I ask her for something."

Patricia, forty-seven, had moved Julie and her older brother from New Hampshire to Nantucket the year before, a few years after she'd gotten divorced from their father. Patricia had a cousin on Nantucket who rented them an apartment. But not long after they moved, Julie's brother left and went to live with their father, and Julie and her mother lived a kind of tensely balanced existence. Julie was glued to video games and seemed precociously savvy about activities more appropriate for teenagers; Patricia had various health complaints and struck her daughter as a somewhat disengaged parent.

"She always had migraines," Julie notes. "She would take a bunch of different medications. She would always be in her bed or lie on the couch watching TV."

That's why the hot chocolate seemed to come out of the blue. "I drank it," Julie recalls. And then, "I felt, like, wicked weird. I felt like I was going to pass out and stuff."

She announced to her mother, "I'm going to lie down in your bed," but before she could make it there, she staggered and clutched herself, "I think you better call the hospital," she whimpered.

Patricia resisted at first. A recovering alcoholic, she had been sober for years, but that night, she'd had a drink, Julie recalls. "Oh, you'll feel better," she told Julie, "and it'll be done." But Julie wasn't feeling better. Patricia ultimately called 911, and an ambulance raced Julie to Nantucket's hospital. There it was discovered that Patricia had laced the hot chocolate with Klonopin, a drug used to treat anxiety disorders. Too much Klonopin can cause confusion, hallucinations, memory loss, mood changes, seizures, even suicidal thoughts or actions. And the Klonopin was mixing with a brew of Julie's other medications: for depression, attention deficit disorder, and sleep problems.

Julie's mother had apparently tried to poison her.

A nurse picked up on the poisoning, and Lepore, standing by, praised him for the quick diagnosis. There wasn't much to be done except to watch Julie until the Klonopin passed from her system. She didn't lose consciousness but was groggy. She stayed hospitalized for several days because in such cases, "you never quite know whether they're on the uphill or the downhill," as Lepore puts it. And "if a kid comes in in that type of situation, you have to come up with a plan." Police and social services agencies have to be called. "Everyone has to be figuring out what happened, why it happened, and what is going to be done immediately."

Julie recalls snatches from that time. "I was so out of it. The guy put the needle in me, and it hurt so bad, and I was like, 'Oh fuck.' And the guy got very mad at me and said, 'Don't ever talk like that again.' I was very paranoid."

Her mother didn't hang around long, as Julie remembers it. Telling her daughter she was "just going to go into another room," she ran out of the hospital. "They caught her at the Essex playground. I haven't seen her since."

That was October 6, 2006. Patricia was arrested and charged with two counts of assault to murder. "This was not a whodunit," recalls Thomas Shack, the prosecutor on the case. "Julie was able to communicate with us what had happened. They got the cup for the hot chocolate from the kitchen, and that was corroborative of what Julie was saying. There were some writings—statements to the police—where Patricia laid out exactly what she had done."

Patricia ultimately reached a plea bargain; in lieu of going to prison, she would serve four years of probation while undergoing psychiatric treatment. She was also barred from having any contact with her daughter until Julie's eighteenth birthday. She went to California and entered a treatment facility, "which I liked because it was 3,000 miles away," Shack says.

Patricia's motive wasn't entirely clear, although Shack says, "basically she was going to use this medication in a dose that would potentially cost Julie her life, and she would commit suicide afterwards."

That's what Julie believes, too, that her mother intended the two of them to be joined together in death. After her arrest, "she wrote a letter that said, 'I want to commit suicide and take her with me,'" Julie says. "She was very depressed."

Julie was immediately removed from her mother's custody. "It was a very difficult case," notes Shack. "I remember thinking the entire time, 'What's in Julie's best interest here?' Is it in the best interest of the child that their parent ends up going to prison? Are we setting the child up for a feeling of, 'Geez, it was my fault that my mother went to prison because if I had just said nothing, nobody would have known?' Julie was at an age where you're not young enough to forget and you're not old enough to understand. We always thought that the best interest is letting her know that her mother was treated for what happened as opposed to her mother was punished for what happened."

Julie was placed with a couple she knew, experienced certified foster parents who took care of her for a year. But it was a rocky experience.

"Julie was like a feral cat," recalls Cathy Lepore, who was Julie's counselor at school, where she was in a special education program. "She was literally addicted to computer games. Nobody had ever said she couldn't watch an R-rated movie. She was watching movies like *Pulp Fiction* at age nine or ten. They got this kid, and, you know, they have rules—most people do."

Julie says that living there was okay at first, "but it started to get hard. When I was living with my mom, I didn't have to do anything, no chores." Now, she was expected to do chores and limit her video gaming. "It was very different to me, and I would get into fights with them a lot."

Eventually, says Cathy, the foster family "just had enough."

But the Department of Children and Families was at a loss. The agency couldn't find anyone on Nantucket willing to take Julie, and she faced the prospect of leaving Nantucket and being placed in foster care elsewhere.

"I was scared," Julie remembers. She confided her fear in Cathy.

"We won't let that happen," Cathy told her. "You can move in with us."

"Oh my gosh," Julie thought. "This is going to be awesome."

Cathy recalls that her feeling was, "this kid has already been through so much. We'll try it for two weeks." Two weeks turned into two months, two years, and more; the Lepores became Julie's foster parents. The doctor had to lock up his guns so the house could pass muster with social workers. And the Lepores began the odyssey of parenting a damaged and difficult child.

Julie's arrival was hardly the first time the Lepores had opened their doors. They have repeatedly taken in people who are down on their luck or need a place to stay. "Lepore's slop house," the doctor sometimes calls it.

"They feel they are very lucky and want to be able to help," says Chris Fraker, their neighbor. "People just sort of drive over here and show up."

While Nantucket is an island with jaw-dropping wealth, the Lepores are hardly affluent. Their home on Prospect Street is modest and not overflowing with space.

But "they were always taking in strays," their daughter, Meredith, says. "It's just part of who they both are."

Their son Nick says he "never realized that that was odd. It was always my family plus whoever was there. I think it then kind of became, like, 'Oh hey, this person needs a place to stay—maybe I can get in touch with the Lepores.'"

One foundling was a high school student named Lynn, who was "having troubles with her mother," Lepore says. After living with the Lepores, she joined the Peace Corps and then became a nurse. A student from Denmark named J.C. was so beloved by the family that "the first time I saw my dad cry was when J.C. left," Nick says.

And a Bosnian Muslim girl, Aida, arrived on a temporary student visa after having hid in a cellar in her home country and cut her hair short to help conceal her identity so she would not be raped. Aida was placed with an older family on Nantucket, "but it wasn't really a good fit, so the sponsor asked us to take her," Lepore says. Later, when Aida returned to Bosnia for what she thought was a Christmas visit, she was told that because she had held a job at a restaurant while being a student on Nantucket, she would not be allowed to leave Bosnia and return to the United States for seven years. The Lepores wrote letters on her behalf and contacted their congressman, but to no avail.

The Lepores have also taken in several nieces and nephews, some of whom were having trouble in school or experiencing stressful home lives. And they have played host to teachers who had come over to do stints in the schools, like Bob Barsanti, a high school English teacher who needed a place to stay for the summer and was supplementing his income by being a bouncer at a club called The Muse.

"If we have room, I'm happy to help people," Lepore says. "It's never been an intrusion." Not every member of his family, however, has always been so sure. Cathy considered Lepore's running buddy, Dickie Brainard, a less than ideal tenant. Brainard lit candles in the basement, setting off the fire alarm in the middle of the night. He ate food that Cathy was saving for the family.

"He was responsible for the infamous Dickie Rule," Meredith says. "Once you cross the Dickie line with my mom, there's no going back."

The Lepores have also given money to people who are struggling, although they are not wealthy themselves. While they earn about $200,000 a year between them, Nantucket is expensive, and Lepore's income is not always consistent. One year, when he bought an ill-fated computer billing program for the office, Lepore made only $25,000 and had to take out a personal line of credit to pay his staff.

Meredith says her father told her, "You're not getting an inheritance," because the family had no resources saved up for that. "But you've got your education."

Pam Michelsen, Cathy's friend, says that growing up in a large working-class Irish Catholic family gave Cathy "a natural empathy for people," making her "just as happy when a kid does something well, even if it's not their kid. I don't know of any two people who are more humane in this often inhuman world."

Their generosity has come at no small cost. At one point it was stressful enough that Meredith told her parents point blank: "I don't want anyone living in the house except us."

One trying situation involved the adopted daughter of one of Cathy's brothers. The Lepores took her in when she was thirteen to help Cathy's brother, whose wife had passed away a couple of years earlier. Cathy says the girl had been diagnosed with attachment disorder and had gotten into trouble stealing things from classmates.

The Lepores thought they could handle it and made sure she had counseling on Nantucket. But "she was a nightmare," Cathy recalls. "The kid was really disturbed. She would lie, and she would smoke weed. I would find pot in her handbag, or she wasn't doing what she was supposed to do for school. She would sneak out at night. She could be very sweet and very nice—you'd say, 'Oh my God, this is such a nice kid'—and then she would turn around and do crazy stuff."

Cathy believes the girl had missed some crucial love and security before being adopted. "Brains develop in layers," she says. "If you do not develop that trust and attachment to a primary caregiver, if that doesn't happen when it's supposed to, the next layer comes in without everything it needs. She had no conscience. She would be upset if she got caught, but not because she did something wrong. She just had no remorse if she did anything. She would just turn around and do it again if she could get away with it."

After about seven months, Cathy came to the troubling realization that it wasn't working, most significantly because "I can't keep her safe." Lepore agreed, and told their niece: "You either come down and talk to us about it, or you pack your bag." The girl packed her bag.

But it was the experience with another niece, Martina, that led to difficult long term fallout for the family. In 1991, when Martina was fifteen, her mother, Lepore's sister, Cheryl Buckley (called Sherry), asked the Lepores to take her for a while. Buckley, who lived in Connecticut, says her marriage was undergoing strain.

"My husband was an alcoholic," says Buckley, whose husband has since sobered up. Her job as a lending broker involved being on the road a lot. "I was working. There was no other money coming in. I made that decision to protect her. Her being alone with him and him being irresponsible and drinking—I couldn't have her home with him drinking and driving."

Lepore offered to pay for his sister to resettle on the island, but she rejected that idea and sent Martina to Nantucket for tenth grade. The Lepores, of course, weren't about to turn Martina away. They had previously let Buckley's sons, Tim and Jonathan, stay during the summer, and Tim Buckley was so inspired that he decided to become a doctor like his uncle Tim. So the precedent was encouraging. And early on, everything was fine.

"I got off the boat, we immediately went to the beach, and I was playing football with T.J. and Nick and my uncle," recalls Martina. "I was like, oh my God. This is what a family was like. I immediately felt loved and immersed in a new family."

Coming from her unstable home life, "I loved Nantucket," she says. "For me there was no chaos. If I ever had problems with things, I'd just go over to the beach, sit, and watch the ocean, and it would rejuvenate my thoughts. Part of it was the whole fact of the island—you were sheltered; you were protected; nobody could get to you."

And that was before her uncle Tim saved her life. Shortly after Martina arrived on Nantucket, "my uncle noticed I was pretty heavyset, and I didn't eat anything. His food bill wasn't really going up, and it didn't make sense."

Lepore was concerned because, as he so delicately put it, "she looked kind of porky." Martina remembers having been like that for a while, but that at home, "my mom was working a lot, and my dad wasn't really aware of what I was doing. Nobody really noticed me."

Martina had undergone a physical in Connecticut before going to Nantucket, and the doctor even "did ultrasound and couldn't see anything," her mother says. "They thought she was fine, but thought she was kind of fat and needed to lose weight." Martina remembers her pediatrician saying, "your stomach's really hard—you must do a lot of sit-ups."

Lepore thought there had to be more to it. Martina told him that "pretty much every time I ate, I had really bad indigestion." He started her on an antacid, but when nothing improved, he took her to the hospital for an ultrasound, thinking she might have gallstones. Oddly, the ultrasound screen was completely black, and the technician assumed the machine was broken. Lepore sent in a radiologist, whose scans showed, alarmingly, that "all of my organs were up in my upper back," Martina recalls. Something was taking up the space in her abdomen.

Amazingly, an ovarian cyst had been growing inside Martina for years, having gotten so large it now weighed thirteen pounds. It had pushed up and compressed her organs. "My kidneys were underneath my shoulder blades."

Martina was dumbstruck: "What are we going to do?" Lepore glanced at her nonchalantly: "Well, tomorrow, at 10:30 AM, we're going to cut you open. We're going to get it out of you."

Lepore called his father, John, still a surgeon in Marlborough, who decided to come to Nantucket to remove the cyst. (Lepore and his father shared a willingness to operate on family members; years earlier, Buckley says, John Lepore operated on his sister, and when she started bleeding and needed a transfusion, "they took blood right from my father and gave it to her.")

But when John Lepore, who had previously had a lung removed to treat his lung cancer, was scrubbing in to perform the surgery on Martina, he began feeling short of breath. He couldn't operate.

"I had to do it," Lepore recalls. Buckley was grateful. "I can't think of anybody else I'd want. Would you like somebody that loves your daughter to do it, or somebody you don't know?"

To put Martina at ease, he cracked Lepore-like jokes. They were crass, she remembers, but they helped. During surgery, he had to remove not only the cyst but an ovary too. And when she woke up, he told her he had also removed her appendix, "'cause I just didn't need it and he was in there."

Martina feared the scar would be "this huge gash on my abdomen, but it ended up being this thin little line." And the next day, Lepore pushed her to get up. "We gotta get you moving," he told her, to jog the organs into shifting back to their rightful abdominal place. Martina learned later that if Lepore hadn't diagnosed her and operated quickly, "my kidney could have burst when nobody was there, and that would have been the end of me."

That wasn't the only benefit, Martina soon discovered. "I went from being 185 pounds on a Monday to 112 pounds on a Tuesday. I remember thinking, 'Holy Cow, I shrank!' I'd never really felt good about myself, and it's like all of a sudden, I'm not obese. All of a sudden, I had a waist and a figure. I felt like Malibu Barbie."

But the Lepores had not counted on raising a life-sized liberated Barbie. "The other children had always been strait-laced—this was the procedure when they were growing up. I didn't have a procedure," Martina admits. Martina was almost a year older than their oldest child, Meredith, and "I didn't have boundaries at home; I didn't have structure; I didn't have too many rules. All of a sudden they got this child who knew how to raise herself and didn't need anybody's input. I think I overwhelmed them because I was the fifteen-year-old girl with the figure and the boys coming. Blam!—they had the instant teenager."

Martina says she didn't drink or do drugs—"I think they thought I did a lot more things than I did." But she spent a lot of time rollerblading around the island and hanging out with a football player she was dating. As an "act of defiance," she didn't do her homework, and "I wasn't a very good student," doing especially poorly in English, which was unfortunate because her English teacher was Bob Barsanti, the friend and former house guest of the Lepores who would visit them all the time.

By the end of the school year, the Lepores had reached their limit. "She's not staying here," Cathy told her sister-in-law. "She needs to be with you now, 'cause I've had it."

Buckley acknowledges now that things weren't handled well. Martina "gave them a tough run for their money. I think it's not what they bargained for."

But back then, Buckley was resentful and took it out on Cathy: "Who are you? Queen of the island?"

To which Cathy replied, "I don't want to talk to you again."

"I was so hurt by the whole thing," Cathy reflects. "Because we always got along, and family is so important to me."

Buckley sent Martina to Nantucket the next year anyway, arranging for someone else, a teacher, to take her in. Martina was dating that teacher's friend's son.

"That was really hard for me," Cathy says. "This teacher was someone that I knew and respected. Nobody called and said, 'Are you okay with this?'" And Cathy couldn't help but come in contact with Martina. "I was the school nurse. She was in the school with me every day. It was awful. There was no love lost, if you will."

At school functions, Martina worried, "Do I go up and say hi, or do I not?" On the island, "everybody knew the Lepores; everybody liked them. I never heard anybody talking negatively ever, which is unusual for an island, because you usually get some nastiness." She considered her uncle, in particular, "a very strong person" who's "done many difficult things in his life that most people could never think about."

Martina wrote to the Lepores and "apologized for whatever I had done," but the tension remained during the year she lived with the teacher and over four subsequent summers when she returned to work as a nanny and lifeguard. "I didn't have any ill will toward the Lepores. I was hurt. I don't know why they didn't like me. I was sad that I screwed up somehow."

Beyond that, Martina says, "I felt that I came between my mom and her brother. I guess I always felt guilty that I had caused all of it."

Buckley says the overt flare-up was "between Cathy and I—my brother does not like to get involved in any controversy." Lepore simply stopped talking to his sister. "I don't like to drag up a lot of what happened," Buckley says. "There were reasons that were legitimate there, and some things that I'm not proud of."

The most painful part for the Lepores was that John Lepore "took my sister's side of this whole thing," Lepore recalls. "My father sent a nasty letter to Cathy."

"Dad, look, this is just untenable," Lepore told his father. It was no use. Direct communication between Lepore and his father had never been extensively emotional. Pam Michelsen, who had gotten to know Lepore's father when she and Cathy would take their children to visit him "in America," says that if John Lepore "doted on his daughter, it was because she always had things go wrong, and Tim was the one who didn't. Tim's dad told me one time: 'Tim's a great doctor, and he loves his children, and he doesn't drink, and I am so proud of him.' But I don't think that Tim heard that, and if he did, he didn't really hear it."

The Martina episode, though, sundered the relationship beyond repair. Lepore did not realize the extent to which his father had abandoned him until John Lepore died in 1995, three years after his son and daughter's feud began.

John Lepore, it turned out, had changed his last will and testament. "My father left everything to my sister. He died and left everything to her."

Buckley had a yard sale of items, including some things that had belonged to Lepore. "I had to buy some of my stuff back," he says incredulously. He sent his friend, Bob DiBuono, to buy several bows. A cousin went to the house with a truck to collect the gun case John Lepore had made for Tim, one of his World War II uniforms in a foot locker, and maps he had used to mark where he had served in North Africa and the Italian campaign.

There were other things of his father's that Lepore would have liked to have: tools, a wine press, a drill press, a jigsaw, a vice. "It didn't have tremendous value. But just having his tools, all the stuff he had"—it would have meant something. As would his father's huge collection of electric motors, his car, his boat. "I don't know what happened to those. The day of the funeral was the last time I was in the house."

Besides the belongings, Lepore knew there was "a bank account in my father's and my name" with $16,000 in it. To get access, he was forced "to get a lawyer to go after my sister."

Buckley says she never tried to keep Lepore from collecting their father's items. "There was always an open door with me: 'What do you want? Take what you want.' No answer. He was more than told many, many times to get what he wanted."

For years there was virtually no contact between Buckley and the Lepores, although the Lepores stayed in touch with Buckley's sons. Then in 2007, Martina, who was married and living in Connecticut, called out of the blue: "Hi, Uncle Tim, it's Martina. I need help."

Martina's eldest child, McKael, then five, was "really, really sick," she recalls. "He couldn't move; he couldn't run. He was crippled, for all intents and purposes. He walked around like he was a ninety-year-old man."

Martina suspected Lyme disease, but her pediatrician disagreed because three Lyme tests had been negative. After nine months of evaluations, Martina's mother suggested she call Lepore. On the phone, he mentioned nothing about the family rift, listened to the symptoms, and urged her to find a doctor who would treat the boy for Lyme. They did, and "within a week and a half, he's a different kid," Martina says. "I remember standing in the kitchen with my husband, and I saw McKael smile. He was always so melancholy and just down; it was so long since I had seen him smile."

Somewhere along the line, the Lepores had made their peace with Martina. "She's a very nice adult," Cathy says. "Realistically, she was a kid, and that's how she coped. People who have alcoholics in their family, that's what they do. They tend to be very manipulative. She felt bad about what had happened."

Detente with Buckley took somewhat longer. In 2009, Buckley's son Tim told her Lepore would be in Guilford, Connecticut, where she had a house, running a race. She called: "I want to see you if only for a minute." Lepore grudgingly agreed and brought Cathy along. Martina, who works as a police officer in Guilford, showed up in uniform, although, she says, "I wasn't there for the Kumbaya moment." Neither was Lepore, who took off running the race, leaving Cathy and Buckley to talk.

"It was like putting two warring factions in a room," Cathy recalls. But Buckley "was very nice, actually." Both women cried.

"We just said, 'What the hell are we doing?'" Buckley remembers. "She experienced losses; I experienced losses. We wasted so much time. We screwed up many, many years."

Not long after that, Buckley went to Nantucket for the Christmas Stroll and again for the Daffodil Festival. "It was a big step," she says. "My brother was rather distant. Did I hang around with my brother? No. But did I enjoy Cathy? Yes."

During the Daffodil Festival visit, Buckley brought five friends, and Lepore "brought them to his office and tried to shock them" with his guns-and-dead-animal decor. "My friends will never forget that."

Cathy is pleased with the rapprochement: "It's not fun to have that monkey on your back. It makes me happier having this relationship work right now. You can carry it all around with you, this anger, and it doesn't really hurt anybody else except you."

Things with Lepore are more of a work in progress. Buckley respects his dedication to the life he's built on Nantucket. "He's very proud of his island," she says. "He's turned into a very beloved, eccentric character on the island, and I think he's a big fish in a relatively little pond, like my father was. It suits his character, and it suits the island type of character."

But they are different people. "I would find it very difficult being there with my brother," Buckley says. "He likes to do what he likes to do, and he's very, very intense with what he does. When he does something, his whole heart, body, and soul is into it."

As for Lepore, his reaction is typically succinct. "It's over," he remarks of the long feud. "Good."

By the time the Lepores took in Julie in November 2007, they figured they'd had enough experience to handle anything. Their own children were grown, and, remarked Lepore, "I view it as we're blessed with having an opportunity. 'Blessed' is a crazy word, but it's an opportunity to help a kid."

At first, they were careful to treat Julie, then thirteen, with kid gloves. After all, this was a child whose mother was believed to have tried to poison her. "I don't want her to feel like if she screws up, we'll get rid of her," was Cathy's philosophy. "She says, 'Other kids get to do this.' I say, 'Julie, these are the rules.' I'll never say to her, 'You need to leave.'"

When she tried to evade the restrictions, going to Lepore to overrule a curfew Cathy had set, for example, they tried to be patient: "She's a good kid, but she can be a meathead sometimes—there's sort of an element of sadness about her," Lepore concluded.

Cathy realized that, "yes, she tries to manipulate me, but sometimes I think she's being that way, and she's not. I've been wrong enough times. She will eventually see this as something that saved her life, because it's given her the opportunity to live with a family who is stable."

As Julie got older—fourteen, fifteen, sixteen—things became more difficult. She bridled at the Lepores' expectations that she help out around the house, get a part-time job, and participate in an athletic activity. They considered that the way to instill a child with responsibility and self-worth. It frustrated them when Julie resisted.

"Julie is bright, very bright—she is also very, very lazy," was Lepore's assessment at one point. "We had her play softball, basketball. We see that as mandatory. And she has to do her schoolwork. If you don't understand the math, go ask the teacher. If she sat down and applied herself . . . if she did her homework . . . She goes in a month before school's over with three Fs, two Ds, and a C. That's what she was heading towards. She passed, but nothing higher than a C."

Lepore was always trying to get Julie to read. "I have this thing about books—you read, you can create the world," he says. "In a video game it makes the world for you. You're a watcher, not a participant. Unplugging the computer is the only way we can get her to get off the Internet."

And they were concerned about what he described as a tendency to "go to school dressed like a hooker." They told her, "Put a shirt on and keep the shirt on."

Julie also tried to ditch one of her few outside jobs, dog walking. "It's a two-hours-a-week job, and she'll put on such histrionics, you'd think she was in the third stage of labor," Lepore observed.

One summer afternoon when she was fifteen was typical.

"I'm supposed to walk my boss's dog, but I don't feel like it today," Julie reported, lounging on the Lepores' couch. "I like dogs that walk with you. This dog, you take it outside, and it just sits there, and you have to pull it really hard. It's a real pain. I just can't deal with it. The dog will be all right for one day."

Julie knew the Lepores would never stand for that. "When Cathy comes home, she's going to ask if I walked the dog. I'm going to say, 'Yes, I walked him.' I hate lying, but if she finds out, she'll be mad, and she'll take away my phone again. I don't really lie, except about little things."

The defiance and clashes worsened. Once, Cathy "got mad because I didn't get out of bed in time," Julie recalls, lamenting that her phone had been confiscated as punishment. "She said I'm not getting it back for two days." Later that day, "Tim wanted me to read my book. I'm like, 'I'm not reading my book right now.' I was so pissed because Cathy took my phone away, and, like, I needed to call my friends and, like, text them and stuff like that."

Julie made amends the next day, promising to be better behaved. "I just went and gave her a hug and said, 'I'm sorry, Cathy,' and she was, like, okay, and then I helped her shuck some corn. I'm, like, a very forgiving person."

That the Lepores were respected and involved members of the community only seemed to amplify the tension. "Everybody knows who they are, so I couldn't really do what I wanted," Julie observed. "If I had wanted to hang out with friends, Cathy was like, 'Oh, that person does drugs, and you can't be friends with them,' 'cause she knows everything." And anything Julie was doing "gets right back to them."

Cathy's role as a school counselor meant that "the teachers know" about "everything I'm doing." And Cathy realized that with Julie around, she was essentially getting no break from her day job of working with troubled teenagers. "I deal with it all day at school, and I don't want to deal with it at home, so that's hard."

Things became even more difficult when, as Julie admits, "I started smoking weed and doing that sort of stuff."

While the Lepores felt deep sympathy for what Julie had been through, they also felt she milked the tragedy and showed little empathy for others. "Julie will say, 'I don't know why people tell me their problems—it's not like my mother didn't try to kill me,'" Cathy reported.

Lepore recognized there would always be an "element of friction. Cathy's not her mother. I think Julie sometimes resents that. Your mother may try and kill you, but she's still your mother." Plus, he observed, the instability in Julie's earlier life may have been chaotic, "but it was excitement, whereas Cathy says, 'Do your homework,' and that isn't quite as much fun."

Although Julie had not had direct contact with her mother, she was in touch through Facebook with her brother, who was living with their mother. "I want to see her. I'm not angry. I'm just kind of like disappointed. But, you know, stuff happens. I miss her."

Cathy consulted Julie's counselor, who told her that Julie targeted Cathy with her anger because she felt safe doing so. "Even though it feels bad, it's a compliment," she told her. But Cathy was not persuaded. "She was not nice to me, and she was only nice to Tim insofar as what she could get. She was just shooting herself in the foot. What has this time been? Has it been meaningless for her?"

Julie was also wondering if she could handle it much longer. "I like it here, but their rules are kind of like so stupid. Sometimes I just get so depressed living here. I don't know if I want to be here till I'm eighteen. I may want to go somewhere more chill."

Nearly three years after moving in with the Lepores, Julie got that chance. Cathy couldn't take it anymore.

"I find it too difficult for me to continue being the parent of a teenager . . . someone else's teenager, specifically," she wrote in an email in late August 2010. "I know it may sound harsh, but I just cannot give her the time that she deserves. In my heart, I am done, done, done."

Without discussing it with Lepore, Cathy called the social worker. "She needs to go," Cathy said. "You need to come and get her out of here."

Cathy says the social worker understood. "I can't thank you enough," she told Cathy. "I was sure she was going to be hospitalized at least three times when she was with you, and she wasn't hospitalized once."

Lepore, on the other hand, was "upset with me because he felt like it wasn't the right thing. I didn't consult with him when I called, and he was upset, and he had a right to be."

But Cathy didn't reconsider her decision: "I don't think he realized the effect it was having on me. He felt it was a failure on his part, but it really wasn't at all. You think that you can bring someone into your house for three years, and you think that some of the values will rub off, and then when they don't, it's very upsetting. It's like planting a tulip and having azaleas come up."

It may be, however, that some of the seeds they planted took root after all. More than a year after she left the Lepores, Julie, seventeen, living with her father in New Hampshire after a couple of unsuccessful foster placements, said she has "definitely changed a lot." She has experienced more tragedy—her brother committed suicide in April 2011. But she said she was attending a high school program in the evenings and getting As and Bs.

Julie doesn't fault the Lepores for ending their foster care arrangement: "I'm not blaming anybody but myself," she says. "I got really lazy when I was living with them. I was just slacking off. I don't really have too many regrets about staying with them. They did teach me a lot, and they taught me the value of education and how important it is and stuff like that. I have a lot of respect for them, you know."

CHAPTER 14

THE LIFE PRESERVER

For a meeting of Nantucket Cottage Hospital's board of trustees, Tim Lepore prepared a PowerPoint presentation. It started off innocuously, with a map of Nantucket, a steel-gray island floating in an ocean of midnight blue. The second slide was a bucolic photograph of a foggy inlet braceleted in scrub oak.

But once Lepore presented his title slide, "Keeping My Finger on the Prostate of Medicine," any pretense of decorum was tossed aside. He showed a photograph of an ivory-billed woodpecker, a creature so prized and rare that scientists have offered rewards for finding one. Lepore explained that a solo general surgeon on an island—someone, as it happens, like himself—is like the woodpecker, "much talked about, seldom seen." Small wonder, he noted, that this special woodpecker is sometimes called the "God Bird."

So much for humility. Lepore had things to say. "I was the skunk at the family picnic."

The family, in this case, had morphed in recent years, adding what Lepore considered a stodgier, less permissive set of in-laws. The hospital had, in 2007, relinquished its independence to merge with a much larger Boston medical system, Massachusetts General Hospital and its parent company, Partners HealthCare.

It was Nantucket's attempt to make its hospital more efficient and financially viable. But to Lepore, it was also a capitulation of sorts to Big Medicine, a world of health care by cost code and corporate-driven consistency.

"I always felt it was better to date larger institutions than marry them" is how Lepore puts it. "When the giant sneezes, the little guy gets a cold."

At the meeting, Lepore wanted to warn the hospital not to get its priorities wrong. "Whether the patient needs something or not is a clinical decision. You deal with the financial decision later. To do it ass-backwards is bad medicine."

Lepore shifted from rare birds to rock bands. "Rolling Stones," read one slide. "'Let It Bleed.' Dr. Tim says: 'Great song, bad public relations.' Nantucket Cottage Hospital is on an island, but not an island. We have to listen to our customers." Customers want a hospital that treats them well.

Lepore said the hospital was charging much more than the mainland for MRIs, CAT scans, and lab testing, creating hardship for islanders without insurance or with copayments that are calculated as a percentage of a procedure's cost. He said he had "brought this up again and again" to billing officials, "and they were treating me like Mickey the Dunce," he said. Told some prices were erroneously high because of computer glitches, he replied, "Fix it, and then make sure you call the people back that paid for it."

But Lepore also told the trustees something that might sound odd for a surgeon. Some board members had discussed adding a second operating room, but Lepore said there wouldn't be enough additional surgical cases to justify the cost of extra anesthetists and nurses to staff another OR. "Where," he wondered aloud, "are you going to get these cases from? We don't have nuclear medicine. We can't really do biopsies for breast cancer. If I can't do what the state of the art is, I don't want to do it." He was not concerned, as some people thought, that a second OR might lead the hospital to hire a second, less maverick surgeon. "If another surgeon came out, great. But I know there isn't enough surgery to keep somebody busy. Plus you got to be a little bit crazy."

There was more. While the hospital is hoping to raise money for a new building, Lepore said some things needed upgrading now. The decor reminded him "of the Soviet era" and was "vaguely reminiscent of Cedar Junction," a Massachusetts maximum security prison. "It is difficult to attract the carriage trade and put them in a barn."

Lepore's last slide was a map showing the hospital and his house, both on Prospect Street, roughly one hundred yards apart. His point was beyond dispute: "This is my vocation and avocation. The hospital is my career and my home."

For Lepore, the big hospital's incursion has been a less-than-seamless work in progress. "It's a pure and simple culture clash," says Margot Hartmann, the hospital's CEO. "I live with it every day. They know that he's outrageous. They would like him to be a party guy. But they also understand that that will never be Tim."

As if to underscore that point, during his board of trustees presentation Lepore displayed the hospital's longtime logo: a silhouette of the island inside a life preserver. Mass General had changed the logo to a shield with a scallop shell on it to homogenize it with the shield logos of other Partners hospitals.

A minor change, one might think. But symbols matter. "They didn't ask us," says Mary Monagle, a nurse. "That's still a huge bone of contention." In fact, in 2010, when Hartmann became CEO, the logo still rankled enough that she made up mugs with the old logo on one side under the words "Honoring the Past," and the new logo on the other side with the words "Celebrating the Future."

For Lepore, though, the changeover is about much more than logos. The new administration wanted Nantucket physicians to join the Massachusetts General Physicians Organization, the MGPO. MGPO doctors get salaries and pay a certain amount to cover management costs. They are subject to rules concerning billing, hours, supplies, and procedures.

The other doctors signed up, but Lepore said no. "I want my employees answering to me. I want to work as hard as I want to work. And if I don't belong to the MGPO, I can stand up and say the emperor has no clothes."

Lepore acknowledges that the MGPO provides "some pluses"—good retirement benefits and malpractice insurance—and some processes can be helped by economies of scale. But there are downsides, like scheduling patients. "If I have a divorced couple, I'm probably not going to schedule them at the same time. That may happen with the MGPO. And nobody's coming in every twenty minutes to tell me that I'm done."

The hospital tracks MGPO physicians' "relative value units" or RVUs, a dollar amount assigned to patient visits, used to calculate how physicians get paid. To Lepore, that's like asking a doctor, "Did you make enough widgets today? I am sink or swim on my own nickel— hopefully swim, just not with sharks."

T.J. Lepore worries the MGPO arrangement could irreversibly cramp his father's style. "It makes it more difficult to get paid in cookies. It's very one-size-fits-all, and Nantucket is a place that doesn't fit all." Tim Lepore is skeptical of the big medical company's impact on Nantucket's scrappy hospital, which he describes as "like a real hospital, except shrunk, Sanforized." The merger, he feels, "is like a Great Dane and a Chihuahua trying to get it on."

And he has bridled as things become more rules-oriented—more Boston Proper, less Wild West. "He always had that free hand, and I think with Mass General, it kind of brings corporate America to the hospital, and with that kind of oversight and stuff, it makes it difficult," T.J. says.

"All of a sudden employees have to sign in," Lepore groused. And when he was told, "Dr. Lepore, we don't want you getting packages at the mail room," his response was, "Hey, bite my ass." When a portable cardiac ultrasound machine was sent over from Cape Cod, a technician complained to Lepore that the patients had not yet been registered. Lepore confronted "the guy in charge of registration, and the son of a bitch wouldn't stop eating his breakfast burrito. He did not view it with quite the intensity that I did. I like to see things made easy for patients because they come in, they are anxious, they have a life."

Lepore also objected to "restricted hours for residents and interns. Sounds good, but do you want to have a guy who actually knows the case and follows it along or do you want to have twelve people do a hand-off because you can only work so many hours?"

It used to be simple, Monagle says, to "call down to the lab and say, 'Dr. Lepore wants you to add on an extra tube of blood.'" Or, if an older patient was scheduled for a colonoscopy, Lepore might admit him to the hospital the night before to make sure he followed the pre-colonoscopy regimen and did not eat or drink the wrong things. "We know the patient lives alone and his daughter has a full-time job, and this way we're able to watch him like a hawk," Monagle recalls. But lab tests and discretionary hospital admissions cost money.

Monagle left in 2011 partly out of frustration with the merger: "Why don't we embrace what makes us unique? What makes us unique is that we are a country hospital. If I wanted to work for Mass General, I would have gone to work for Mass General. I wanted to work with Dr. Lepore, the way he does it."

The way Lepore does it has earned him respect from many in the community. "Sometimes he plays role of canary in the coal mine, so when he sees something he doesn't like that the administration is doing, he can be vocal about it," says Michelle Whelan, executive director of Sustainable Nantucket.

"He would like to see the hospital be better than it is, offering more things," says Louise Hourihan, a patient, whose husband, Bill, a bank executive, is on the hospital board. "He's controversial because he doesn't sugarcoat things and he's very opinionated."

Some board members have learned to take Lepore on his own terms. "That's Tim. He doesn't want anybody to pay his salary and tell him what to do," says Bruce Chabner, a board member who, as director of clinical research at Mass General's Cancer Center, has followed the merger from both sides.

Chabner remembers Lepore's board presentation as "a little distasteful" and says some trustees and hospital officials "think he's an unusual sort of person. He doesn't want to be fenced in. But he's a respected clinician. I don't think anybody says he's not a good doctor."

In fact, says Chabner, who has summered on Nantucket for decades and whose wife has been treated by Lepore, "the first years I knew Tim, we had a sort of cool relationship. Politically, he's on the other end. He likes guns. He's sort of a swashbuckling character. But I respect him as a doctor, so I got to know him. And I wouldn't hesitate to send a patient to him."

If hospital officials object when Lepore becomes what he calls "the archetypal loose cannon," he doesn't care. "They are not ordained. I didn't see tongues of fire on their heads. I have to say what's on my mind. If people don't like it, they don't like it."

No one is more involved in choreographing the Lepore–Mass General pas de deux than Margot Hartmann, who has known Lepore since 1999, when she was a summer visitor feeling disgruntled about her primary care practice in a Boston suburb.

"He likes to say that I walked slowly past the hospital and he reached out," Hartmann says. "Actually I think I reached out to him." She began working in Nantucket's emergency room and remembers when she first called Lepore to get his opinion on a complicated patient. She presented the facts over the phone in the rubric physicians learn: medical history, symptoms, test results, etc.

"I, of course, wanted to do a good job and show that I knew what I was talking about, that I wasn't bothering him or trying to interrupt his life for something that wasn't worth his time. So I'm launching into my thing with this guy, and I think I'm doing fine."

"Margot, Margot, Margot," Lepore interrupted. Hartmann stopped cold.

"What?" she thought. "Have I missed something major?"

"Margot. You cannot polish a meatball."

"What? Meatball? Why are we talking about meatballs? That is not in the code at all."

But she realized "what he was actually saying to me was, this man had so many things wrong with him that basically don't get your hopes up too high about what the therapeutic goal can be. That was my first real insight into the kind of brilliance and outrage of working with Tim Lepore. What he was saying was, 'I have heard you. I have taken in all the info, and this is my assessment, and we're not going to get all bent out of shape about it.'"

It was the first of many experiences. "Tim has this pithy phrase which comes out of who knows where, but what he says has a pearl of truth always. If he wasn't a good enough clinician to be able to back it up, you wouldn't care that he has a *Readers' Digest* funny phrase of the month."

Lepore can usually take a joke at his expense—when the Anglican minister dressed as Lepore for Halloween, or when a pumpkin carving contest featured a Lepore look-alike skeleton in a lab coat and running socks, holding an X-ray, a tick crawling across its pumpkin head.

"You must admit I'm an easy target," Lepore shrugs. Hartmann says Lepore fesses up to mistakes, unlike "some clinicians, who handle the weight of the responsibility by making their colleagues wrong. Tim never does that, and that's a class act."

Still, she says, "sometimes he'll play, 'I'm the surgeon; I'm going to nail everybody with the most esoteric question in public.' It's a gladiatorial combat kind of game."

Hartmann recalls one meeting when she was running the emergency room. "Tim asked a very, very nasty question of me, a kind of show-off question that was designed to set me up: 'Could you comment on the fact, Dr. Hartmann, that blah, blah, blah? . . .' I felt so wrong-footed by this, in front of my peers and the people that I oversee."

The next day, when Hartmann asked, "Tim, what was that about?" he apologized and sent flowers. She later told Cathy Lepore that the flowers were greatly appreciated. "Oh," Cathy said, "he has their number on speed dial."

Now, as the hospital's CEO, Hartmann has inherited a hospital in strained financial straits. At the hospital's annual meeting in 2011, which was also the hospital's centennial, the numbers were sobering. The hospital's loss from operations the previous year was $8.8 million, compared with $6.4 million in 2009. The cost of providing free care to poor and uninsured patients had grown by 60 percent; 18 percent of adults under sixty-five on Nantucket had no health insurance, twice the percentage in the rest of the state.

These problems reflect upheaval in America's health system, and they are being felt in hospitals and communities across the country, especially in small towns. "Health care changed around us, and we were too small and really didn't have the resources and probably didn't want to know it," Hartmann says. "We did not keep up. We kept up with the medical care, but not with the business of medical care."

Nantucket's hospital gets no financial support from local government, unlike some small community hospitals, and relies significantly on private donors, some not as flush as they once were. The number of patients is declining, as some people move off-island and others go off-island for medical care.

"The little procedures that used to help keep the system afloat, those have been whittled and whittled and whittled away," Hartmann says. Some patients are going elsewhere because "the technology has advanced so much that we can't keep up," says Jane Bonvini, director of nursing at the hospital until she was let go in 2010.

The hospital building, erected in 1957, is in the worst shape and is the least efficient to heat, cool, light, and operate of any in the Partners system, Hartmann says. It costs about a million dollars a year just to keep things repaired and maintained, and Hartmann thinks the building may only be usable for another five years. "I'm pretty sure Florence Nightingale used that sink," noted Monagle one afternoon in the hospital. "That shade of green is from 1958."

A 2011 national report gave Nantucket high ratings as a place where people are healthy, ranking it first among Massachusetts counties on measures like health outcomes, mortality, and healthy behaviors. But Nantucket ranked near the bottom in two categories: its high number of uninsured adults and its low number of physicians. Lepore told the local paper that winning healthiest county in the state was like "being the tallest midget."

Indeed, a few months later came another rating, from the American Trauma Society, which listed Nantucket among the country's "danger" zones because it can take more than an hour to reach a hospital with advanced trauma care.

Hartmann is in a tough spot. She heads what she calls "an improbably sophisticated facility for the size of the year-round population" and faces bean counters who believe the hospital should be stripped down to "basically a first aid center and a helipad." Other islanders want "the intimacy of a small place, but they want the cutting-edge delivery of care. People choose to be out on Nantucket probably because they don't trust and don't like the way it's done on the mainland."

Chabner says "the real issue for Nantucket is how much should they try to do out there versus how much should they refer. I think it has to offer very good emergency service, very good family care, routine internal medicine care, and has to have some capability for emergency surgery. That's why Tim's so important. It's very hard to find a person with his kind of background."

Recruiting and retaining staff of any kind is "a nightmare," Hartmann says. "Our costs of living are probably 127 percent of anybody else's. Everyone's enchanted in the beginning, and it's all wonderful. But the island, for the person, let alone their family, it's a whole different kind of commitment. It either clicks or it doesn't, and more often than not it doesn't. Some people, they want the mall and the multiplex cinema, and they want the chain store, and they get island fever very quickly."

Also nurses and doctors these days want to specialize, but Nantucket needs them to do everything. "You get people saying, 'I only work in the ER, and I can't do anything else.' Well, we can't hire you then," former nursing director Bonvini says.

Hartmann says Nantucket needs "a particular kind of person that likes to live this remotely, and is comfortable enough with their skills to function without all the layers of subspecialists, somebody who already knows what they don't know, and is very good at identifying that and knowing who to call."

All these tensions are playing out in economic ways. In 2011, the hospital cafeteria was shut because of deteriorating plumbing, reopening after a $50,000 repair bill months later, but only in a scaled-down version. Programs like home health nursing have been eliminated or contracted out to off-island organizations.

For Lepore, the cutbacks are "very stressful," T.J. says. "He recognizes when things are being lost that shouldn't be lost. At a hospital that size when you start peeling away services, where does that end?" In the past, "he's always had people over a barrel who demand things because he's the only show in town. I'm not sure Mass General really understands that. I think in a lot of ways they see it as a normal feeder hospital, and it's not."

Hartmann sees both sides, saying, "We're really just trying to stabilize the hospital and figure out whether we can be sustainable, which I think we can be." Hartmann hopes that a fundraising campaign will generate enough to build a new facility on hospital grounds.

But for now, with the resources it has, the hospital is renovating some areas, hoping to improve outpatient clinics, and increasing telemedicine, with mainland doctors giving virtual consultations to patients with strokes, skin conditions, and other problems.

Telemedicine concerns Lepore, especially teleradiology because relying on off-island radiologists could limit his ability to offer input and get scan results quickly. "Other people practice very effectively waiting for the X-ray report. I don't. You could say, 'Well, Tim, in the grand scheme of things, this isn't good for the hospital or the country or the world.' I don't care about that. My concern is that particular patient."

Lepore knows his value to the hospital. "I'm a little bit like an amulet. If I croak, there are problems." Besides his own medical activities, he mentors young staff members, popping in on a new lab technician and saying, "Can you take my blood?" The technician was so nervous she was practically shaking, but when she finished, Lepore told her, "You're going to do great."

He regularly contributes his own money to the hospital, sometimes as much as $25,000, and has purchased equipment on his own dime, including an advanced blood sugar monitor. He recruits donations from his wealthy patients for equipment like a laryngoscope. "The hospital may not see it as a need, but I do, and that's it. If I think it's important, I put my money where my mouth is."

But Lepore can be headstrong even with Hartmann. When one of his dogs, Buddy, a Nova Scotia Duck-Tolling Retriever, had a kidney tumor, Lepore wanted to use the hospital's ultrasound. He was rebuffed. "They got their undies in a bundle," says Lepore, who took Buddy to Boston. "It cost them money to cover me when I had to go off-island. And I did not appreciate it."

Hartmann saw it differently. "If Tim wants to bring a dog into the ultrasound suite, and frankly if he's feeling the need to make an iconoclastic point, then he will swagger in and do it in the middle of day when everybody is there, which sets me up and sets everybody up. My feeling is 'if you're going to do this, fine, I'll help you. Let's do it at a time when people aren't around.' He didn't need to be so visible. He set it up so that somebody had to come down and say no, which makes the suits look like the suits and Tim look like the good guy who's on the side of right."

Hartmann sees Lepore as "basically a libertarian, maybe with a small *l*. He's always going to try and take pot shots at those of us who are not, and he enjoys that. If I'm in the mood, I will play. But if not, I will say, 'Tim, I am fighting for the survival of this hospital. I don't need that kind of pot shot.' And he stops."

In truth, Lepore doesn't always pick a fight. His goal, usually, is not to break the fine china but to quietly use his own tried-and-true set of plates. When he transfers a patient off-island, he doesn't necessarily adhere to the administration's preference that he send them to Mass General or another Partners hospital. "I send them where I want," based on what he feels a particular hospital excels in and where "I can make one phone call and the patient's well taken care of." Some hospitals "can be a bit of a black hole. I deal with quality people who I trust. I know the patients are going to be treated well, and I know I'm going to hear back." Besides, it's a small victory in his crusade to maintain independence from the corporate suits. "It gets their noses out of joint, which makes me happy."

Chabner, who makes sure that when Lepore calls his office for a cancer patient, "I get him in right away," would like to see more Nantucket patients sent to Mass General. But he understands that other hospitals "have provided very good service for him when he's needed it in the past. To suddenly drop those people and establish relationships elsewhere is hard."

Lepore doesn't complain about everything in the new hospital landscape. "He doesn't trust any of it, but on the other hand he's the first one to tell you that in some ways Mass General has brought good things," Hartmann reports. "Well, he won't be the first one to tell you, but if you hang in long enough in the conversation, he will tell you that."

In fact, says Lepore, "some of the people from Mass General are recognizing that there are some things we need. Once, I wanted to get a psychiatrist to see one of the patients. The reimbursement issues were very unclear. The financial guy said, 'Look, get the psychiatrist. We'll deal with the reimbursement later.'"

He has also made accommodations to the new culture, in his own way. He doesn't wear his hunting vest so much anymore or the clothes from his favorite military surplus store. But sometimes he dresses to the other extreme, going beyond the casual clothing other doctors wear. "I wanted to drive people crazy by switching. For a while I was wearing a tie and jacket. People were making fun of me, particularly when I had my initials on my pocket. I just thought I'd spiff up a little, just to separate myself."

Lepore intends to remain separate. "If they pressure me" to sign up with the MGPO, he says, "I just say I'll take a month off. They can't do anything to me. I'm fairly bulletproof."

Cathy thinks some of that is bravado, and she fears that "things are getting narrower for him with this MGPO. I think he feels like a dinosaur."

But no one on Nantucket wants Lepore to become extinct. Chabner, whose father was a small-town doctor in Illinois, says people like Lepore "have a different relationship with patients. You become an intimate friend of the family; you go through all sorts of trauma with them, medical and psychological."

Plus Chabner knows Lepore's knowledge of tick-borne diseases is invaluable to Nantucket. "He's really an expert at it, something really unique in medicine."

As a surgeon, Lepore is unusual too, because he'll perform so many different operations but also turn down surgical opportunities if he thinks patients should go elsewhere.

"You don't find many surgeons that are willing to open up a big family practice," T.J. observes. "He is one of the few surgeons I know that would make that choice. It's going to be hard to find a young person, certainly, who's going to want to come and do very little surgery and maintain their skill level, but it's going to be hard to find an older surgeon who wants to work the hours he does. I think that's one thing that's going to make it very hard when he retires, if he does retire. He's practicing a brand of medicine that is hard to do these days, and it's rare."

In fact, while Richard H. Koehler, a laparoscopic surgeon, comes to Nantucket to cover when Lepore goes off-island, neither Koehler nor anyone he can think of would fill Lepore's running shoes. "You will never find a general surgeon who's going to do primary care. Never. Maybe in the outskirts of rural Montana or Manitoba. I would be stunned. He's two people. Then, when he acts as an obstetrician, he's three. He also does endoscopies," inserting a scope into the body to look inside. Many general surgeons don't do that either, Koehler says. "He's four people."

All of which means, says Pam Michelsen, that if Lepore ever stops doctoring, the island "will be like the rest of the world, and that's just not Nantucket."

Lepore, at sixty-seven, shows no sign of retiring, but the hospital is dreading the possibility. "That's a very serious issue now," Chabner asserts.

It's a question other small communities across the country are confronting in their own way: what to do when the kinds of doctors people have always relied on can no longer make a living practicing medicine that way. What to do when medical care becomes less personal, more expensive, farther away, more cookie cutter, less Lepore-like?

"How can you replace a guy like that?" Chabner asks.

Hartmann thinks that, at least for Nantucket, it's virtually impossible.

"My personal nightmare is succession planning for Tim Lepore," she says. "There are no Tims out there. There probably really isn't another Tim Lepore in the whole country."

One day, a DVD arrives in Lepore's mailbox. Its title is *Trees Inn: The Next Best Trespass*. It says it is "a film by Dug Underwood" about "another handmade home by Forest Green."

Lepore is intrigued. Dug Underwood and Forest Green were two aliases of Underground Tom, who built illegal hovels and hideaways all over Nantucket, but whom Lepore has not seen in a while. The video turns out to be nearly two hours long, a molasses-paced montage with shots of trees and birds. But to Lepore it is invaluable because it gives a fascinating update on his mysterious patient.

"This is Dick Human," Johnson says, appearing on screen dressed in camouflage pants and cap with netting pulled over his face. "You're watching the *Forest Green* show. In this episode, we're going pioneering."

What follows is a documentary of Johnson building a new illegal abode, a tree house on stilts somewhere on Cape Cod. Filmed around Christmastime and spiced with country and reggae music, the film shows Johnson under the gun to build his new residence before authorities disconnect utilities in a place he had been squatting.

"Six days 'till they're shutting the water off," Johnson grumbles. "Only thirteen more chopping days till Christmas."

Some days Johnson doesn't chop because he fears the noise will attract attention. He carefully arranges brush and trees. "As I go along, I camouflage." One day, he mourns: "Broke my axe. This thing has helped me build so many places." Still, he presses on, working from before dawn till moonrise: "When you've done this as many times as I have, there are few wasted steps or opportunities or wasted materials."

The first snowstorm of winter arrives, making him fear being discovered if his feet leave "leading tracks back out of here." Plus, "everything's frozen solid," so it is it harder to use his primary tools, a pruning saw and a machete. On Christmas, Johnson sings, "It's beginning to look a lot like Trespass," then mutters, "So glad that Christmas is over. All those goddamn songs stuck in my head."

The house, finished in six weeks for $195.17, has neatly crisscrossed logs, glass-paned windows, a peaked roof. Johnson builds a wood stove from an ash can and empty soup cans. "I'll never be done with this place, always be doing something. But no one heard or saw me, and I didn't get hurt, which is saying a lot with these sharp tools and being accident prone. . . . But I am bone tired. I feel like my whole body has carpal tunnel syndrome."

Watching, Lepore worries about Johnson, out in the elements, eating and drinking who-knows-what. Even someone used to reclusive wilderness life is at risk for disease and deterioration. Johnson mentions smoking pot several times, and in at least one scene it appears that he is. He's contracted poison ivy so bad that his eyes are swollen and his face puffed up. "This is why I live in a swamp all alone," he says, laughing maniacally, as he stares into the camera. "I got a face like an ass. I got the P.I. as bad as you could hope to have it."

Johnson's "Trees Inn" location is a mystery, though he refers to a specific highway, suggesting southern Cape Cod. Later, the house gets discovered by state public works employees. "Somebody lives there," one says. Johnson replies, "Yeah man, that's me, dude. Any chance of keeping that cool?" The worker is awestruck: "Unbelievable craftsmanship . . . unfreakin' real."

Johnson, afraid of being ratted out, tells him, "I'm freaking out right now, man. . . . I'm homeless you know."

"Well," the worker says, "obviously you need some camouflage. I'm going to cut cedar branches for you."

Another worker tells Johnson: "I read about you on that Nantucket. . . . We're going to cut back on what we're doing . . . let you be and let it be our secret."

Johnson shows them around, proudly displaying a decorative carving of a rat, duck, and shore bird that he creates "in all my places." He asks that they dispel any rumors about him or the house by saying, "Nah, we just met some guy that was in there for a few days." A worker readily agrees, saying that would be "a damn believable story. It's almost more believable than what you're doing."

After they leave, Johnson can hardly believe his luck. "Well, I got away with it. To my health, stealth, and wealth."

At one point in the film, Johnson is briefly on Nantucket, visiting a tree house he built in 1998. It is weathered and some of what appear to be corrugated metal panels are peeling away from the tree house frame. But Johnson looks on with pride. "Still standing after ten years, for all the high winds and storms," he says, as another storm starts brewing. "And there's the ironic thunder rumbling in my life."

At the end, before the credits roll ("construction consultant: Frank Load Right"), Johnson as "Dick Human, hobo semipro" does a mock commercial for the "Trees Inn. . . . They got everything a bum on the run needs." For a movie by a hermit with barely a nickel to his name, it is a tour-de-force.

The film prompts Lepore to try a cell phone number Johnson had given him once, but it is disconnected. He pays another visit to Johnson's Nantucket "twigloo," which he finds to still be outfitted with crammed-in creature comforts, giving the impression that Johnson may return.

"He sort of comes and goes with the wind," Lepore muses. Then, after returning home, Lepore has a thought. Firing up Google Maps on his computer, he searches to see if the Hidden Forest house is visible on the satellite images. He doesn't want people intruding on it, destroying it like they did the Nantucket tree house, which, Lepore discovered when he went to check on it , was pulled down to make way for a Frisbee golf course.

Of course, Lepore figures somebody will stumble upon the twigloo one day. In fact, eventually it will not only be discovered, but dismantled, stripped of its accoutrements, hauled out of the forest on bamboo poles, and set up in a schoolyard—an empty shell to be used as a children's playhouse. Not a very Tom-like denouement.

But for now, this patient's secret is safe, zealously guarded by the only person with a key to his hidden homestead. Zooming in as far as possible on the satellite maps, Lepore spots a white smudge and wonders if it is the twigloo. The doctor cocks his head, squinting carefully at the screen. It's as though he is scanning an X-ray, an X-ray of the life of a patient who trusts almost no one else.

ACKNOWLEDGMENTS

"What's your book about?" people ask. When I give them a summary, I often get this reaction: "It's fiction, right? This stuff doesn't really happen, does it?"

It's true, I tell them. But I can understand the impulse behind the question. Often while working on this book I had the same feeling. Toe-tourniquet syndrome? A horse with cyanide poisoning? Knitting with dog hair? Really? Sometimes in exploring the world of Tim Lepore, I could understand how Cathy Lepore felt when she talked about why she married him: "I want to have someone interesting . . . I think I went over the top."

In fact, the biggest challenge was one that every writer should be fortunate enough to have, that every time I spoke with Tim there would be something else: another fascinating patient, an anecdote he'd forgotten to tell me, a comment that was just too funny or quirky to ignore. It was a challenge I exuberantly accepted.

In truth, a writer could not ask for a better relationship with a subject or his family. Tim and Cathy opened their lives to me, were unfailingly honest, and exceedingly generous. They shared their time, their family, their friends, their work, their home, and even their car (the one with the driver's seat frozen into a position so far back I could barely reach the gas pedal). Cathy made me more than a few delicious meals, and in countless other ways went the extra mile to assist my work.

The Lepores shared their painful stories as well as their successes. They never tried to airbrush anything or turn the book into hagiography.

They were always the way I hope they come across here: real people involved in real, if sometimes extraordinary, situations in an unusual and intriguing place. I cannot thank them enough.

The Lepore children—Meredith, T.J., and Nick—were also extremely helpful, bringing Tim, Cathy, and the community to life with wit and understanding. I am thankful to them for their openness and for making me laugh with their colorful memories and razor-sharp characterizations of their father.

I am grateful to Sherry Buckley and Martina Jakober, Tim's sister and niece, for their willingness to talk about sometimes-difficult family matters that provided invaluable depth to the book. And to Bob DiBuono, the childhood friend whom Tim nicknamed "the Weasel," but who was anything but weaselly in his forthright recollections.

Many Nantucketers, too many to mention here, gave of their time, their stories, and their insight. I am appreciative of all of them, as well as to those I did not have a chance to meet but whose day-to-day lives and work make the island the special place it is and helped inform this book in indirect ways.

In particular, I would like to express my profound gratitude to the families who have suffered the terrible agony of losing a child. Because of the sensitivity of these tragedies, I took great care to consult with these families and to respect their wishes concerning information that would be included about their experiences in the chapter called The Lost. Some family members chose to share their stories openly and in detail and were comfortable with being fully identified in the book. Others preferred that less information be disclosed. And ultimately, although national and local media had previously published the full names of the young people who passed away, I decided to publish only their first names in an effort to be especially compassionate to the ongoing pain that these losses have caused their families, their friends, and their community. My heart goes out to them.

A number of people showed tremendous courage in revealing difficult, delicate, or emotional experiences that will undoubtedly help inspire other people in similar circumstances. They include Alexandra McLaughlin, Justin Curry, Sean Kehoe, Alison Stark, Morgan Browne, Louise Hourihan, Linda Peterson, and others who preferred to not be fully identified but who deserve recognition as well. Thank you to Julie, who lived with the Lepores, for being candid about her family and her struggles.

Barbara Rives, Doug Kenward, Michelle Whelan, Elliot Norton, Rob McMullen, Laura Mueller, Doreen Goodwin, Michael Miller, Shelley Foulkes, Tom Foley, Lulie Gund, Edmund and Doris Reggie, Foley Vaughan, John Kerry, Chris Matthews, George Hull, John Gardner, Carolyn Condon, Eileen Howard, Genevieve Gordon, and Christine Kopanski were remarkably generous and open in sharing their experiences as patients or relatives of patients.

The members of Tim Lepore's excellent office staff were always welcoming. Diana Hull and Katie Pickman offered their reflections and allowed me to witness the devoted care they give to patients. Laura Kohtio-Graves provided useful background. Duncan MacDonald cheerfully gave me more than one ride to the ferry. Others deserving recognition include Carla Ray, Alicia Labrie, Diane Pittman, Shane Peters, Connie Holgate, Michelle Nee, and Beth Tornovish.

Several other medical professionals on and off the island, as well as current and former employees of Nantucket Cottage Hospital, deserve great thanks. Margot Hartmann, Diane Pearl, Bruce Chabner, Mary Murray, Mary Monagle, and Richard H. Koehler were especially giving of their time and insight. Others who were helpful include Wayne Wilbur, Jane Bonvini, Suzanne Duncan, Judy Divoll, Mary Kendall, Chris Iller, Chuck Gifford, and Charlene Chadwick.

Sam Telford III, Dean Belanger, Rob Deblinger, Ronnie Conway, James Cardoza, and the members of Nantucket's tick-borne disease committee, among others, helped educate me about ticks, deer, and associated diseases.

I am extremely indebted to the multifaceted and meaningful conversations I've had with Richard Ray, Jim Lentowski, Rhoda Weinman,

Steve Tornovish, Pam Michelsen, Chris Fraker, Peter Swenson, Martina Richards, Robin Rowland, Mariellen Scannell, Tristram Dammin, Paul and Brenda Johnson, David Goodman, Kim Horyn, Peter MacKay, Jeffrey Drazen, John Lochtefeld, Janine Mauldin, Michael Kopko, Steve Meadow, Bruce Watts, Jenny Garneau, and Thomas Shack, among others.

Thank you to Underground Tom, wherever he is, and to Henry, the cookie man, for a strikingly entertaining interview and recipes you're unlikely to see on Top Chef.

And I am deeply honored that the wonderful Nathaniel Philbrick not only supplied some colorful Tim Lepore stories but offered to write a foreword that poetically blended his vast knowledge of history with humor, sobriety, and a touch of magical realism.

A number of resources were valuable to my reporting. I am a subscriber to the Nantucket *Inquirer and Mirror*, which, under the impressive direction of its editor and publisher, Marianne Stanton, actively covers all things Nantucket. It provided an important avenue for keeping up on island life, and I thank all of the people who contribute to this publication, perhaps especially Jason Graziadei, who seems to regularly write more than half the paper.

Other resources included the *Nantucket Independent*, the *Cape Cod Times*, Plum TV, and a host of blogs including yackon.com, Mahon About Town, DiscoverNantucket.com, Boating Local, and Wicked Local Nantucket. I gleaned useful information from the *Vineyard Gazette*, *Martha's Vineyard Magazine*, *The Boston Globe*, *The Washington Post*, and *The New York Times*.

The staff of the Nantucket Atheneum, especially Lincoln Thurber, was helpful in providing old newspaper clippings. Other sources included the Nantucket Historical Association, Nantucket District Court, the Cape and Islands District Attorney's office, the Nantucket Police Department, the Massachusetts Division of Fisheries and Wildlife, the Massachusetts Department of Health, the Centers for Disease Control and Prevention, and the Food and Drug Administration. I used a number of medical journals including the *New England Journal of Medicine*, the *Harvard Public Health Review*, *Science*, and the *American Journal of Tropical Medicine and Hygiene*. I found several books helpful, including Nathaniel Philbrick's *Abram's Eyes* and *Away Off Shore*, Robert F. Mooney's *Nantucket Only Yesterday* and *The Nantucket Way*, and Robert Desowitz's *New Guinea Tapeworms and Jewish Grandmothers*.

I owe tremendous gratitude to my employer, *The New York Times*, and to way too many of my colleagues to name here. Special thanks to Bill Keller and Jill Abramson, and to Joe Lelyveld before them, for the remarkable opportunities they have given me, and for their inspiration and the exceptional journalism they have produced. Thanks to the editors on the National desk whose idea it was, in 2007, to have me, as New England bureau chief, write a piece about "someone who is doing something interesting in an interesting place." Had they picked any of the other ideas on my list—the art gallery owner/pro wrestler in Maine, for instance—this book might never have happened.

Thanks to Jack Kadden for editing that first story and for making me cut only a few of my favorite lines, some of which, he will notice, now see the light of day in this book. Thanks to my colleague Katie Zezima for holding down the fort in Boston while I spent time on Nantucket, and for being an all-around great person to have in the New England bureau. And thanks to Stephen Crowley, who spent several days with me on Nantucket taking photographs and video for that piece. Later, Cary Hazlegrove, a skilled Nantucket photographer, took pictures for a second article I wrote. And Alain Delaqueriere of *The Times*'s research department dug up background information.

My current colleagues on the Science staff of *The Times* embody the ideal combination of intelligence, collegiality, and just enough quirkiness to keep things interesting. The amazing Barbara Strauch, the Science editor, has been extraordinarily supportive and magnanimous during the book writing process. Her admirable predecessor, Laura Chang, also gave me encouragement. And the excellent health editor, Celia Dugger, has been wonderfully patient in allowing me to take time away from my day job. The terrific David Corcoran, who is a poet in addition to being a crackerjack editor, read many chapters, providing incisive comments and a dose of much-appreciated positive reinforcement.

Other colleagues who kindly gave their time to read portions of the book include Dennis Overbye, Donald G. McNeil Jr., and Cornelia Dean. Many others, including Soo-Jeong Kang, Nancy Donaldson, Todd Heisler, Jennifer Kingson, Michael Mason, Dabrali Jimenez, Thomas Lin, Jill Taylor, Toby Bilanow, Karen Barrow, James Gorman, Gina Kolata, Kenneth Chang, Tara Parker-Pope, Lawrence Altman, James Glanz, and Benedict Carey all provided encouragement in one way or another.

Denise Grady is not only an always-gracious colleague who read part of the book, but she added a dose of fun to some pretty intense days and once even gave me a gigantic piece of chocolate carved to look like two aspirin tablets. And William J. Broad, a true class act, provided invaluable advice about writing books, and became one of my cheerleaders as he listened enthusiastically to several outlandish Tim Lepore stories.

I'd like to thank my colleagues in the Knight Science Journalism Fellowship—Boyce Rensberger, Kathy Boisvert, Molly Seamans, Julie Robotham, Cathy Clabby, Jonathan Fahey, John Mangels, Ivan Semeniuk, Keith Seinfeld, Zarina Khan, Esther Nakkazi, Pere Estupinyà—who not only cheered me on, but took it in stride in Costa Rica when I spent several long, bumpy bus rides and insect-filled nights in the rain forest working away on what would become the Moby-Tick chapter.

And I'm grateful to Anne Bernays and the members of the Neiman writing group for helping launch me on the book-writing path and always believing I could do it.

Someone else who never lost faith is my terrific agent, Michael Carlisle, who spotted my initial article on Tim Lepore and contacted me about writing this book. Michael's warmth and his excitement about ideas are infectious, and he assisted me in navigating several challenging decisions along the way. Michael's affection for this book is part of what carried me through, and his kindness and decency are something to treasure.

I owe thanks to the people who have worked with Michael at Inkwell Management, especially Lauren Smythe and Ethan Bassoff for their responsiveness and guidance. I was also lucky that Jenny Witherell at Inkwell just happens to be a Nantucketer, and her reading of several chapters added valuable perspective and several additional details.

My publisher, PublicAffairs, has provided an excellent home for this book, understanding what it could be and endorsing the writer's voice and ideas all along the way. I am indebted to Peter Osnos, the founder and editor-at-large; Susan Weinberg, the publisher; Pete Garceau, the jacket designer; Timm Bryson, the text designer; Lindsay Fradkoff in marketing; and Renee Caputo, the proofer. Melissa Raymond, the managing editor, has been organized, patient, and responsive. Beth Wright was a careful and conscientious copyeditor. Emily Lavelle has been an energetic and creative publicist. Thanks also to Jeffrey Miller for his legal advice.

My editor, Clive Priddle, has been (almost) unfailingly understanding of the life of a *New York Times* writer juggling a book and her day job, relocating from one state to another, moving three times while selling and buying houses, and raising two little girls. He fielded phone calls and emails from me while I was on assignment in places like South Korea, Colombia, and Arizona's Navajo reservation, and while I was jugging parental responsibilities in skating rinks and piano recitals.

He didn't always say much, but (once he learned how to pronounce the name of our main character) what he said was perceptive and he made several suggestions that were nothing short of wise. You could try to chalk it up to the fact that his British accent makes him sound preternaturally smart. But in truth, he actually is. Just as important for me, he let me make him laugh or did a good job feigning amusement at my bad puns and silly jokes. This more than made up for his attempts to sneak Britishisms into the text (Americans, Clive, do not "pop round" to visit neighbors).

Once, when I was teasing Clive about his Dickensian name, he pointed out that his namesake was none other than Clive of India, the baron and military officer who established British colonial supremacy in India. This august figure had a campaign slogan—"Clive For Ever, Hurrah!"—and Priddle told me, "If you find yourself flagging, you may shout it with vim." My response was "Clive For Ever? Perish the thought." Now, though, when one thinks about the special gift of having an editor who helps a writer's work become better, that sentiment doesn't seem like such a bad idea.

I am very grateful to the talented Warren St. John for reading my work, and to Mark Russi, who cast his intelligent eye over several chapters. My wonderful friends Andy Meyers and Chris Leh also read the manuscript, just another way that their humor and wisdom has enriched my life over the years. Other friends provided enthusiastic support, patience with my overbooked schedule, and fountains of laughter and positive feelings that sustained me through this process. They include Deborah Scroggins, Margaret Usdansky, Peter Bass, Beth Haase, Jodi Cahn, Steve Wasserman, Ellen Clegg, and Alicia Anstead.

I have many musical acknowledgments to make because music gives my life unparalleled joy and meaning. The members of my jazz group, Equilibrium—Terry Schwadron, Frederic Gilde, Rich Russo, Dan Silverstone, and Brad Baker—helped me more than they know. So did other musicians, including Matt Buttermann, Kenneth Kuo, Fred Ury, Kevin Foxman, Micah Grand, Alexei Tsiganov, Jamie Stewardson, David Zoffer, Heather Stewart Fishman, and my friend Pete Muller. Natalie Ryshna Maynard, a marvelously dedicated pianist and teacher, was always inquisitive and engaged, and she will be dearly missed.

Thanks to the awesome June Clark for her enthusiasm and for loving our daughters almost as much as we do; to Kathleen Murphy and

Latiesha Gay for helping me make the time to write and report; and to the admirable coaches and parents from the Skyliners Synchronized Skating Team, who never seemed to mind that I was perpetually the mom in the rink with a laptop, tapping away with fingers that sometimes got cold enough to turn Skyliner blue.

It's impossible to capture the gratitude I feel toward my parents, Frances and Raymond. They are incomparable role models of integrity and earnestness, hard work and commitment, fairness, kindness, and love. They are at the root of all my joys and anything I have managed to accomplish in life.

My brother David has always held a stature for me that justifies every inch of his six-foot-five frame, inspiring me with his intelligence, dedication, achievement, and great generosity. I thank my sister-in-law Jocelyn as well. My brother Joseph is someone I greatly admire and respect, a person who sticks to his principles and has a keen devotion to family and friends. And I am grateful for the caring friendship of my sister-in-law, Laura, with whom I feel a special kinship.

Now for our daughters, Arielle and Jillian, who sparkle with wonder and exuberance; approach all they do with creativity, energy, humor, and imagination; dazzle me with their insights and observations every day; and thrill my heart with the most indescribable love in the world.

And finally to the person with whom I share life and love: my husband Bill. His support and encouragement have been beyond extraordinary. There were quotidian things: computer help and carpooling, lawn mowing and laundry and sending me lunch deliveries at work. There was the way he held things together at home when I traveled or worked way too late or spent what seemed like months hibernating to write and revise.

There was his hands-on assistance with the book: helping me track down phone numbers for sources, sending me multiple copies of the Associated Press style guide, fact-checking small details (who knew that Lipton Cup O' Noodles stopped using the O' in 1993?), listening to one anecdote after another, and reading and offering suggestions for chapter after chapter.

There was the animated and irrepressible way he shared his journalistic talent, his humor, and his honesty. And there was always his unwavering love and belief in me. This has been an amazing journey and Bill has been the most important person with me for every discovery along the way.

Pam Belluck has been a staff writer for the *New York Times* for more than fifteen years, during which she has written about everything from cattle rustling to embryo adoption and reported from places as diverse as Medellín, Colombia, and Seongham, South Korea. She served for more than a decade as a national bureau chief, covering some of the biggest stories for the paper. She is currently a health and medical writer for the *Times*. She has won several awards, a Knight fellowship, and a Fulbright, and her work has been selected for *The Best American Science Writing* and *The Best American Sports Writing* anthologies.

PublicAffairs is a publishing house founded in 1997. It is a tribute to the standards, values, and flair of three persons who have served as mentors to countless reporters, writers, editors, and book people of all kinds, including me.

I. F. STONE, proprietor of *I. F. Stone's Weekly*, combined a commitment to the First Amendment with entrepreneurial zeal and reporting skill and became one of the great independent journalists in American history. At the age of eighty, Izzy published *The Trial of Socrates*, which was a national bestseller. He wrote the book after he taught himself ancient Greek.

BENJAMIN C. BRADLEE was for nearly thirty years the charismatic editorial leader of *The Washington Post*. It was Ben who gave the *Post* the range and courage to pursue such historic issues as Watergate. He supported his reporters with a tenacity that made them fearless and it is no accident that so many became authors of influential, best-selling books.

ROBERT L. BERNSTEIN, the chief executive of Random House for more than a quarter century, guided one of the nation's premier publishing houses. Bob was personally responsible for many books of political dissent and argument that challenged tyranny around the globe. He is also the founder and longtime chair of Human Rights Watch, one of the most respected human rights organizations in the world.

·　·　·

For fifty years, the banner of Public Affairs Press was carried by its owner Morris B. Schnapper, who published Gandhi, Nasser, Toynbee, Truman, and about 1,500 other authors. In 1983, Schnapper was described by *The Washington Post* as "a redoubtable gadfly." His legacy will endure in the books to come.

Peter Osnos, *Founder and Editor-at-Large*